LOGISTIC REGRESSION

USING THE SAS° SYSTEM

Theory and Application

Paul D. Allison

Comments or Questions?

The author assumes complete responsibility for the technical accuracy of the content of this book. If you have any questions about the material in this book, please write to the author at this address:

SAS Institute
Books by Users
Attn: Paul D. Allison
SAS Campus Drive
Cary, NC 27513

If you prefer, you can send e-mail to sasbbu@sas.com with "comments for Paul D. Allison" as the subject line, or you can fax the Books by Users program at (919)677-4444.

The correct bibliographic citation for this manual is as follows: Paul D. Allison, *Logistic Regression Using the SAS® System: Theory and Application,* Cary, NC: SAS Institute Inc., 1999. 304 pp.

Logistic Regression Using the SAS® System: Theory and Application

Copyright © 1999 by SAS Institute Inc., Cary, NC, USA.

ISBN 1-58025-352-0

1st printing, October 1999
2nd printing, April 2000

Note that text corrections may have been made at each printing.

Table of Contents

Acknowledgments

For their detailed comments and suggestions, I wish to thank Nicholas Christakis, Roger Johnson, Andrew Karp, Scott Long, Michael Patetta, David Schlotzhauer, Anita Weber, and Christopher Winship. For permission to use their data in examples, I am indebted to Nicholas Christakis, Mordecai Garelick, David Hensher, Anne Keane, and Steve Metraux. Finally, I am deeply grateful to my editor, Judy Whatley, for her great patience and encouragement in bringing this book to fruition.

Chapter 1

Introduction

1.1   What This Book Is About

When I began graduate study at the University of Wisconsin in 1970, categorical data analysis consisted of chi-square tests for cross-tabulated data, a technique introduced around the turn of the century by the great Karl Pearson. This methodology was viewed with scorn by most of my quantitatively oriented cohorts. It was the province of old fogies who hadn't bothered to learn about REGRESSION ANALYSIS, the new universal tool for social science data analysis. Little did we realize that another revolution was taking place under our noses. By the time I left Wisconsin in 1975, the insanely great new thing was LOGLINEAR ANALYSIS, which made it possible to analyze complicated contingency tables in ways that Karl Pearson never dreamed of. But loglinear analysis was a rather different animal from linear regression and I, for one, never felt entirely comfortable working in the loglinear mode.

In the years after I left Wisconsin, these dissimilar approaches to data analysis came together in the form of LOGIT ANALYSIS, also known as logistic regression analysis. The logit model is essentially a regression model that is tailored to fit a categorical dependent variable. In its most widely used form, the dependent variable is a simple dichotomy, and the independent variables can be either quantitative or categorical. As we shall see, the logit model can be generalized to dependent variables that have more than two categories, both ordered and unordered. Using the method of conditional logit analysis, it can also be extended to handle specialized kinds of data such as discrete-choice applications, matched-pair analysis, and longitudinal data. Logit models for longitudinal data can also be analyzed with a method called generalized estimating equations.

This book is an introduction to the logit model and its various extensions. Unlike most introductory texts, however, this one is heavily focused on the use of the SAS System to estimate logit and related models. In my judgment, you can't fully understand and appreciate a new statistical technique without carefully considering the practical details of estimation. To accomplish that, it's necessary to choose a particular software system to carry out the computations. Although there are many good statistical packages for doing logit regression, SAS is certainly among the best in terms of the range of estimation methods, available features and options, efficiency and stability of the algorithms, and quality of the documentation. I find I can do almost anything I want to do in SAS and, in the process, I encounter few of the annoying software problems that seem to crop up frequently in other packages.

In addition to the logit model, I also write briefly about two alternatives for binary data, the probit model and the complementary log-log model. The last chapter is about loglinear analysis, a close cousin to logit analysis. Because some kinds of contingency table analysis are awkward to handle with the logit model, the loglinear model can be a useful alternative. I don't pretend to give a comprehensive treatment of loglinear analysis, however. The emphasis is on how to do it with the GENMOD procedure, and to show examples of the type of applications where a loglinear analysis might be particularly useful. The penultimate chapter is about Poisson regression for count data. I've included this topic partly for its intrinsic interest, but also because it's a useful preparation for the loglinear chapter. In PROC GENMOD, loglinear analysis is accomplished by way of Poisson regression.

Besides GENMOD, this book gives extensive coverage to the LOGISTIC procedure. The chapter on multinomial logit analysis focuses on the CATMOD procedure, and the chapters that use conditional logit analysis make heavy use of the PHREG procedure. However, this book is not intended to be a comprehensive guide to these SAS procedures. I discuss only those features that are most widely used, most potentially useful, and most likely to cause problems or confusion. You should always consult the official documentation in the *SAS/STAT User's Guide* or in later updates, such as *SAS/STAT Software: Changes and Enhancements through Release 6.12.*

1.2   What This Book Is Not About

This book does *not* cover a variety of categorical data analysis known as Cochran-Mantel-Haenszel (CMH) statistics, for two reasons. First, I have little expertise on the subject and it would be presumptuous for me to try to teach others. Second, while CMH is widely used in the biomedical sciences, there have been few applications in the social sciences. This disuse is not necessarily a good thing. CMH is a flexible and well-founded approach to categorical data analysis—one that I believe has many potential applications. While it accomplishes many of the same objectives as logit analysis, it is best suited to those situations where the focus is on the relationship between one independent variable and one dependent variable, controlling for a limited set of additional variables. Statistical control is accomplished in a nonparametric fashion by stratification on all possible combinations of the control variables. Consequently, CMH is less vulnerable than logit regression to certain kinds of specification error but at the expense of reduced statistical power. Stokes et al. (1995) give an excellent and thorough introduction to CMH methods as implemented with the FREQ procedure in SAS.

1.3   What You Need to Know

To understand this book, you need to be familiar with multiple linear regression. That means that you should know something about the assumptions of the linear regression model and about estimation of the model via ordinary least squares. Ideally, you should have a substantial amount of practical experience using multiple regression on real data and should feel comfortable interpreting the output from a regression analysis. You should be acquainted with such topics as multicollinearity, residual analysis, variable selection, nonlinearity, interactions, and dummy variables. As part of this knowledge, you must certainly know the basic principles of statistical inference: standard errors, confidence intervals, hypothesis tests, *p*-values, bias, efficiency, and so on. In short, a two-semester sequence in statistics ought to provide the necessary statistical foundation for most people.

I have tried to keep the mathematics at a minimal level throughout the book. Except for one section on maximum likelihood estimation (which can be skipped without loss of continuity), there is no calculus and little use of matrix notation. Nevertheless, to simplify the presentation of regression models, I occasionally use the vector notation

$\beta \mathbf{x} = \beta_0 + \beta_1 x_1 + ... + \beta_k x_k$. While it would be helpful to have some knowledge of maximum likelihood estimation, it's hardly essential. However, you should know the basic properties of logarithms and exponential functions.

With regard to SAS, the more experience you have with SAS/STAT and the SAS DATA step, the easier it will be to follow the presentation of SAS programs. On the other hand, the programs presented in this book are fairly simple and short, so don't be intimidated if you're just beginning to learn SAS.

1.4 Computing

All the computer input and output displayed in this book was produced by and for Release 6.12 of the SAS System. Occasionally, I point out differences between the syntax of 6.12 and earlier releases. I use the following convention for presenting SAS programs: All SAS keywords are in uppercase. All user-specified variable names and data set names are in lowercase. In the main text, both SAS keywords and user-specified variables are in uppercase. In the output displays, nonessential output lines are often edited out to conserve space.

1.5 References

Most of the topics in this book can be found in any one of several textbooks on categorical data analysis. In preparing this book, I have particularly benefited from consulting Agresti (1990, 1996), Hosmer and Lemeshow (1989), Long (1997), Fienberg (1980), and Everitt (1992). I have generally refrained from giving references for material that is well established in the textbook literature, but I do provide references for any unusual, nonstandard, or controversial claims. I also give references whenever I think the reader might want to pursue additional information or discussion. This book should not be regarded as a substitute for official SAS documentation. As of this writing, the most complete and up-to-date documentation for the LOGISTIC, GENMOD, and PHREG procedures can be found in *SAS/STAT Software: Changes and Enhancements through Release 6.12* (SAS Institute 1996). For PROC CATMOD, consult the *SAS/STAT User's Guide*, volume 1 (SAS Institute 1989).

Chapter 2

Binary Logit Analysis: Basics

2.1. Introduction

A great many variables in the social sciences are dichotomous—employed vs. unemployed, married vs. unmarried, guilty vs. not guilty, voted vs. didn't vote. It's hardly surprising, then, that social scientists frequently want to estimate regression models in which the dependent variable is a dichotomy. Nowadays, most researchers are aware that there's something wrong with using ordinary linear regression for a dichotomous dependent variable, and that it's better to use logit or probit regression. But many of them don't know what it is about linear regression that makes dichotomous variables problematic, and they may have only a vague notion of why other methods are superior.

In this chapter, we focus on logit analysis (a.k.a. logistic regression analysis) as an optimal method for the regression analysis of dichotomous (binary) dependent variables. Along the way, we'll see that logit analysis has many similarities to ordinary linear regression analysis. To understand and appreciate the logit model, we first need to see why ordinary linear regression runs into problems when the dependent variable is dichotomous.

2.2. Dichotomous Dependent Variables: Example

To make things tangible, let's start with an example. Throughout this chapter, we'll be examining a data set consisting of 147 death penalty cases in the state of New Jersey. In all of these cases, the defendant was convicted of first-degree murder with a recommendation by the prosecutor that a death sentence be imposed. Then a penalty trial was conducted to determine whether the defendant would receive a death sentence or life imprisonment. Our dependent variable DEATH is coded 1 for a death sentence and 0 for a life sentence. The aim is to determine how this outcome was influenced by various characteristics of the defendant and the crime.

Many potential independent variables are available in the data set, but let's consider three of special interest:

BLACKD   Coded 1 if the defendant was black, otherwise 0.

WHITVIC   Coded 1 if the victim was white, otherwise 0.

SERIOUS   A rating of the seriousness of the crime, as evaluated by a panel of judges.

The variable SERIOUS was developed in an auxiliary study in which panels of trial judges were given written descriptions of each of the crimes in the original data set. These descriptions did not mention the race of the defendant or the victim. Each judge evaluated 14 or 15 cases and ranked them from least serious to most serious. Each case was ranked by four to six judges. As used in this chapter, the SERIOUS score is the average ranking given to each case, ranging from 1 (least serious) to 15 (most serious).

Using the REG procedure in SAS, I estimated a linear regression model that uses DEATH as the dependent variable and the other three as independent variables. The SAS code is:

```
PROC REG DATA=my.penalty;
   MODEL death=blackd whitvic serious;
RUN;
```

Results are shown in Output 2.1. Neither of the two racial variables have coefficients that are significantly different from 0. Not surprisingly, the coefficient for SERIOUS is highly significant—more serious crimes are more likely to get the death penalty.

Should we trust these results, or should we ignore them because the statistical technique is incorrect? To answer that question we need to see *why* linear regression is regarded as inappropriate when the dependent variable is a dichotomy. That's the task of the next section.

Output 2.1 *Linear Regression of Death Penalty on Selected Independent Variables*

```
Dependent Variable: DEATH

                        Analysis of Variance

                      Sum of        Mean
Source          DF    Squares      Square    F Value    Prob>F

Model            3    2.61611     0.87204     4.105     0.0079
Error          143   30.37709     0.21243
C Total        146   32.99320


     Root MSE         0.46090     R-square         0.0793
     Dep Mean         0.34014     Adj R-sq         0.0600
     C.V.           135.50409


                      Parameter Estimates

                Parameter       Standard     T for H0:
Variable   DF    Estimate          Error   Parameter=0    Prob > |T|

INTERCEP    1   -0.054924     0.12499281      -0.439        0.6610
BLACKD      1    0.121974     0.08224415       1.483        0.1403
WHITVIC     1    0.053309     0.08411308       0.634        0.5272
SERIOUS     1    0.038403     0.01200143       3.200        0.0017
```

2.3. Problems with Ordinary Linear Regression

Not so long ago, it was common to see published research that used ordinary least squares (OLS) linear regression to analyze dichotomous dependent variables. Some people didn't know any better. Others knew better but didn't have access to good software for alternative methods. Now, virtually every major statistical package includes procedures for logit or probit analysis, so there's no excuse for applying inferior methods. No reputable social science journal would publish an article that used OLS regression with a dichotomous dependent variable.

Should all the earlier literature that violated this prohibition be dismissed? Actually, most applications of OLS regression to dichotomous variables give results that are qualitatively quite similar to results obtained using logit regression. There are exceptions, of course, so I certainly wouldn't claim that there's no need for logit analysis. But as an approximate method, OLS linear regression does a surprisingly good job with dichotomous variables, despite clear-cut violations of assumptions.

What are the assumptions that underlie OLS regression? While there's no single set of assumptions that justifies linear regression, the list in the box is fairly standard. To keep things simple, I've included only a single independent variable x, and I've presumed that x is "fixed" across repeated samples (which means that every sample has the same set of x values). The i subscript distinguishes different members of the sample.

Assumptions of the Linear Regression Model

1. $y_i = \alpha + \beta x_i + \varepsilon_i$
2. $E(\varepsilon_i) = 0$
3. $\mathrm{var}(\varepsilon_i) = \sigma^2$
4. $\mathrm{cov}(\varepsilon_i, \varepsilon_j) = 0$
5. $\varepsilon_i \sim Normal$

Assumption 1 says that y is a linear function of x plus a random disturbance term ε, for all members of the sample. The remaining assumptions all say something about the distribution of ε. What's important about assumption 2 is that $E(\varepsilon)$ (the expected value of ε) does *not* vary with x, implying that x and ε are uncorrelated. Assumption 3, often called the *homoscedasticity* assumption, says that the variance of ε is the same for all observations. Assumption 4 says that the random disturbance for one observation is uncorrelated with the random disturbance for any other observation. Finally, assumption 5 says that the random disturbance is normally distributed. If all five assumptions are satisfied, ordinary least squares estimates of α and β are unbiased and have minimum sampling variance (minimum variability across repeated samples).

Now suppose that y is a dichotomy with possible values of 1 or 0. It's still reasonable to claim that assumptions 1, 2, and 4 are true. But if 1 and 2 are true for a dichotomy, then 3 and 5 are *necessarily* false. First, let's consider assumption 5. Suppose that $y_i=1$. Then assumption 1 implies that $\varepsilon_i=1-\alpha-\beta x_i$. On the other hand, if $y_i=0$, we have $\varepsilon_i=-\alpha-\beta x_i$. Because ε_i can only take on two values, it's impossible for it to have a normal distribution (which has a continuum of values and no upper or lower bound). So assumption 5 must be rejected.

To evaluate assumption 3, it's helpful to do a little preliminary algebra. The expected value of y_i is, by definition,

$$E(y_i) = 1 \times \Pr(y_i = 1) + 0 \times \Pr(y_i = 0).$$

If we define $p_i = \Pr(y_i=1)$, this reduces to

$$E(y_i) = p_i$$

In general, for any dummy variable, its expected value is just the probability that it is equal to 1. But assumptions 1 and 2 also imply another expression for this expectation. Taking the expected values of both sides of the equation in assumption 1, we get

$$\begin{aligned} E(y_i) &= E(\alpha + \beta x_i + \varepsilon_i) \\ &= E(\alpha) + E(\beta x_i) + E(\varepsilon_i) \\ &= \alpha + \beta x_i. \end{aligned}$$

Putting these two results together, we get

$$p_i = \alpha + \beta x_i, \tag{2.1}$$

which is sometimes called the *linear probability model*. As the name suggests, this model says that the probability that $y=1$ is a linear function of x. Regression coefficients have a straightforward interpretation under this model. A 1-unit change in x produces a change of β in the probability that $y=1$. In Output 2.1, the coefficient for SERIOUS was .038. So we can say that each 1-point increase in the SERIOUS scale (which ranges from 1 to 15) is associated with an increase of .038 in the probability of a death sentence, controlling for the other variables in the model. The BLACKD coefficient of .12 tells us that the estimated probability of a death sentence for black defendants is .12 higher than for non-black defendants, controlling for other variables.

Now let's consider the variance of ε_i. Because x is treated as fixed, the variance of ε_i is the same as the variance of y_i. In general, the variance of a dummy variable is $p_i(1-p_i)$. Therefore, we have

$$\mathrm{var}(\varepsilon_i) = p_i(1 - p_i) = (\alpha + \beta x_i)(1 - \alpha - \beta x_i).$$

We see, then, that the variance of ε_i must be different for different observations and, in particular, it varies as a function of x. The disturbance variance is at a maximum when $p_i=.5$ and gets small when p_i is near 1 or 0.

We've just shown that a dichotomous dependent variable in a linear regression model necessarily violates assumptions of homoscedasticity (assumption 3) and normality (assumption 5) of the error term. What are the consequences? Not as serious as you might think. First of all, we don't need these assumptions to get *unbiased* estimates. If just assumptions 1 and 2 hold, ordinary least squares will produce unbiased estimates of α and β. Second, the normality assumption is not needed if the sample is reasonably large. The central limit theorem assures us that coefficient estimates will have a distribution that is approximately normal even when ε is *not* normally distributed. That means that we can still use a normal table to calculate p-values and confidence intervals. If the sample is small, however, these approximations could be poor.

Violation of the homoscedasticity assumption has two undesirable consequences. First, the coefficient estimates are no longer *efficient*. In statistical terminology, this means that there are alternative methods of estimation with smaller standard errors. Second, and more serious, the standard error estimates are no longer *consistent* estimates of the true standard errors. That means that the estimated standard errors could be biased (either upward or downward) to unknown degrees. And because the standard errors are used in calculating test statistics, the test statistics could also be biased.

In addition to these technical difficulties, there is a more fundamental problem with the assumptions of the linear model. We've seen that when the dependent variable is a dichotomy, assumptions 1 and 2 imply the linear probability model

$$p_i = \alpha + \beta x_i,$$

While there's nothing intrinsically wrong with this model, it's a bit implausible, especially if x is measured on a continuum. If x has no upper or lower bound, then for any value of β there are values of x for which p_i is either greater than 1 or less than 0. In fact, when estimating a linear probability model by OLS, it's quite common for predicted values generated by the model to be outside the $(0, 1)$ interval. (That wasn't a problem with the regression in Output 2.1, which implied predicted probabilities ranging from .03 to .65). Of course, it's impossible for the true values (which are probabilities) to be greater than 1 or less than 0. So the only way the model could be true is if a ceiling and floor are somehow imposed on p_i, leading to considerable awkwardness both theoretically and computationally.

These problems with the linear model led statisticians to develop alternative approaches that make more sense conceptually and also have better statistical properties. The most popular of these approaches is the logit model, which is estimated by maximum likelihood. Before considering the full model, let's examine one of its components—the *odds* of an event.

2.4. Odds and Odds Ratios

To appreciate the logit model, it's helpful to have an understanding of *odds* and *odds ratios*. Most people regard probability as the "natural" way to quantify the chances that an event will occur. We automatically think in terms of numbers ranging from 0 to 1, with a 0 meaning that the event will certainly not occur, and a 1 meaning that the event certainly will occur. But there are other ways of representing the chances of event, one of which—the odds—has a nearly equal claim to being "natural."

Widely used by professional gamblers, the odds of an event is the ratio of the expected number of times that an event will occur to the expected number of times it will not occur. An odds of 4 means we expect 4 times as many occurrences as non-occurrences. An odds of 1/5 means that we expect only one-fifth as many occurrences as non-occurrences. In gambling circles, odds are sometimes expressed as, say, "5 to 2," but that corresponds to the single number 5/2.

There is a simple relationship between probabilities and odds. If p is the probability of an event and O is the odds of the event, then

$$O = \frac{p}{1-p} = \frac{probability\ of\ event}{probability\ of\ no\ event}$$

(2.2)

$$p = \frac{O}{1+O}.$$

This functional relationship is illustrated in Table 2.1.

Table 2.1   *Relationship between Odds and Probability*

Probability	Odds
.1	.11
.2	.25
.3	.43
.4	.67
.5	1.00
.6	1.50
.7	2.33
.8	4.00
.9	9.00

Note that odds less than 1 correspond to probabilities below .5, while odds greater than 1 correspond to probabilities greater than .5. Like probabilities, odds have a lower bound of 0. But unlike probabilities, there is no upper bound on the odds.

Why do we need the odds? Because it's a more sensible scale for multiplicative comparisons. If I have a probability of .30 of voting in the next election, and your probability of voting is .60, it's reasonable to claim that your probability is twice as great as mine. But if my probability is .60, it's impossible for your probability to be twice as great. There's no problem on the odds scale, however. A probability of .60 corresponds to odds of .60/.40=1.5. Doubling that yields odds of 3. Converting back to probabilities gives us 3/(1+3)=.75.

This leads us to odds ratios, a widely used measure of the relationship between two dichotomous variables. Consider Table 2.2, which shows the cross-tabulation of race of defendant by death sentence for the 147 penalty-trial cases. The numbers in the table are the actual numbers of cases that have the stated characteristics.

Table 2.2   *Death Sentence by Race of Defendant for 147 Penalty Trials*

	Blacks	Nonblacks	Total
Death	28	22	50
Life	45	52	97
Total	73	74	147

Overall, the estimated odds of a death sentence are 50/97= .52. For blacks, the odds are 28/45 = .62. For nonblacks, the odds are 22/52 = .42. The ratio of the black odds to the non-black odds is 1.47. We may say, then, that the odds of a death sentence for blacks are 47% greater than for nonblacks. Note that the odds ratio in a 2 × 2 table is also equal to the *cross-product ratio*, which is the product of the two main-diagonal frequencies divided by the product of the two off-diagonal frequencies. In this case, we have (52 × 28)/(22 × 45) = 1.47.

Of course, we can also say that the odds of a death sentence for nonblacks are 1/1.47 = .63 times the odds of a death sentence for blacks. Similarly, the odds of a *life sentence* for blacks are .63 times the odds for nonblacks. So, depending on which categories we're comparing, we either get an odds ratio greater than 1 or its reciprocal, which is less than 1.

Implicit in much of the contemporary literature on categorical data analysis is the notion that odds ratios (and various functions of them) are less sensitive to changes in the marginal frequencies (for example, the total number of death and life sentences) than other measures of association. In this sense, they are frequently regarded as fundamental descriptions of the relationship between the variables of interest. As we shall see, odds ratios are directly related to the parameters in the logit model.

2.5. The Logit Model

Now we're ready to introduce the logit model, otherwise known as the logistic regression model. As we discussed earlier, a major problem with the linear probability model is that probabilities are bounded by 0 and 1, but linear functions are inherently unbounded. The solution is to transform the probability so that it's no longer bounded.

Transforming the probability to an odds removes the upper bound. If we then take the logarithm of the odds, we also remove the lower bound. Setting the result equal to a linear function of the explanatory variables, we get the logit model. For k explanatory variables and $i = 1,\ldots, n$ individuals, the model is

$$\log\left[\frac{p_i}{1-p_i}\right] = \alpha + \beta_1 x_{i1} + \beta_2 x_{i2} + \ldots + \beta_k x_{ik} \tag{2.3}$$

where p_i is, as before, the probability that $y_i=1$. The expression on the left-hand side is usually referred to as the *logit* or *log-odds*. (Natural logarithms are used throughout this book. However, the only consequence of switching to base-10 logarithms would be to change the intercept α.) As in ordinary linear regression, the x's may be either interval-level variables or dummy (indicator) variables.

Unlike the usual linear regression model, there is no random disturbance term in the equation for the logit model. That doesn't mean that the model is deterministic because there is still room for random variation in the probabilistic relationship between p_i and y_i. Nevertheless, as we shall see later, problems may arise if there is unobserved heterogeneity in the sample.

We can solve the logit equation for p_i to obtain

$$p_i = \frac{\exp(\alpha + \beta_1 x_{i1} + \beta_2 x_{i2} + ... + \beta_k x_{ik})}{1 + \exp(\alpha + \beta_1 x_{i1} + \beta_2 x_{i2} + ... + \beta_k x_{ik})} \tag{2.4}$$

Exp(x) is the exponential function, equivalent to e^x. In turn, e is the exponential constant, approximately equal to 2.71828. Its defining property is that $\log(e^x)=x$. We can simplify further by dividing both the numerator and denominator by the numerator itself:

$$p_i = \frac{1}{1 + \exp(-\alpha - \beta_1 x_{i1} - \beta_2 x_{i2} - ... - \beta_k x_{ik})} \tag{2.5}$$

This equation has the desired property that no matter what values we substitute for the β's and the x's, p_i will always be a number between 0 and 1.

If we have a single x variable with $\alpha = 0$ and $\beta = 1$, the equation can be graphed to produce the S-shaped curve in Figure 2.1. As x gets large or small, p gets close to 1 or 0 but is never equal to these limits. From the graph, we see that the effect of a unit change in x depends on where you start. When p is near .50, the effect is large; but when p is near 0 or 1, the effect is small. More specifically, the slope of the curve is given by

$$\frac{\partial p_i}{\partial x_i} = \beta p_i (1 - p_i). \tag{2.6}$$

When $\beta=1$ and $p=.5$, a 1-unit increase in x produces an increase in the probability of .25. When β is larger, the slope of the S-shaped curve at $p=.5$ is steeper. When β is negative, the curve is flipped horizontally so that p is near 1 when x is small and near 0 when x is large.

There are alternative models that have similar S-shaped curves, most notably the probit and complementary log-log models. I'll discuss them briefly in the next chapter. But, for several reasons, the logit model is more popular:

- The coefficients have a simple interpretation in terms of odds ratios.
- The logit model is intimately related to the loglinear model, which is discussed in Chapter 10.
- The logit model has desirable sampling properties, which are discussed in Section 3.12.
- The model can be easily generalized to allow for multiple, unordered categories for the dependent variable.

Figure 2.1 *Graph of Logit Model for a Single Explanatory Variable*

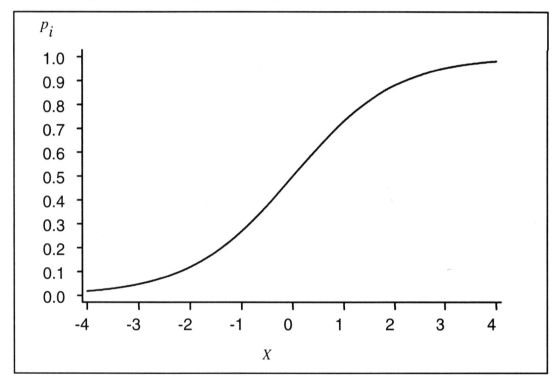

2.6. Estimation of the Logit Model: General Principles

Now that we have a model for dichotomous dependent variables, the next step is to use sample data to estimate the coefficients. How that's done depends on the type of data you're working with. If you have *grouped data*, there are three readily available methods: ordinary least squares, weighted least squares, and maximum likelihood.

Grouped data occurs when the explanatory variables are all categorical and the data is arrayed in the form of a contingency table. We'll see several examples of grouped data in

Chapter 4. Grouped data can also occur when data is collected from naturally occurring groups. For example, suppose that the units of analysis are business firms and the dependent variable is the probability that an employee is a full-time worker. Let P_i be the observed proportion of employees who work full-time in firm i. To estimate a logit model by OLS, we would simply take the logit transformation of P, which is $\log[P/(1-P)]$, and regress that transformation on characteristics of the firm and on the average characteristics of the employees. A weighted least squares (WLS) analysis would be similar, except that the data would be weighted to adjust for heteroscedasticity. The SAS procedure CATMOD does WLS estimation for grouped data (in addition to maximum likelihood).

Maximum likelihood (ML) is the third method for estimating the logit model for grouped data and the *only* method in general use for *individual-level data*. This is data for which we simply observe a dichotomous dependent variable for each individual along with measured characteristics of the individual. OLS and WLS can't be used with this kind of data unless the data can be grouped in some way. If y_i can only have values of 1 and 0, it's impossible to apply the logit transformation—you get either minus infinity or plus infinity. To put it another way, any transformation of a dichotomy is still a dichotomy.

Maximum likelihood is a very general approach to estimation that is widely used for all sorts of statistical models. You may have encountered it before with loglinear models, latent variable models, or event history models. There are two reasons for this popularity. First, ML estimators are known to have good properties in large samples. Under fairly general conditions, ML estimators are consistent, asymptotically efficient, and asymptotically normal. Consistency means that, as the sample size gets larger, the probability that the estimate is within some small distance of the true value also gets larger. No matter how small the distance or how high the specified probability, there is always a sample size that yields an even higher probability that the estimator is within that distance of the true value. One implication of consistency is that the ML estimator is approximately unbiased in large samples. Asymptotic efficiency means that, in large samples, the estimates will have standard errors that are, approximately, at least as small as those for any other estimation method. And, finally, the sampling distribution of the estimates will be approximately normal in large samples, which means that you can use the normal and chi-square distributions to compute confidence intervals and p-values.

All these approximations get better as the sample size gets larger. The fact that these desirable properties have only been proven for large samples does *not* mean that ML has bad properties for small samples. It simply means that we usually don't *know* what the small-sample properties are. And in the absence of attractive alternatives, researchers routinely use ML estimation for both large and small samples. Although I won't argue against that practice, I do urge caution in interpreting *p*-values and confidence intervals when samples are small. Despite the temptation to accept *larger p*-values as evidence against the null hypothesis in small samples, it is actually more reasonable to demand *smaller* values to compensate for the fact that the approximation to the normal or chi-square distributions may be poor.

The other reason for ML's popularity is that it is often straightforward to derive ML estimators when there are no other obvious possibilities. One case that ML handles very nicely is data with categorical dependent variables.

The basic principle of ML is to choose as estimates those parameter values which, if true, would maximize the probability of observing what we have, in fact, observed. There are two steps to this: (1) write down an expression for the probability of the data as a function of the unknown parameters, and (2) find the values of the unknown parameters that make the value of this expression as large as possible.

The first step is known as constructing the *likelihood function*. To accomplish this, you must specify a model, which amounts to choosing a probability distribution for the dependent variable and choosing a functional form that relates the parameters of this distribution to the values of the explanatory variables. In the case of the logit model, the dichotomous dependent variable is presumed to have a binomial distribution with a single "trial" and parameter p_i. Then p_i is assumed to depend on the explanatory variables according to equation (2.3), the logit model. Finally, we assume that the observations are independent across individuals.

The second step—maximization—typically requires an iterative numerical method, which means that it involves successive approximations. Such methods are often computationally demanding, which explains why ML estimation has become popular only in the last two decades. For those who are interested, I work through the basic mathematics of constructing and maximizing the likelihood function in Chapter 3. Here I focus on the practical aspects of ML estimation with SAS.

2.7. Maximum Likelihood Estimation with PROC LOGISTIC

SAS has four procedures that will estimate a binary logit model via maximum likelihood: LOGISTIC, GENMOD, PROBIT and CATMOD. I won't discuss the PROBIT procedure at all because its capabilities are mostly duplicated by the LOGISTIC procedure, except for certain specialized bioassay statistics. I'll postpone a discussion of the CATMOD procedure until Chapter 4 because it's most useful for estimating the *multinomial* logit model. That leaves the LOGISTIC and GENMOD procedures for this chapter. PROC LOGISTIC has been around longer and, as a result, is more widely used. But PROC GENMOD has features that make it attractive for many applications, especially the analysis of contingency tables. GENMOD's capabilities are also available with a point-and-click interface by using SAS/INSIGHT software. LOGISTIC can be used in a point-and-click mode in SAS/ASSIST software or the SAS Analyst Application. In my own work, I often switch back and forth between GENMOD and LOGISTIC. I'll begin by discussing PROC LOGISTIC.

Let's estimate a logit model analogous to the linear probability model that we examined in Section 2.2. Minimal SAS code for this model is

```
PROC LOGISTIC DATA=my.penalty DESCENDING;
   MODEL death=blackd whitvic serious;
RUN;
```

Of course, there are also numerous options and special features that we'll consider later.

One option that I've specified in the PROC statement is DESCENDING. The default in LOGISTIC is to estimate a model predicting the *lowest* value of the dependent variable. Consequently, if I had omitted the DESCENDING option, the result would be a logit model predicting the probability that the dependent variable DEATH is equal to 0. The DESCENDING option (which can be abbreviated DES) reverses this so that the model predicts the probability of the *highest* value. If you forget this option, the only consequence is to change the intercept and the signs of the coefficients. As long as you realize what you've done, you shouldn't need to rerun the model.

Results are shown in Output 2.2. After some preliminary information, we find a section titled "Testing Global Null Hypothesis: BETA=0." Within this section there are two chi-square statistics, one with a value of 12.206, the other with a value of 11.656. Both of these statistics are testing the same null hypothesis—that *all* the explanatory variables have coefficients of 0. (In a linear regression, this hypothesis is usually tested by means of an overall *F*-test.) The three degrees of freedom for each of these statistics correspond to the three coefficients for the independent variables. In this case, the associated *p*-value is less than .01, so we reject the null hypothesis and conclude that at least one of the coefficients is not 0.

Output 2.2 *PROC LOGISTIC Output for Death Penalty Data*

```
                         The LOGISTIC Procedure
        Data Set: MY.PENALTY
        Response Variable: DEATH
        Response Levels: 2
        Number of Observations: 147
        Link Function: Logit


                              Response Profile

                            Ordered
                             Value    DEATH      Count

                               1        1         50
                               2        0         97

                     Testing Global Null Hypothesis: BETA=0

                                  Intercept
                      Intercept     and
        Criterion       Only      Covariates    Chi-Square for Covariates


        AIC            190.491     184.285            .
        SC             193.481     196.247            .
        -2 LOG L       188.491     176.285       12.206 with 3 DF  (p=0.0067)
        Score             .           .          11.656 with 3 DF  (p=0.0087)


                     Analysis of Maximum Likelihood Estimates

                      Parameter Standard    Wald       Pr >     Standardized    Odds
        Variable DF   Estimate   Error   Chi-Square Chi-Square    Estimate      Ratio

        INTERCPT 1     -2.6516   0.6748    15.4425     0.0001         .           .
        BLACKD   1      0.5952   0.3939     2.2827     0.1308      0.164628     1.813
        WHITVIC  1      0.2565   0.4002     0.4107     0.5216      0.069548     1.292
        SERIOUS  1      0.1871   0.0612     9.3343     0.0022      0.329478     1.206


             Association of Predicted Probabilities and Observed Responses
                        Concordant = 67.2%     Somers' D = 0.349
                        Discordant = 32.3%     Gamma     = 0.351
                        Tied       =  0.5%     Tau-a     = 0.158
                        (4850 pairs)           c         = 0.675
```

Why do we need two chi-square statistics? The first one is the *likelihood ratio chi-square* obtained by comparing the log-likelihood for the fitted model with the log-likelihood for a model with *no* explanatory variables. It is calculated by taking twice the positive difference in the two log-likelihoods. In fact, LOGISTIC reports $-2 \times$ log-likelihood for each of those models, and the chi-square is just the difference between those two numbers. The *score* statistic is a function (a quadratic form) of the first and second derivatives of the log-likelihood function under the null hypothesis. In large samples, there's no reason to prefer either of these statistics, and they will generally be quite close. In small samples or samples with extreme data patterns, there is some evidence that the likelihood ratio chi-square is superior (Jennings 1986).

In this section of the output, we also see two other statistics that are useful in comparing the relative fit of different models. *Akaike's information criterion* (labeled AIC) is calculated as $-2 \times$ log-likelihood $+ 2k$ where k is the number of estimated parameters (4 in this case). The *Schwartz criterion* (labeled SC) is equal to $-2 \times$ log-likelihood $+ k \log n$ where n is the sample size. This second statistic is more familiar to social scientists as the *BIC* statistic (which is an acronym for Bayesian information criterion). Both statistics "penalize" the log-likelihood for estimating more parameters, with the Schwartz criterion producing the more severe penalization. In general, lower values of these statistics correspond to more desirable models.

Next we get to the heart of the matter—the "Analysis of Maximum Likelihood Estimates." As with linear regression, we get coefficient estimates, their estimated standard errors, and test-statistics for the null hypotheses that each coefficient is equal to 0. The test statistics are labeled "Wald chi-squares". They are calculated by dividing each coefficient by its standard error and squaring the result. If we omitted the squaring operation, we could call them t or z statistics, and the *p*-values calculated from a normal table would be exactly the same as the chi-square *p*-values reported here.

For this data, we see that the variable SERIOUS has a highly significant coefficient, while the value for the variable WHITVIC is clearly not significant. With a *p*-value of .13, BLACKD is approaching conventional significance levels but doesn't quite make it. Now compare these *p*-values with those in Output 2.1 for an ordinary regression analysis. While not identical, they are remarkably similar. In this case at least, logistic regression and OLS regression lead us to exactly the same qualitative conclusions. It's more difficult to compare coefficient estimates across the two methods, however, and I won't attempt that here.

The last two columns are labeled "Standardized Estimate" and "Odds Ratio." As in linear regression, the standardized estimates measure the relative importance of the explanatory variables. I'll postpone discussing them further until Section 3.9, which deals with a latent variable interpretation of the logit model. The odds ratios are obtained by simply exponentiating the coefficients in the first column, that is, computing $\exp(\beta)$. I'll have a lot more to say about them in Section 2.9, which presents interpretation of coefficients.

The last section of the output, labeled "Association of Predicted Probabilities and Observed Responses," is an attempt to measure the explanatory power of the model. I'll discuss these measures in Section 3.7.

2.8. Maximum Likelihood Estimation with PROC GENMOD

GENMOD is a relatively new SAS procedure that's designed to estimate *generalized linear models* (McCullagh and Nelder 1989), which include the standard linear model, logit and probit models, loglinear models, Poisson regression models, and many other less familiar models. It's very similar in features and syntax to the famous GLIM program introduced by the Royal Statistical Society in the early 1970s.

Here's how to use PROC GENMOD to estimate the same logit model that we fit with PROC LOGISTIC in the previous section. The code for Release 6.12 and later is

```
PROC GENMOD DATA=my.penalty;
  MODEL death=blackd whitvic serious / DIST=BINOMIAL;
RUN;
```

(Earlier releases of SAS require that the dependent variable be specified as DEATH/N, where N is a variable that is always equal to 1). Although PROC GENMOD doesn't need the DESCENDING option, it does require the DIST=BINOMIAL option (which can be abbreviated D=B) in the MODEL statement. This tells PROC GENMOD that the dependent variable is dichotomous with a binomial distribution. For dichotomous data, the default in GENMOD is to fit a logit model. In Section 3.10, we'll see how to use the LINK option to fit probit and complementary log-log models.

Results are shown in Output 2.3. The first section of the output, labeled "Model Information," is largely self-explanatory. The third section, "Analysis of Parameter Estimates," reports the same numbers we got with LOGISTIC. However, we don't get standardized estimates or odds ratios. This section also contains a line labeled SCALE, along with a note saying that "the scale parameter was held fixed." This information can be ignored for binary regression models unless you're working with grouped data and want to allow for something called *overdispersion* (see Section 4.6).

In the middle section of Output 2.3 under "Criteria for Assessing Goodness of Fit," we find the *deviance* and the Pearson chi-square. (For now, we can ignore the scaled versions of these statistics.) For individual-level data, the deviance is just –2 times the log-likelihood, which we also saw in the LOGISTIC output. In logit analysis, the deviance plays the same role as the residual sum of squares in linear regression analysis.

By adding $2k$ to the deviance (where k is the number of parameters), you can calculate the Akaike Information Criterion. Or by adding $k \log n$ to the deviance (n being the sample size), you get the BIC statistic. You can also use the *difference* in deviances for two *nested* models as a chi-square test for whether the simpler model is valid or not. We'll see many examples of this later on. What you *cannot* do (at least not legitimately) is treat the deviance itself as a goodness of fit chi-square statistic and compute a p-value for the model. That may be appropriate for grouped data (as we'll see in Chapter 4), but for individual-level data the deviance does *not* have a chi-square distribution. The Pearson chi square is even worse for individual-level data.

Output 2.3 *PROC GENMOD Output for Death Penalty Data*

```
                    The GENMOD Procedure

                     Model Information

          Description                 Value

          Data Set                    MY.JUDGE
          Distribution                BINOMIAL
          Link Function               LOGIT
          Dependent Variable          DEATH
          Observations Used           147
          Number Of Events            50
          Number Of Trials            147



            Criteria For Assessing Goodness Of Fit

     Criterion             DF        Value      Value/DF

     Deviance              143     176.2850       1.2328
     Scaled Deviance       143     176.2850       1.2328
     Pearson Chi-Square    143     149.5144       1.0456
     Scaled Pearson X2     143     149.5144       1.0456
     Log Likelihood          .     -88.1425          .



              Analysis Of Parameter Estimates

  Parameter    DF    Estimate    Std Err    ChiSquare  Pr>Chi

  INTERCEPT     1     -2.6516     0.6748     15.4424    0.0001
  BLACKD        1      0.5952     0.3939      2.2827    0.1308
  WHITVIC       1      0.2565     0.4002      0.4107    0.5216
  SERIOUS       1      0.1871     0.0612      9.3343    0.0022
  SCALE         0      1.0000     0.0000         .         .

  NOTE:  The scale parameter was held fixed.
```

Unlike PROC LOGISTIC, PROC GENMOD does not report a global test for the null hypothesis that all the coefficients are 0. The best way to get that statistic is to fit a model with no explanatory variables (MODEL death=/D=B;), sometimes called a *null* model. For this data, the deviance for the null model is 188.49. Taking the difference between 188.49 and 176.3 (the deviance for the model in Output 2.3), we get 12.2, which is the likelihood-ratio chi square reported by PROC LOGISTIC.

Now that you've seen the basic syntax and output for both the LOGISTIC and GENMOD procedures, you may well ask why we need GENMOD? After all, GENMOD doesn't produce some of the useful statistics reported by LOGISTIC. The answer is that GENMOD has several features that are absent in LOGISTIC—features that are extremely useful for some applications, especially the analysis of contingency tables. Here are some of GENMOD's features that I find particularly valuable:

CLASS variables. As with the GLM, LIFEREG, and PROBIT procedures, GENMOD has a CLASS statement that allows you to specify that a variable is to be treated as categorical (nominal). When a CLASS variable is included as an explanatory variable in the MODEL statement, GENMOD automatically creates a dummy variable for each distinct value of the original variable. To accomplish the same thing in LOGISTIC, you must create the dummy variables yourself in a DATA step.

Here's an example with the death-penalty data. The data set contains the variable CULP, which has the integer values 1 to 5 (5 denotes high culpability and 1 denotes low culpability, based on a large number of aggravating and mitigating circumstances defined by statute). Although we could treat this variable as an interval scale, we might prefer to treat it as a set of categories. To do this, we run the program

```
PROC GENMOD DATA=my.penalty;
  CLASS culp;
  MODEL death = blackd whitvic culp / D=B;
RUN;
```

which produces the results in Output 2.4.

Output 2.4 *Use of a CLASS Variable in PROC GENMOD*

Parameter		DF	Estimate	Std Err	ChiSquare	Pr>Chi
INTERCEPT		1	0.5533	0.7031	0.6193	0.4313
BLACKD		1	1.7246	0.6131	7.9141	0.0049
WHITVIC		1	0.8385	0.5694	2.1687	0.1408
CULP	1	1	-4.8670	0.8251	34.7926	0.0001
CULP	2	1	-3.0547	0.7754	15.5185	0.0001
CULP	3	1	-1.5294	0.8400	3.3153	0.0686
CULP	4	1	-0.3610	0.8857	0.1662	0.6835
CULP	5	0	0.0000	0.0000	.	.

Analysis Of Parameter Estimates

Because the variable CULP has 5 possible values, GENMOD has created four dummy variables, one for each of the values 1 through 4. As in other procedures that have CLASS variables, the default in GENMOD is to take the highest value as the omitted category. Thus, each of the four coefficients for CULP is a comparison between that particular value and the highest value. More specifically, each coefficient can be interpreted as the log-odds for that particular value of CULP minus the log-odds for CULP=5, controlling for other variables in the model. The pattern for the four coefficients is just what we'd expect. Defendants with CULP=1 are much less likely to get the death sentence than those with CULP=5. Each increase of CULP is associated with an increase in the probability of a death sentence. Note that when CULP is included in the model, the coefficient for BLACKD (black defendant) is much larger than it was in Output 2.3 and is now statistically significant.

Multiplicative terms in the MODEL statement. Regression analysts often want to build models that have *interactions* in which the effect of one variable depends on the level of another variable. The most popular way of doing this is to include a new explanatory variable in the model, one that is the product of the two original variables. With PROC LOGISTIC, you have to create the product variables in a DATA step. With PROC GENMOD, you just specify the product in the MODEL statement. For example, some criminologists have argued that black defendants who kill white victims may be especially likely to receive a death sentence. We can test that hypothesis for the New Jersey data with this program:

```
PROC GENMOD DATA=my.penalty;
  MODEL death = blackd whitvic culp blackd*whitvic / D=B;
RUN;
```

This produces the table in Output 2.5.

Output 2.5 *Multiplicative Variables in PROC GENMOD*

```
                Analysis Of Parameter Estimates

Parameter        DF    Estimate    Std Err   ChiSquare   Pr>Chi

INTERCEPT         1     -5.4047     1.1627     21.6073    0.0001
BLACKD            1      1.8723     1.0463      3.2021    0.0735
WHITVIC           1      1.0727     0.9877      1.1794    0.2775
CULP              1      1.2704     0.1968     41.6881    0.0001
BLACKD*WHITVIC    1     -0.3274     1.1782      0.0772    0.7811
SCALE             0      1.0000     0.0000         .         .
```

With a *p*-value of .78, the product term is clearly not significant and can be excluded from the model.

The product syntax in GENMOD also makes it easy to construct polynomial functions. For example, to estimate a *cubic* equation you can specify a model of the form

```
MODEL y = x x*x x*x*x / D=B;
```

This fits the model $\log(p/(1-p)) = \alpha + \beta_1 x + \beta_2 x^2 + \beta_3 x^3$.

Likelihood-ratio tests for individual coefficients. While PROC LOGISTIC reports a likelihood-ratio test for the null hypothesis that *all* coefficients are 0, the tests for the *individual* coefficients are Wald statistics. That's because Wald statistics are so easy to compute: just divide the coefficient by its estimated standard error and square the result. By contrast, to get likelihood ratio tests, you must refit the model multiple times, deleting each explanatory variable in turn. You then compute twice the positive difference between the log-likelihood for the full model and for each of the reduced models. Despite the greater computational burden, there is mounting evidence that likelihood ratio tests are superior (Hauck and Donner 1977, Jennings 1986), especially in small samples or samples with unusual data patterns, and many authorities express a strong preference for them (for example, Collett 1991).

As with PROC LOGISTIC, PROC GENMOD reports Wald statistics for the individual coefficients. But you can *also* get likelihood-ratio statistics by putting the TYPE3 option in the MODEL statement. For the model in Output 2.5, we can modify the MODEL statement to read

```
MODEL death = blackd whitvic culp blackd*whitvic / D=B TYPE3;
```

which produces the likelihood-ratio tests in Output 2.6. While similar to the Wald statistics, there are some noteworthy differences. In particular, the likelihood-ratio chi square for CULP is nearly twice as large as the Wald chi square.

Output 2.6 *Likelihood-ratio Tests in GENMOD*

```
LR Statistics For Type 3 Analysis

Source            DF    ChiSquare   Pr>Chi

BLACKD             1       3.6132    0.0573
WHITVIC            1       1.2385    0.2658
CULP               1      75.3762    0.0001
BLACKD*WHITVIC     1       0.0775    0.7807
```

The TYPE3 option does not produce likelihood-ratio tests for the individual coefficients of a CLASS variable. Instead, a single chi square for the entire set is reported, testing the null hypothesis that all the coefficients in the set are equal to 0. To get individual likelihood-ratio tests, use the CONTRAST statement described in Section 4.5.

Generalized Estimating Equations. With Release 6.12, GENMOD provides an optional estimation method—known as GEE—that's ideal for longitudinal and other *clustered data*. For conventional logit analysis, a crucial assumption is that observations are independent—the outcome for one observation is completely unrelated to the outcome for any other observation. But suppose you follow people over a period of time, measuring the same dichotomous variable at regular intervals. It's highly unlikely that a person's response at one point in time will be independent of earlier or later responses. Failure to take such correlations into account can lead to seriously biased standard errors and test statistics. The GEE method—invoked by using the REPEATED statement—solves these problems in a convenient, flexible way. We'll discuss this method in some detail in Chapter 8.

What the GENMOD procedure lacks. Despite these desirable features, GENMOD lacks some important capabilities of PROC LOGISTIC that prevent it from being the universal logit procedure in SAS. Most importantly, LOGISTIC has

- **The cumulative logit model.** LOGISTIC can estimate logit models where the dependent variable has more than two ordered categories. We'll discuss such models extensively in Chapter 6. This capability will be added to GENMOD in Version 7.

- **Influence statistics.** These statistics, discussed in Section 3.8, tell you how much the coefficients change with deletion of each case from the model fit. They can be very helpful in discovering problem observations.

- **Automated variable selection methods.** LOGISTIC has a variety of methods for selecting variables into a model from a pool of potential explanatory variables. But because I'm not a fan of such methods, I won't discuss them in this book.

2.9. Interpreting Coefficients

When logit analysis first became popular, a major complaint by those who resisted its advance was that the coefficients had no intuitive meaning. Admittedly, they're not as easy to interpret as coefficients in the linear probability model. For the linear probability model, a coefficient of .25 tells you that the predicted probability of the event increases by .25 for every 1-unit increase in the explanatory variable. By contrast, a logit coefficient of .25 tells you that the log-odds increases by .25 for every 1-unit increase in the explanatory variable. But who knows what a .25 increase in the log-odds means?

The basic problem is that the logit model assumes a nonlinear relationship between the probability and the explanatory variables, as shown in Figure 2.1. The change in the probability for a 1-unit increase in an independent variable varies according to where you start. Things become much simpler, however, if we think in terms of odds rather than probabilities.

In Output 2.7, we see the coefficients and associated statistics that were displayed in Output 2.2. The numbers in the "Parameter Estimate" column are the β's in the logit model. Except for their sign, they *are* hard to interpret. Let's look instead at the numbers in the

"Odds Ratio" column, which are obtained from the parameter estimates by computing e^{β}. These might be better described as *adjusted* odds ratios because they control for other variables in the model. Recall that BLACKD has a value of 1 for black defendants and 0 for everyone else. The odds ratio of 1.813 tells us that the predicted odds of a death sentence for black defendants are 1.813 times the odds for nonblack defendants. In other words, the odds of a death sentence for black defendants are 81% *higher* than the odds for other defendants. This compares with an *unadjusted* odds ratio of 1.47 found in Table 2.2.

Output 2.7 *Excerpt from Output 2.2*

```
              Analysis of Maximum Likelihood Estimates

              Parameter Standard    Wald      Pr >   Standardized  Odds
    Variable DF  Estimate   Error  Chi-Square Chi-Square  Estimate    Ratio

    INTERCPT 1    -2.6516   0.6748   15.4425    0.0001        .          .
    BLACKD   1     0.5952   0.3939    2.2827    0.1308     0.164628    1.813
    WHITVIC  1     0.2565   0.4002    0.4107    0.5216     0.069548    1.292
    SERIOUS  1     0.1871   0.0612    9.3343    0.0022     0.329478    1.206
```

For the dummy variable WHITVIC, which indicates white victim, the odds ratio is 1.292. This implies that the predicted odds of death are about 29% higher when the victim is white. Of course, the coefficient is far from statistically significant so we wouldn't want to put much confidence in this value. What about the coefficient for the variable SERIOUS? Remember that this variable is measured on a 15-point scale. For quantitative variables, it's helpful to subtract 1 from the odds ratio and multiply by 100 or, equivalently, take $100(e^{\beta}-1)$. This tells us the *percent change* in the odds for each 1-unit increase in the independent variable. In this case, we find that a 1-unit increase in the SERIOUS scale is associated with a 21% increase in the predicted odds of a death sentence.

With GENMOD, of course, you have to calculate the odds ratios yourself. Consider Output 2.4. There the coefficient for CULP 2 is –3.0547. Exponentiating this yields an odds ratio of .047. This means that the odds of a death sentence for someone at culpability level 2 are only about 5% of the odds for someone at culpability level 5, the omitted category. Equivalently, if we take 1/.047 = 21.3, we can say that the odds of a death sentence for someone at level 5 are about 21 times the odds for someone at level 2.

Interpretation of coefficients in terms of odds ratios is certainly the easiest way to approach the logit model. On the other hand, odds ratios can sometimes be misleading if the probabilities are near 1 or 0. Suppose that in a wealthy suburban high school, the probability of graduation is .99, which corresponds to odds of 99. When financial aid is increased for needy students, the probability of graduation goes up to .995, which implies odds of 199. Apparently, the odds of graduation have *doubled* under the new program even though only half a percent more students are graduating. Is this a meaningful increase? That depends on many nonstatistical issues.

For those who insist on interpreting logit models in terms of probabilities, there are several graphical and tabular methods available (Long 1996). Perhaps the simplest approach is to make use of equation (2.6):

$$\frac{\partial p_i}{\partial x_i} = \beta p_i (1 - p_i).$$

This equation says that the change in the probability for a 1-unit increase in x depends on the logit regression coefficient for x, as well as on the value of the probability itself. For this to be practically useful, we need to know what probability we are starting from. If we have to choose one value, the most natural is the overall proportion of cases that have the event. In our example, 50 out of 147 defendants got the death penalty, so the overall proportion is .34. Taking .34 times 1–.34, we get .244. We can multiply each of the coefficients in Output 2.7 by .244, and we get:

BLACKD	.133
WHITVIC	.057
SERIOUS	.046

We can then say that, on the average, the probability of a death sentence is .133 higher if the defendant is black compared with nonblacks, .057 higher if the victim is white compared with nonwhites, and .046 higher for a 1-unit increase on the SERIOUS scale. Of course, these numbers only give a rough indication of what actually happens for a given change in the x variable. Note, however, that they are very similar to the coefficients obtained with the OLS regression in Output 2.1.

Chapter 3

Binary Logit Analysis: Details and Options

3.1   Introduction

In this chapter, we continue with the binary logit model and its implementation in
LOGISTIC and GENMOD. We'll examine several optional features of these procedures,
consider some potential problems that might arise, and pursue the details of the estimation
process in greater depth. You might get by without this chapter, but you'd miss some useful
and enlightening stuff.

3.2   Confidence Intervals

It's standard practice in social science journals to report only *point estimates* and hypothesis
tests for the coefficients. Most statisticians, on the other hand, hold that *confidence intervals*
give a better picture of the sampling variability in the estimates.

Conventional confidence intervals for logit regression coefficients are easily computed by hand. For an approximate 95% confidence interval around a coefficient, simply add and subtract the standard error multiplied by 1.96 (2.00 is close enough for most purposes). But you can save yourself the trouble by asking LOGISTIC or GENMOD to do it for you. In LOGISTIC, the option in the MODEL statement for conventional (Wald) confidence intervals is CLPARM=WALD. In GENMOD, the corresponding MODEL option is WALDCI. The default is a 95% confidence interval. To change that to a 90% interval, put the option ALPHA=.10 in the MODEL statement.

There's another method, called *profile likelihood confidence intervals*, that may produce better approximations, especially in smaller samples. This method involves an iterative evaluation of the likelihood function and produces intervals that are not generally symmetric around the coefficient estimate. GENMOD computes profile likelihood confidence intervals with the MODEL option LRCI (likelihood ratio confidence intervals). In LOGISTIC, the model option is CLPARM=PL (for profile likelihood). The profile likelihood method is computationally intensive so you may want to use it sparingly for large samples.

Here's an example of both kinds of confidence intervals using LOGISTIC with the death-penalty data set:

```
PROC LOGISTIC DATA=my.penalty DES;
  MODEL death = blackd whitvic culp / CLPARM=BOTH;
RUN;
```

Besides the usual results, we get the numbers shown in Output 3.1. The intervals produced by the two methods are very similar but not identical.

Output 3.1   *Confidence Intervals Produced by LOGISTIC*

```
Parameter Estimates and 95% Confidence
Intervals

                                      Wald
                                Confidence Limits
                 Parameter
Variable         Estimate        Lower        Upper

INTERCPT          -5.2182       -7.0407      -3.3957
BLACKD             1.6360        0.4689       2.8031
WHITVIC            0.8477       -0.2427       1.9381
CULP               1.2709        0.8863       1.6555


                                Profile Likelihood
                                Confidence Limits
                 Parameter
Variable         Estimate        Lower        Upper

INTERCPT          -5.2182       -7.2485      -3.5710
BLACKD             1.6360        0.5289       2.8890
WHITVIC            0.8477       -0.2190       1.9811
CULP               1.2709        0.9187       1.6953
```

The output from GENMOD is sufficiently different that it's worth examining as well. The program is:

```
PROC GENMOD DATA=my.penalty;
  MODEL death = blackd whitvic culp / D=B WALDCI LRCI;
RUN;
```

In the top half of Output 3.2, we see the Wald confidence intervals, labeled "Normal" because they are based on the normal distribution. Unfortunately, variable names aren't given so you have to remember that PRM1 (parameter 1) is the intercept, PRM2 is the coefficient for BLACKD, and so on.

In the lower portion of the output, we find the profile likelihood results. The first column of numbers is the one to pay attention to. The remaining columns can usually be ignored, but here's a brief explanation. When GENMOD is evaluating the profile likelihood function, it varies not only the parameter of interest but also the other parameters in the model. The additional columns tell us what values the other parameters took on when the parameter of interest was at its lower (or upper) limit.

Output 3.2   *Confidence Intervals Produced by GENMOD*

```
                  Normal Confidence Intervals For Parameters

                  Two-Sided Confidence Coefficient: 0.9500
                  Parameter        Confidence Limits


                  PRM1           Lower          -7.0408
                  PRM1           Upper          -3.3956
                  PRM2           Lower           0.4689
                  PRM2           Upper           2.8031
                  PRM3           Lower          -0.2427
                  PRM3           Upper           1.9381
                  PRM4           Lower           0.8863
                  PRM4           Upper           1.6555



          Likelihood Ratio Based Confidence Intervals For Parameters

                  Two-Sided Confidence Coefficient: 0.9500
    Param      Confidence Limits            Parameter Values
                                    PRM1      PRM2      PRM3      PRM4


    PRM1   Lower    -7.2485      -7.2485    2.6226    1.5941    1.6140
    PRM1   Upper    -3.5710      -3.5710    0.8248    0.1857    1.0038
    PRM2   Lower     0.5289      -4.0304    0.5289    0.4032    1.1420
    PRM2   Upper     2.8890      -6.8385    2.8890    1.3096    1.5126
    PRM3   Lower    -0.2190      -4.2409    1.1922   -0.2190    1.2389
    PRM3   Upper     1.9811      -6.6011    2.1640    1.9811    1.4047
    PRM4   Lower     0.9187      -3.9489    1.1767    0.6457    0.9187
    PRM4   Upper     1.6953      -6.8361    2.3064    1.1261    1.6953
```

We've seen how to get confidence intervals for the β parameters in a logistic regression. What about confidence intervals for the odds ratios? LOGISTIC can compute them for you. In the MODEL statement, the CLODDS=WALD option requests the conventional Wald confidence intervals, and the CLODDS=PL option requests the profile likelihood intervals. Output 3.3 shows the results for the model just estimated. The "Unit" column indicates how much each independent variable is incremented to produce the estimated odds ratio. The default is 1 unit. For the variable CULP, each 1-point increase on the culpability scale multiplies the odds of a death sentence by 3.564.

Output 3.3   *Odds Ratio Confidence Intervals in LOGISTIC*

```
 Conditional Odds Ratios and 95% Confidence Intervals

                                     Profile Likelihood
                                      Confidence Limits
                            Odds
 Variable       Unit        Ratio      Lower       Upper

 BLACKD         1.0000      5.135      1.697      17.976
 WHITVIC        1.0000      2.334      0.803       7.251
 CULP           1.0000      3.564      2.506       5.448


 Conditional Odds Ratios and 95% Confidence Intervals

                                            Wald
                                      Confidence Limits
                            Odds
 Variable       Unit        Ratio      Lower       Upper

 BLACKD         1.0000      5.135      1.598      16.495
 WHITVIC        1.0000      2.334      0.784       6.945
 CULP           1.0000      3.564      2.426       5.236
```

If you want odds ratios for different increments, you can easily calculate them by hand. If O is the odds ratio for a 1-unit increment, O^k is the odds ratio for a k-unit increment. If that's too much trouble, you can use the UNITS statement to produce "customized" odds ratios. For example, to get the odds ratio for a 2-unit increase in CULP, include the following statement in the LOGISTIC procedure:

```
UNITS culp=2 / DEFAULT=1;
```

The DEFAULT option tells SAS to print odds ratios and their confidence intervals for a one-unit increase in each of the other variables in the model.

Because GENMOD doesn't compute odds ratios, it won't produce confidence intervals for them. However, they're easy to get with a hand calculator. The first step is to get confidence intervals for the original parameters. Let β be a parameter estimate, and let U and L be the upper and lower confidence limits for this parameter. The odds ratio estimate is e^{β}. The upper and lower odds ratio limits are e^{U} and e^{L}. This works for either conventional confidence intervals or profile likelihood confidence intervals. If you want confidence intervals for the transformation $100(e^\beta - 1)$, discussed in Section 2.9, just substitute the upper and lower limits for β in this formula.

3.3 Details of Maximum Likelihood Estimation

In Section 2.6, I discussed some general properties of maximum likelihood estimators. Here, we consider the details of the construction and maximization of the likelihood function. Although this section can be skipped without loss of continuity, I strongly encourage you to work through it to the best of your ability. A basic understanding of maximum likelihood for the logit model can help to remove much of the mystery of the technique. It can also help you understand how and why things sometimes go wrong.

Let's start with some notation and assumptions. We have data for n individuals ($i=1,....,n$) who are assumed to be statistically independent. For each individual i, the data consists of y_i and $\mathbf{x}_i$, where y_i is a random variable with possible values of 0 and 1, and $\mathbf{x}_i = [1\ x_{i1}\ ...\ x_{ik}]'$ is a vector of explanatory variables (the 1 is for the intercept). Vector notation is helpful here, otherwise the equations get messy. For simplicity, we treat $\mathbf{x}_i$ as a set of fixed constants for each individual rather than as random variables. (We could get equivalent results with $\mathbf{x}_i$ treated as random and y_i expressed conditional on the values of $\mathbf{x}_i$, but that would just complicate the notation.)

Letting p_i be the probability that $y_i=1$, we assume that the data is generated by a logit model, which says that

$$p_i = \frac{1}{1 + e^{-\beta \mathbf{x}_i}}\ , \tag{3.1}$$

which is equivalent to equation (2.5).

We now construct the likelihood function, which expresses the probability of observing the data in hand as a function of the unknown parameters. The likelihood of observing the values of y for all the observations can be written as

$$L = \Pr(y_1, y_{2,}..., y_n).$$

Because we are assuming that observations are independent, the overall probability of observing all the y_i's can be factored into the product of the individual probabilities:

$$L = \Pr(y_1)\Pr(y_2)...\Pr(y_n) = \prod_{i=1}^{n} \Pr(y_i), \tag{3.2}$$

where Π indicates repeated multiplication.

By definition, $\Pr(y_i=1)=p_i$ and $\Pr(y_i=0)=1-p_i$. That implies that we can write

$$\Pr(y_i) = p_i^{y_i}(1-p_i)^{1-y_i}. \tag{3.3}$$

In this equation, y_i acts like a switch, turning parts of the equation on or off. When $y_i=1$, p_i raised to the y_i power is just p_i. But $1-y_i$ is then 0, and $(1-p_i)$ raised to the 0 power is 1. Things are reversed when $y_i=0$. Substituting equation (3.3) into equation (3.2) and doing a little algebra yields

$$L = \prod_{i=1}^{n} p_i^{y_i}(1-p_i)^{1-y_i} = \prod_{i=1}^{n} \left(\frac{p_i}{1-p_i}\right)^{y_i}(1-p_i).$$

At this point we take the logarithm of both sides of the equation to get

$$\log L = \sum_i y_i \log\left(\frac{p_i}{1-p_i}\right) + \sum_i \log(1-p_i). \tag{3.4}$$

It is generally easier to work with the logarithm of the likelihood function because products get converted into sums and exponents become coefficients. Because the logarithm is an increasing function, whatever maximizes the logarithm will also maximize the original function.

Substituting our expression for the logit model (equation 3.1) into equation (3.4), we get

$$\log L = \sum_i \beta x_i y_i - \sum_i \log(1+e^{\beta x_i}), \tag{3.5}$$

which is about as far as we can go in simplifying the likelihood function.

This brings us to step 2, choosing values of β that make equation (3.5) as large as possible. There are many different methods for maximizing functions like this. One well-known approach is to find the derivative of the function with respect to β, set the derivative equal to 0, and then solve for $\boldsymbol{\beta}$. Taking the derivative of equation (3.5) and setting it equal to 0 gives us:

$$\frac{\partial \log L}{\partial \boldsymbol{\beta}} = \sum_i \mathbf{x}_i y_i - \sum_i \mathbf{x}_i (1 + e^{-\boldsymbol{\beta} \mathbf{x}_i})^{-1}$$

$$= \sum_i \mathbf{x}_i y_i - \sum_i \mathbf{x}_i \hat{y}_i = 0 \tag{3.6}$$

where

$$\hat{y}_i = \frac{1}{1 + e^{-\boldsymbol{\beta} \mathbf{x}_i}},$$

the predicted probability of y for a given value of $\mathbf{x}_i$. Because $\mathbf{x}_i$ is a vector, equation (3.6) is actually a system of $k+1$ equations, one for each element of $\boldsymbol{\beta}$.

Those familiar with OLS theory may recognize the second line of equation (3.6) as identical to the *normal equations* for the linear model. The difference is that $\hat{y}$ is a linear function of $\boldsymbol{\beta}$ in the linear model but a nonlinear function of $\boldsymbol{\beta}$ in the logit model. Consequently, except in special cases like a single dichotomous x variable, there is no explicit solution to equation (3.6). Instead, we must rely on iterative methods, which amount to successive approximations to the solution until the approximations "converge" to the correct value. Again, there are many different methods for doing this. All give the same solution, but they differ in such factors as speed of convergence, sensitivity to starting values, and computational difficulty at each iteration.

One of the most widely-used iterative methods is the Newton-Raphson algorithm, which can be described as follows: Let $\mathbf{U}(\boldsymbol{\beta})$ be the vector of first derivatives of $\log L$ with respect to $\boldsymbol{\beta}$ and let $\mathbf{I}(\boldsymbol{\beta})$ be the matrix of second derivatives of $\log L$ with respect to $\boldsymbol{\beta}$. That is,

$$\mathbf{U}(\boldsymbol{\beta}) = \frac{\partial \log L}{\partial \boldsymbol{\beta}} = \sum_i \mathbf{x}_i y_i - \sum_i \mathbf{x}_i \hat{y}_i$$

$$\mathbf{I}(\boldsymbol{\beta}) = \frac{\partial^2 \log L}{\partial \boldsymbol{\beta} \partial \boldsymbol{\beta}'} = -\sum_i \mathbf{x}_i \mathbf{x}_i' \, \hat{y}_i (1 - \hat{y}_i)$$

The vector of first derivatives $\mathbf{U}(\boldsymbol{\beta})$ is sometimes called the *gradient* or *score*. The matrix of second derivatives $\mathbf{I}(\boldsymbol{\beta})$ is called the *Hessian*. The Newton-Raphson algorithm is then

$$\boldsymbol{\beta}_{j+1} = \boldsymbol{\beta}_j - \mathbf{I}^{-1}(\boldsymbol{\beta}_j) \mathbf{U}(\boldsymbol{\beta}_j) \tag{3.7}$$

where $\mathbf{I}^{-1}$ is the inverse of $\mathbf{I}$. In practice, we need a set of starting values $\boldsymbol{\beta}_0$, which GENMOD gets with a variation of least squares. LOGISTIC simply starts with all coefficients equal to 0. These starting values are substituted into the right-hand side of equation (3.7), which yields the result for the first iteration, $\boldsymbol{\beta}_1$. These values are then substituted back into the right-hand side, the first and second derivatives are recomputed, and the result is $\boldsymbol{\beta}_2$. This process is repeated until the maximum change in each parameter estimate from one step to the next is less than some criterion. If the absolute value of the current parameter estimate β_j is less than or equal to .01, the default criterion for convergence is

$$\left| \beta_{j+1} - \beta_j \right| < .0001$$

If the current parameter estimate is greater than .01 (in absolute value), the default criterion is

$$\left| \frac{\beta_{j+1} - \beta_j}{\beta_j} \right| < .0001$$

After the solution $\hat{\boldsymbol{\beta}}$ is found, a byproduct of the Newton-Raphson algorithm is an estimate of the covariance matrix of the coefficients, which is just $-\mathbf{I}^{-1}(\hat{\boldsymbol{\beta}})$. This matrix, which can be printed by putting COVB as an option in the MODEL statement (for either GENMOD or LOGISTIC), is often useful for constructing hypothesis tests about linear combinations of coefficients. Estimates of the standard errors of the coefficients are obtained by taking the square roots of the main diagonal elements of this matrix.

3.4 Convergence Problems

As explained in the previous section, maximum likelihood estimation of the logit model is an iterative process of successive approximations. When the change in the coefficient estimates from one iteration to the next is very small, the computations stop and the algorithm is said to have converged. Usually this process goes smoothly with no special attention needed. However, sometimes the iterative process breaks down so that convergence is not achieved. Dealing with convergence failures can be one of the more frustrating problems encountered by users of logit regression.

LOGISTIC has a default limit of 25 iterations and GENMOD has a default limit of 50. If the algorithm hasn't converged by this limit, both procedures give a warning message and print out the results at the last iteration. While it's possible to raise the iteration limit (with the MAXITER= option in the MODEL statement), this rarely solves the problem. Models that haven't converged in 25 iterations will usually never converge.

In most cases of convergence failure, the maximum likelihood estimates simply don't exist. Consider the following SAS program, which inputs six observations on *x* and *y* and then performs a logit regression of *y* on *x*:

```
DATA compsep;
  INPUT x y;
  DATALINES;
1 0
2 0
3 0
4 1
5 1
6 1
;
PROC LOGISTIC DES;
  MODEL y = x;
RUN;
```

LOGISTIC doesn't produce any estimates in this case. Instead, it simply prints the message

```
WARNING: There is a complete separation in the sample points. The
maximum likelihood estimate does not exist.
```

Complete separation means that there is some linear combination of the explanatory variables that perfectly predicts the dependent variable. In this example, whenever *x* is greater than 3.5, *y* is equal to 1. Whenever *x* is less than 3.5, *y* is equal to 0. If you examine the iteration process for this data (which you can do by putting the ITPRINT option in the MODEL statement), you'll find that the coefficient for *x* gets larger at every iteration. In effect, the maximum likelihood coefficient for *x* is infinite.

GENMOD isn't quite so informative. If you run the program,

```
PROC GENMOD DATA=compsep;
 MODEL y = x / D=B;
RUN;
```

you get the results shown in Output 3.4. Although no warning message is given, there are three indications that something is wrong:

- The log-likelihood and deviance are 0, even though there are 4 degrees of freedom.
- The coefficient for *x* is very large.
- Its standard error is humongous.

Output 3.4   *GENMOD Results for Data with Complete Separation*

```
Criteria For Assessing Goodness Of Fit

   Criterion              DF        Value        Value/DF

   Deviance                4       0.0000         0.0000
   Scaled Deviance         4       0.0000         0.0000
   Pearson Chi-Square      4       0.0000         0.0000
   Scaled Pearson X2       4       0.0000         0.0000
   Log Likelihood          .       0.0000             .


Analysis Of Parameter Estimates

Parameter    DF    Estimate     Std Err    ChiSquare   Pr>Chi

INTERCEPT     1    -265.6316   905480840     0.0000    1.0000
X             1      76.0588   277001554     0.0000    1.0000
```

More common than complete separation is something called *quasi-complete separation*. We can illustrate this by adding a single observation to the previous data set.

```
DATA quasisep;
   INPUT x y;
   DATALINES;
1 0
2 0
3 0
4 0
4 1
5 1
6 1
;
PROC LOGISTIC DES;
   MODEL y = x;
```

```
PROC GENMOD;
   MODEL y = x /D=B;
RUN;
```

The only difference between this and the earlier example is that when *x*=4, there is one observation that has *y*=0 and another observation that has *y*=1. In general, quasi-complete separation occurs whenever there is complete separation except for a single value of the predictor for which both values of the dependent variable occur.

For this example, LOGISTIC prints the message

```
WARNING: There is possibly a quasicomplete separation in the sample
points. The maximum likelihood estimate may not exist.
WARNING: The LOGISTIC procedure continues in spite of the above
warning. Results shown are based on the last maximum likelihood
iteration. Validity of the model fit is questionable.
```

Numerical results shown in Output 3.5 show a very large coefficient and an extremely large standard error.

Output 3.5   *LOGISTIC Results under Quasi-Complete Separation*

```
WARNING: The validity of the model fit is questionable.

              Analysis of Maximum Likelihood Estimates

              Parameter Standard    Wald       Pr >     Standardized     Odds
Variable DF   Estimate   Error  Chi-Square Chi-Square    Estimate       Ratio

INTERCPT 1    -33.2785   181.1    0.0337     0.8542         .             .
X        1      8.3196  45.2858   0.0338     0.8542      7.881348     999.000
```

GENMOD prints the following warning messages *in the LOG file, not the OUTPUT file:*

```
WARNING: The negative of the Hessian is not positive definite. The
convergence is questionable.
WARNING: The procedure is continuing but the validity of the model
fit is questionable.
WARNING: The specified model did not converge.
```

GENMOD also produces the statistics shown in Output 3.6. Unlike complete separation, we now get nonzero values for the deviance and log likelihood. The parameter estimate is again very large, but the standard error is reported as 0 and chi-square and *p*-values are not reported. As with complete separation, the true maximum likelihood estimate for the coefficient of *x* is infinite.

Output 3.6   *GENMOD Results under Quasi-Complete Separation*

```
              Criteria For Assessing Goodness Of Fit

        Criterion            DF        Value      Value/DF

        Deviance              5        2.7726       0.5545
        Scaled Deviance       5        2.7726       0.5545
        Pearson Chi-Square    5        2.0000       0.4000
        Scaled Pearson X2     5        2.0000       0.4000
        Log Likelihood        .       -1.3863         .

               Analysis Of Parameter Estimates

   Parameter   DF     Estimate     Std Err   ChiSquare  Pr>Chi

   INTERCEPT    1    -109.7190      1.4142   6019.1312  0.0001
   X            0      27.4298      0.0000       .         .
```

In my experience, the most common cause of quasi-complete separation is a dummy independent variable that has the following property: at one level of the dummy variable either every case has a 1 on the dependent variable or every case has a 0. To illustrate this, let's restrict the sample of death penalty cases to those with nonblack defendants. Then, using GENMOD, we'll fit a model with two independent variables, CULP and SERIOUS. We'll treat CULP as a categorical independent variable (with 5 categories) by putting it in a CLASS statement:

```
PROC GENMOD DATA=my.penalty;
  WHERE blackd=0;
  CLASS culp;
  MODEL death = culp serious / D=B TYPE3;
RUN;
```

GENMOD sets up four dummy variables corresponding to the first four categories of CULP. Parameter estimates and associated statistics are shown in Output 3.7.

Output 3.7   *GENMOD Estimates for Nonblack Defendants Only*

```
              Analysis Of Parameter Estimates

   Parameter       DF    Estimate     Std Err   ChiSquare  Pr>Chi

   INTERCEPT        1      3.1273      1.7545     3.1772   0.0747
   CULP     1       1    -29.4757  157276.996     0.0000   0.9999
   CULP     2       1     -3.8366      1.2267     9.7819   0.0018
   CULP     3       1     -0.7645      1.1312     0.4568   0.4991
   CULP     4       1     -0.9595      1.0587     0.8213   0.3648
   CULP     5       0      0.0000      0.0000       .        .
   SERIOUS          1     -0.1693      0.1385     1.4950   0.2214
```

Unlike the previous example, GENMOD gives no warning messages about convergence. Nevertheless, Output 3.7 contains the telltale signs of quasi-complete separation: the estimate for CULP 1 is very large in magnitude, and the standard error is extremely large. To see the cause, take a look at Table 3.1, which shows the cross-classification of DEATH by CULP for the 74 nonblack defendants. Quasi-complete separation occurs because all 30 defendants at level 1 of CULP got life sentences.

Table 3.1   *Cross-Classification of Death Penalty by Culpability, Nonblack Defendants*

	DEATH		
CULP	0	1	Total
1	30	0	30
2	14	2	16
3	2	4	6
4	3	6	9
5	3	10	13
Total	52	22	74

What can you do about complete or quasi-complete separation? The first task is to figure out which variable (or variables) is causing the problem. As we've seen, they're likely to be the variables with large coefficients and even larger standard errors. To be sure of which variables are causing the problem, you should delete individual variables or sets of variables from the model until you make the problem go away. It's also very helpful to look at cross-classifications of any categorical independent variables with the dependent variable, as we did in Table 3.1. If you find a cell frequency of 0 in any of these tables, you've pinpointed a cause of quasi-complete separation.

After you've found the problem variables, what do you do about them? The answer depends on whether you have complete or quasi-complete separation. If separation is complete, there's no way to get estimates for the coefficients of the other variables as long as the problem variables are in the model. Because the problem variables completely account for the variation in the dependent variable, nothing is left for additional variables to explain. On the other hand, excluding the problem variables from the model isn't very appealing either. The reason they're problematic is that they're *too good* at predicting the dependent variable. Leaving out the strongest predictors can misleadingly suggest that they are unimportant and can also bias the coefficients for remaining variables. If you decide to present results for a model without the problem variables, you should also report that the problem variables perfectly predicted the dependent variable.

If the problem is *quasi*-complete separation, there are additional options to consider:

Recode the problem variables. Consider the model that has quasi-complete separation as shown in Output 3.7. The problem occurred because all persons with CULP=1 got life sentences. One way to eliminate this problem is to take CULP out of the CLASS statement and treat it as a quantitative variable. Of course, this assumes that the effect of CULP is linear, an assumption that may be too restrictive for the data. Another method is to collapse categories 1 and 2 of CULP so that the combined category has 2 death sentences and 44 life sentences:

```
DATA;
   SET my.penalty;
   IF culp=1 THEN culp=2;
PROC GENMOD;
   WHERE blackd=0;
   CLASS culp;
   MODEL death=culp serious /D=B;
RUN;
```

This produced the results shown in Output 3.8.

Output 3.8   *Collapsing Categories to Eliminate Quasi-Complete Separation*

Parameter		DF	Estimate	Std Err	ChiSquare	Pr>Chi
INTERCEPT		1	2.7033	1.6868	2.5682	0.1090
CULP	2	1	-4.9386	1.2423	15.8037	0.0001
CULP	3	1	-0.7032	1.1205	0.3939	0.5303
CULP	4	1	-0.8606	1.0452	0.6781	0.4103
CULP	5	0	0.0000	0.0000	.	.
SERIOUS		1	-0.1329	0.1340	0.9831	0.3214

Exclude cases from the model. When there is quasi-complete separation, we know that the model perfectly predicts the outcome for some subset of the cases. For example, we just saw that when CULP=1, everyone gets a life sentence. For those individuals, there's nothing left for the other variables to explain, so we might as well restrict the analysis to those cases where CULP > 1. For example,

```
PROC GENMOD DATA=my.penalty;
   WHERE blackd=0 AND culp > 1;
   CLASS culp;
   MODEL death=culp serious /D=B;
RUN;
```

Results are shown in Output 3.9. If you take the approach of excluding cases, you should also report the cross-tabulation of the problem variable with the dependent variable, along with an appropriate test of significance (for example, the Pearson chi-square test for independence).

Output 3.9   *Excluding Cases to Eliminate Quasi-Complete Separation*

Parameter		DF	Estimate	Std Err	ChiSquare	Pr>Chi
INTERCEPT		1	3.1273	1.7545	3.1772	0.0747
CULP	2	1	-3.8366	1.2267	9.7819	0.0018
CULP	3	1	-0.7645	1.1312	0.4568	0.4991
CULP	4	1	-0.9595	1.0587	0.8213	0.3648
CULP	5	0	0.0000	0.0000	.	.
SERIOUS		1	-0.1693	0.1385	1.4950	0.2214

Retain the model with quasi-complete separation but use likelihood-ratio tests. A third option is to stick with the GENMOD model that produced quasi-complete separation. This model controls for the variable that produced the problem, and there is no reason to be suspicious of the results for the *other* variables. As a matter of fact, the results for the SERIOUS variable are identical in Output 3.9, which excluded cases and in Output 3.7, which yielded quasi-complete separation. Of course, the coefficient for CULP 1 in Output 3.7 is useless; in research reports, I suggest listing it as ∞. The reported standard error and Wald chi-square for this variable are also useless. Nevertheless, we can still get valid likelihood-ratio tests. (This is one instance where likelihood-ratio tests are far superior to Wald tests). As previously noted, the TYPE3 option in the MODEL statement produces likelihood-ratio statistics. For the model in Output 3.7, the likelihood-ratio statistics are shown in Output 3.10.

Output 3.10   *Likelihood-Ratio Statistics for Model in Output 3.7*

```
LR Statistics For Type 3 Analysis

Source         DF    ChiSquare   Pr>Chi

CULP            4      41.8937    0.0001
SERIOUS         1       1.5984    0.2061
```

For CLASS variables like CULP, the TYPE3 option reports only a global test for the null hypothesis that all the coefficients for CULP are 0 (including the problematic coefficient for CULP 1). To get a likelihood-ratio test for the hypothesis that the CULP 1 coefficient is 0, we can use a CONTRAST statement in GENMOD. The full program is:

```
PROC GENMOD DATA=my.penalty;
   WHERE blackd=0;
   CLASS culp;
   MODEL death=culp serious /D=B;
   CONTRAST 'culp1 v. culp5' CULP 1 0 0 0 -1;
RUN;
```

The CONTRAST statement (described more fully in Section 4.5) must have a user-specified label that is enclosed within single quotes. The name of the CLASS variable is then followed by a set of numbers, one for each level of the variable. These numbers must sum to 0. In this case, putting a 1 for level 1 and a −1 for level 5 tells GENMOD to test for a difference between level 1 and level 5. The result is a likelihood ratio chi-square of 30.

Estimate the model with LogXact. While I'm reluctant to admit that you can't do everything with SAS, there's a specialized program for logistic regression that has no real competitors. Called LogXact (www.cytel.com), the program does two things that, to my knowledge, are not available in any other commercial software:

- It produces *exact p*-values and confidence intervals for logit regression models by a method that generalizes Fisher's exact test.
- It can produce parameter estimates (not maximum likelihood) for variables that induce quasi-complete separation.

The algorithm is very computationally intensive, and it only works for relatively small data sets that have extreme splits on the dependent variable. Fortunately, these are just the situations in which quasi-complete separation is likely to occur and the usual asymptotic approximations are poor.

3.5 Multicollinearity

One of the nice things about logit analysis is that it's so much like ordinary linear regression analysis. Unfortunately, some of the less pleasant features of linear regression analysis also carry over to logit analysis. One of these is multicollinearity, which occurs when there are strong linear dependencies among the explanatory variables.

For the most part, everything you know about multicollinearity for ordinary regression also applies to logit regression. The basic point is that, if two or more variables are highly correlated with one another, it's hard to get good estimates of their distinct effects on some dependent variable. Although multicollinearity doesn't bias the coefficients, it does make them more unstable. Standard errors may get large, and variables that appear to have weak effects, individually, may actually have quite strong effects as a group. Fortunately, the consequences of multicollinearity only apply to those variables in a model that are collinear.

How do you diagnose multicollinearity? Examining the correlation matrix produced by PROC CORR may be helpful but is not sufficient. It's quite possible to have data in which no pair of variables has a high correlation, but several variables together may be highly interdependent. Much better diagnostics are produced by PROC REG with the options TOL, VIF, and COLLINOINT. But PROC LOGISTIC and PROC GENMOD don't have these options, so what can you do? The thing to remember is that multicollinearity is a property of the explanatory variables, not the dependent variable. So whenever you suspect multicollinearity in a logit model, just estimate the equivalent model in PROC REG and specify the collinearity options.

Here's an example using the death-penalty data. There are actually two versions of
the SERIOUS variable used for the logit model shown in Output 2.2. SERIOUS1 (the one
used before) is based on rankings of death penalty cases and SERIOUS2 is based on a 5-
point rating scale. They have a correlation of .92. Obviously, no sensible person would put
both these variables in the same model, but let's see what happens if we do. Output 3.11
shows the results from fitting the model with LOGISTIC. None of the variables is
statistically significant even though SERIOUS1 was highly significant in Output 2.2. On the
other hand, the global chi-square of 12.76 is significant at nearly the .01 level. When none of
the individual variables is significant but the entire set is significant, multicollinearity is a
likely culprit.

Output 3.11   *Model with Highly Correlated Explanatory Variables*

```
        Model Fitting Information and Testing Global Null Hypothesis BETA=0

                                  Intercept
                      Intercept     and
       Criterion        Only     Covariates    Chi-Square for Covariates

       AIC            190.491     185.732           .
       SC             193.481     200.684           .
       -2 LOG L       188.491     175.732       12.759 with 4 DF (p=0.0125)
       Score             .           .          12.063 with 4 DF (p=0.0169)


                    Analysis of Maximum Likelihood Estimates

                   Parameter Standard    Wald       Pr >      Standardized  Odds
        Variable DF Estimate   Error  Chi-Square Chi-Square     Estimate    Ratio

        INTERCPT 1  -3.1684   0.9867   10.3117     0.0013          .          .
        BLACKD   1   0.5854   0.3942    2.2054     0.1375       0.161921    1.796
        WHITVIC  1   0.2842   0.4029    0.4978     0.4805       0.077078    1.329
        SERIOUS1 1   0.0818   0.1532    0.2852     0.5933       0.144152    1.085
        SERIOUS2 1   0.3967   0.5347    0.5503     0.4582       0.204835    1.487
```

Let's check it out with PROC REG:

```
PROC REG DATA=my.penalty;
   MODEL death = blackd whitvic serious1 serious2 / TOL VIF;
RUN;
```

Output 3.12 gives the collinearity diagnostics. (There's little point in looking at the coefficients and test statistics because that's not the point of this analysis). The tolerance is computed by regressing each variable on all the other explanatory variables, calculating the R^2, then subtracting that from 1. Low tolerances correspond to high multicollinearity. While there's no strict cutoff, I begin to get concerned when I see tolerances below .40. Here we find high tolerances for BLACKD and WHITVIC, but very low tolerances for the two versions of the SERIOUS variable. The variance inflation factor is simply the reciprocal of the tolerance. It tells you how "inflated" the variance of the coefficient is, compared to what it would be if the variable were uncorrelated with any other variable in the model. We see, for example, that the variance of the SERIOUS1 coefficient is 7 times what it would be in the absence of collinearity, implying that its standard error is $\sqrt{7}=2.6$ times as large.

Output 3.12   *Multicollinearity Diagnostics Obtained from PROC REG*

```
                                 Variance
   Variable  DF    Tolerance    Inflation

   INTERCEP   1       .         0.00000000
   BLACKD     1    0.85427957   1.17057698
   WHITVIC    1    0.84547793   1.18276298
   SERIOUS1   1    0.14290048   6.99787696
   SERIOUS2   1    0.14386813   6.95080953
```

This approach to diagnosis should be entirely satisfactory in the vast majority of cases, but occasionally it can miss serious multicollinearity (Davis et al. 1986). That's because the linear combinations should actually be adjusted by the weight matrix used in the maximum likelihood algorithm. If you really want to do it right, here's how:

```
PROC LOGISTIC DES DATA=my.penalty;
   MODEL death = blackd whitvic serious1 serious2;
   OUTPUT OUT=a PRED=phat;
DATA b;
   SET a;
   w = phat*(1-phat);
PROC REG DATA=b;
   WEIGHT w;
   MODEL death = blackd whitvic serious1 serious2 / TOL VIF;
RUN;
```

The OUTPUT statement in LOGISTIC creates a new data set that contains all the variables in the MODEL statement plus the variable PHAT that contains the predicted probabilities of the dependent variable. These predicted values are then used in a DATA step to construct the weight variable W. Finally, a weighted least squares regression is performed, using W as the weight variable. For these data, the collinearity diagnostics were only trivially different from those shown in Output 3.12, so I won't bother displaying them.

Diagnosis of multicollinearity is easy. The big problem is what to do about it. The range of solutions available for logit regression is pretty much the same as for linear regression, such as dropping variables, combining variables into an index, and testing hypotheses about sets of variables. Usually, none of the potential fix-ups is very satisfying. For a detailed discussion of how to deal with multicollinearity in linear models see Fox (1991).

3.6 Goodness-of-Fit Statistics

The LOGISTIC and GENMOD procedures produce many different statistics that can help you evaluate your models. We've already examined some of the default statistics, notably the global chi-square tests produced by LOGISTIC (Section 2.7) and the deviance chi-square produced by GENMOD (Section 2.8). In this section, we'll look at some of the optional statistics.

It's essential to keep in mind that there are many ways of approaching model evaluation, and statistics that appear to be similar may actually answer quite different questions. For example, LOGISTIC's global chi-square addresses the question "Is this model better than nothing?" A significant chi-square signals a "yes" answer, suggesting that the model is acceptable. By contrast, GENMOD's deviance chi-square answers the question "Is there a better model than this one?" Again, a significant chi-square corresponds to a "yes" answer, but that leads to *rejection* of the model.

The deviance is often described as a goodness-of-fit statistic. Such statistics implicitly involve a comparison between the model of interest and a "maximal" model that is more complex. The maximal model always fits better than the model of interest—the question is whether the difference in fit could be explained by chance.

In calculating the deviance for a logit model, the maximal model is often referred to as the *saturated* model. A saturated model has one parameter for every predicted probability and therefore produces a perfect fit to the data. As a likelihood ratio statistic, the deviance is equal to twice the positive difference between the log-likelihood for the fitted model and the log-likelihood for the saturated model. With individual-level data, the log-likelihood for the saturated model is necessarily 0, so the deviance is just –2 times the log-likelihood for the fitted model.

Unfortunately, with individual-level data the deviance doesn't have a chi-square distribution, for two reasons:

- The number of parameters in the saturated models increase with sample size, thereby violating a condition of asymptotic theory.
- The predicted frequencies for each observation are small (between 0 and 1) .

As a result, it's incorrect to compute a *p*-value for the deviance when working with individual-level data (which is why a *p*-value isn't automatically reported in GENMOD).

If the number of explanatory variables is small and each variable has a small number of values, you can use the AGGREGATE and SCALE options in LOGISTIC to get a deviance that *does* have a chi-square distribution. Consider the model we used in Section 3.2 as an example of computing confidence intervals. Two of the explanatory variables WHITVIC and BLACKD are dichotomous. The other variable CULP has five values. If we fit this model in GENMOD, we get a deviance of 110.65 with 143 d.f. Because the deviance is less than the degrees of freedom, this seems like a decent fit. But we can't be confident because we can't compute a valid *p*-value. Now let's do it in LOGISTIC, and use the AGGREGATE option:

```
PROC LOGISTIC DES DATA=my.penalty;
  MODEL death = blackd whitvic culp / AGGREGATE SCALE=NONE;
RUN;
```

The SCALE=NONE option tells LOGISTIC *not* to adjust the goodness-of-fit statistics for overdispersion, a topic we'll pursue in Chapter 4.

These options don't change any of the standard output—all they do is produce the new statistics shown in Output 3.13. The *p*-value for the new deviance is .81 indicating a very good fit.

Output 3.13 *Statistics from the AGGREGATE Option*

```
      Deviance and Pearson Goodness-of-Fit Statistics


                                                    Pr >
   Criterion      DF      Value    Value/DF    Chi-Square

   Deviance       15    10.0834     0.6722        0.8145
   Pearson        15     8.4680     0.5645        0.9037

         Number of unique profiles: 19
```

How is this deviance calculated? Under the AGGREGATE option, LOGISTIC forms the cross-classification of all levels of all the explanatory variables. In this case, we get a $2 \times 2 \times 5$ table, but one of those 20 combinations has no cases, leaving us with 19 "unique profiles." For each of those 19 profiles, the observed and expected frequencies for each of the two outcomes of the dependent variable are calculated based on the fitted model. The deviance is then computed as

$$Deviance = 2\sum_j O_j \log\left(\frac{O_j}{E_j}\right) \tag{3.8}$$

where O_j is the observed frequency and E_j is the expected frequency in cell j. In this example, the sum is taken over all 38 cells. The 15 degrees of freedom come from the 19 profiles minus the 4 estimated parameters in the model.

What is this statistic testing? As before, the deviance is implicitly contrasting the fitted model with a saturated model. But here the saturated model has one parameter for each of the 19 profiles, not one parameter for each of the 147 cases. In GENMOD, we could fit the saturated model by using the program:

```
PROC GENMOD DATA=my.penalty;
CLASS culp;
MODEL death = blackd whitvic culp blackd*whitvic blackd*culp
              whitvic*culp blackd*whitvic*culp / D=B;
```

The saturated model treats CULP as a categorical variable and includes all possible interactions among the explanatory variables. If we take twice the positive difference between the log-likelihood for this model and for the model with only main effects and CULP treated as quantitative, we would get the deviance shown in Output 3.13. Hence, that deviance can be interpreted as a test of the null hypothesis that (a) the effect of CULP is linear and (b) all the interactions among the three explanatory variables are 0. It is *not* testing whether the inclusion of other variables could improve the fit.

What about the Pearson chi-square? It's an alternative test of the same null hypothesis, calculated by the well-known formula

$$X^2 = \sum_j \frac{(O_j - E_j)^2}{E_j}$$ (3.9)

As with the deviance, Pearson's chi-square does not have a chi-square distribution when applied to individual-level data.

While the AGGREGATE option is often useful, it doesn't help if there are many explanatory variables or if some of them are measured on a continuum—situations that are typical in social science research. In those cases, there will be nearly as many profiles as original observations and nothing is accomplished by aggregating. To remedy this deficiency, Hosmer and Lemeshow (1989) proposed a test that has rapidly gained widespread use. It is implemented in LOGISTIC with the LACKFIT option in the MODEL statement. Let's apply it to the model we've just been evaluating:

```
PROC LOGISTIC DES DATA=my.penalty;
  MODEL death = blackd whitvic culp / LACKFIT;
RUN;
```

The resulting *p*-value of .82, shown in Output 3.14, suggests that the model fits very well.

Output 3.14 *Results from LACKFIT Option in LOGISTIC*

```
              Hosmer and Lemeshow Goodness-of-Fit Test

                         DEATH = 1              DEATH = 0
                    ---------------------   ---------------------
  Group    Total    Observed    Expected    Observed    Expected

    1        6          0         0.11          6         5.89
    2       24          0         1.03         24        22.97
    3        6          1         0.39          5         5.61
    4       22          2         1.98         20        20.02
    5       10          1         1.38          9         8.62
    6       18          3         3.38         15        14.62
    7       16          8         5.56          8        10.44
    8       16         10        10.30          6         5.70
    9       16         13        13.52          3         2.48
   10       13         12        12.34          1         0.66

  Goodness-of-fit Statistic = 4.3929 with 8 DF (p=0.8201)
```

The Hosmer-Lemeshow (HL) statistic is calculated in the following way. Based on the estimated model, predicted probabilities are generated for all observations. These are sorted by size, then grouped into approximately 10 intervals. Within each interval, the expected frequency is obtained by adding up the predicted probabilities. Expected frequencies are compared with observed frequencies by the conventional Pearson chi-square statistic. The degrees of freedom is the number of intervals minus 2.

The HL statistic has become popular because it fills a major need and has no serious competition. But it's a rather *ad hoc* statistic and its behavior has not been extensively investigated. Hosmer and Lemeshow (1989) reported simulations showing that the statistic has approximately a chi-square distribution under the null hypothesis that the fitted model is correct. That may be true, but my own simulations suggest that it is not a very powerful test. I generated 100 samples of 500 cases each. The model used to produce the data had two explanatory variables and included main effects and an interaction term,

$$\log\left(\frac{p}{1-p}\right) = \beta_0 + \beta_1 x + \beta_2 z + \beta_3 xz \ ,$$

with $\beta_0 = 0$, $\beta_1 = 1$, $\beta_2 = 1$, and $\beta_3 = .5$. The variables x and z were drawn from standard normal distributions with a correlation of .50. In each sample, I estimated a logit model *without* the interaction term and applied the HL test. The model was rejected at the .05 level in only 25% of the samples. In other words, in 75% of the samples the HL test failed to reject a model known to be incorrect. I then fitted a logit model *with* an interaction term in each of the 100 samples. The Wald test for the interaction was significant at the .05 level in 75% of the samples. While this hardly constitutes a definitive study, it suggests caution in concluding that a model is OK just because the HL test is not significant.

3.7   Statistics Measuring Predictive Power

Another class of statistics describes how well you can predict the dependent variable based on the values of the independent variables. This is a very different criterion from the goodness-of-fit measures that we've just been considering. It's entirely possible to have a model that predicts the dependent variable very well, yet has a terrible fit as evaluated by the deviance or the HL statistic. Nor is it uncommon to have a model that fits well, as judged by either of those goodness-of-fit statistics, yet has very low predictive power.

For least squares linear regression, predictive power is usually measured by the coefficient of determination, commonly known as R^2. Many different R^2 measures have been proposed for logit analysis, but LOGISTIC only calculates one of them. Fortunately, it's the one I like best. It's based on the likelihood ratio chi-square for testing the null hypothesis that all the coefficients are 0 (Cox and Snell 1989), which is the statistic reported by LOGISTIC under the heading "Testing Global Null Hypothesis." If we denote that statistic by L^2 and let n be the sample size, the *generalized R^2* is

$$R^2 = 1 - \exp\left\{ -\frac{L^2}{n} \right\}$$

(3.10)

Although this is easy to compute with a hand calculator, LOGISTIC will do it for you if you put the RSQ option in the MODEL statement.

Here's the rationale for the generalized R^2. For an OLS linear regression model, it's possible to calculate a likelihood-ratio chi-square for the hypothesis that all coefficients are 0. That statistic is related to the conventional R^2 by the formula (3.10). In other words, the formula used for logit regression is identical to the formula that applies to linear regression. In fact, this formula can be used for any regression model estimated by maximum likelihood, including the probit model, the Poisson regression model, and the Cox regression model.

In addition to its appeal as a generalization of the conventional R^2, the generalized R^2 has several things going for it:

- It's based on the quantity being maximized, namely the log-likelihood.

- It's invariant to grouping. You get the same R^2 whether you're working with grouped or individual-level data (as long as cases are only grouped together if they're identical on all the independent variables).

- It's readily obtained with virtually all computer programs because the log-likelihood is nearly always reported by default.

- It never diminishes when you add variables to a model.

- The calculated values are usually quite similar to the R^2 obtained from fitting a linear probability model to dichotomous data by ordinary least squares.

As an example of the last point, the generalized R^2 for the model that has CULP, WHITVIC, and BLACKD is .41. When I fit a linear probability model to this data, the R^2 was .47. I also calculated predicted values of the dependent variable based on a logistic regression model and computed the squared correlation between the predicted and observed values. The result was .48. Keep in mind that while the generalized R^2 may behave quite similarly to the linear model R^2, it *cannot* be interpreted as a proportion of variance "explained" by the independent variables.

A possible drawback of the generalized R^2 is that its upper bound is less than 1 because the dependent variable is discrete. To fix this, LOGISTIC also reports something labeled the "Max-rescaled Rsquare," which divides the original R^2 by its upper bound (Nagelkerke 1991). For the model just considered, the rescaled R^2 is .57.

Long before the generalized R^2 was introduced to LOGISTIC, the procedure printed statistics based on ordinal measures of association. I rarely look at these, but because they're always reported, I guess it's worth a little space to explain them. Output 3.15 shows the results for the model we've been examining. Four measures of association are shown in the right-hand column. The left-hand column gives the intermediate calculations on which those four statistics are based.

Output 3.15 *Ordinal Measures of Association from LOGISTIC*

```
Association of Predicted Probabilities and Observed
Responses

Concordant = 88.3%        Somers' D = 0.800
Discordant =  8.4%        Gamma     = 0.827
Tied       =  3.3%        Tau-a     = 0.361
(4850 pairs)              c         = 0.900
```

Here's the idea. For the 147 observations in the sample there are $147(146)/2 = 10732$ different ways to pair them up (without pairing an observation with itself). Of these, 5881 pairs have either both 1's on the dependent variable or both 0's. These we ignore, leaving 4850 pairs in which one case has a 1 and the other case has a 0. For each pair, we ask the question "Does the case with a 1 have a higher predicted value (based on the model) than the case with a 0?" If the answer is yes, we call that pair *concordant*. If no, the pair is *discordant*. If the two cases have the same predicted value, we call it a tie. Let C be the number of concordant pairs, D the number of discordant pairs, T the number of ties, and N the total number of pairs (before eliminating any). The four measures of association are then

$$Tau - a = \frac{C - D}{N}$$

$$Gamma = \frac{C - D}{C + D}$$

$$Somer's\, D = \frac{C - D}{C + D + T}$$

$$c = .5\,(1 + Somer's\, D).$$

All four measures vary between 0 and 1, with large values corresponding to stronger associations between the predicted and observed values. Of the four statistics, Tau-a tends to be closest to the generalized R^2.

3.8 Predicted Values, Residuals, and Influence Statistics

Next, we turn to diagnostic statistics that are computed for each individual observation. GENMOD and LOGISTIC produce a large number of case-wise statistics that can either be printed in the output display or written to a separate file. Here are the ones produced by both procedures:

- **Linear predictor**—Predicted log-odds for each case. In matrix notation, this is $\mathbf{x\beta}$, so it's commonly referred to as XBETA.

- **Standard error of linear predictor**—Used in generating confidence intervals.

- **Predicted values**—Predicted frequency of the event, based on the estimated model and values of the explanatory variables. For individual-level data, this is a predicted probability.

- **Confidence intervals for predicted values**—Confidence intervals are first calculated for the linear predictor by adding and subtracting an appropriate multiple of the standard error. Then, to get confidence intervals around the predicted values, the upper and lower bounds on the linear predictor are substituted into $1/(1+e^{-x})$, where x is either an upper or a lower bound.

- **Raw residual**—For each observation, the observed frequency minus the expected frequency.

- **Deviance residuals**—Contribution of each observation to the deviance chi-square.

- **Pearson residuals**—Contribution of each observation to the Pearson chi-square.

Obviously, the residuals are useful in determining which observations are most poorly fit by the model.

In addition to the statistics shared by the two procedures, each procedure can produce some statistics not found in the other procedure. The ones unique to GENMOD (available in Release 6.11 and later) are:

- **Standardized Pearson residual**—Pearson residual modified to have a standard deviation of 1.

- **Standardized deviance residual**—Deviance residual modified to have a standard deviation of 1.

- **Likelihood residual**—A combination of the standardized Pearson residual and the standardized deviance residual.

- **Diagonal of Hessian weight matrix**—These are the weights given to each observation in the maximum likelihood algorithm.

The LOGISTIC procedure has several statistics that are designed to measure the *influence* of each observation. Basically, influence statistics tell you how much some feature of the model changes when a particular observation is deleted from the model fit. For linear models, influence statistics are exact. Exact computations in logit models would be very intensive, however, so only approximations are used. The available statistics in LOGISTIC are:

- **DFBETAS**—These statistics tell you how much each regression coefficient changes when a particular observation is deleted. The actual change is divided by the standard error of the coefficient.

- **DIFDEV**—Change in deviance with deletion of the observation.

- **DIFCHISQ**—Change in Pearson chi-square with deletion of the observation.

- **C and CBAR**—Measures of overall change in regression coefficients, analogous to Cook's distance in linear regression.

- **Hat matrix diagonal**—A measure of how extreme the observation is in the "space" of the explanatory variables.

Now let's see how to get these statistics. In GENMOD, the OBSTATS option in the MODEL statement prints out all the statistics except for three: the two standardized residuals and the likelihood residual. To get these additional residuals, you must also put the RESIDUALS option in the MODEL statement. To write all these statistics onto a separate SAS data set, you use the MAKE statement. The following program both prints the statistics to the output display and writes them to a data set called A:

```
PROC GENMOD DATA=my.penalty;
  MODEL death = culp blackd whitvic / D=B OBSTATS RESIDUALS;
  MAKE 'OBSTATS' OUT=a;
RUN;
```

Output 3.16 prints out the first seven observations in data set A. The first person received a death sentence (YVAR1=1) and had a predicted probability of a death sentence of .879. The 95% confidence interval for this prediction was (.72, .95). Not surprisingly, all the residuals were on the small side. The third person also received a death sentence but had a predicted probability of only .36. In this case, the residuals are much larger, but not large enough to raise any flags. In general, standardized residuals less than 2 aren't worth mentioning, and only those approaching 3 or greater merit serious attention. For this data, the largest residuals were for the 86th observation (a person got a life sentence but had a predicted probability of

.94 of getting a death sentence). This produced a standardized deviance residual of –2.41148, a standardized Pearson residual of –4.05175, and a likelihood residual of –2.46732. What you do with these large residual cases is beyond the scope of this book, although the issues are much the same as with linear models. For extensive discussion about the treatment of residuals, see Hosmer and Lemeshow (1989).

Output 3.16 *Output from OBSTATS Option in GENMOD*

OBS	YVAR1	PRED	XBETA	STD	HESSWGT	LOWER	UPPER
1	1	0.87910	1.98394	0.52791	0.10628	0.72096	0.95341
2	0	0.01894	-3.94731	0.78593	0.01858	0.00412	0.08265
3	1	0.36405	-0.55784	0.37250	0.23152	0.21620	0.54295
4	0	0.01894	-3.94731	0.78593	0.01858	0.00412	0.08265
5	1	0.75699	1.13626	0.63233	0.18396	0.47425	0.91495
6	0	0.04312	-3.09963	0.55399	0.04126	0.01499	0.11776
7	0	0.04312	-3.09963	0.55399	0.04126	0.01499	0.11776

OBS	RESRAW	RESCHI	RESDEV	STRESDEV	STRESCHI	RESLIK
1	0.12090	0.37085	0.50765	0.51534	0.37646	0.51177
2	-0.01894	-0.13895	-0.19556	-0.19670	-0.13975	-0.19614
3	0.63595	1.32170	1.42160	1.44500	1.34346	1.44185
4	-0.01894	-0.13895	-0.19556	-0.19670	-0.13975	-0.19614
5	0.24301	0.56659	0.74619	0.77525	0.58865	0.76308
6	-0.04312	-0.21229	-0.29692	-0.29882	-0.21364	-0.29789
7	-0.04312	-0.21229	-0.29692	-0.29882	-0.21364	-0.29789

In LOGISTIC, you can get printed output by putting the INFLUENCE option in the MODEL statement. This does not contain the linear predictor and its standard error, or the predicted value and its confidence limits. But because it produces everything else, the output can be voluminous. For 147 cases and three independent variables, there were 23 pages of output (55 lines and 75 columns per page). Output 3.17 displays the output for the first five cases in the data set. The star graphs can help you quickly identify those cases that have extreme values in any of the statistics.

Output 3.17 *Output from the INFLUENCE Option in LOGISTIC*

```
                          Regression Diagnostics

                                                   Pearson Residual
                         Covariates
        Case                                       (1 unit =  0.5)
        Number    WHITVIC      BLACKD      CULP     Value    -8  -4  0 2 4 6 8

           1      1.0000          0      5.0000    0.3708    |          |*         |
           2           0          0      1.0000   -0.1389    |         *|          |
           3      1.0000          0      3.0000    1.3217    |          |   *      |
           4           0          0      1.0000   -0.1389    |         *           |
           5           0          0      5.0000    0.5666    |          |*         |

                     Deviance Residual                   Hat Matrix Diagonal

        Case              (1 unit =  0.3)                  (1 unit = 0.01)
        Number    Value   -8  -4  0 2 4 6 8     Value      0 2 4 6 8  12  16

           1     0.5077    |          |  *     |  0.0296    |     *           |
           2    -0.1956    |       *|        |  0.0115    |  *              |
           3     1.4216    |          |    *   |  0.0321    |     *           |
           4    -0.1956    |       *|        |  0.0115    |  *              |
           5     0.7462    |          |  *     |  0.0736    |              *  |

                      INTERCPT Dfbeta                      WHITVIC  Dfbeta

        Case              (1 unit = 0.07)                   (1 unit = 0.06)
        Number    Value   -8  -4  0 2 4 6 8     Value      -8  -4  0 2 4 6 8

           1    -0.0245    |          *      |   0.0211    |          *        |
           2    -0.0149    |          *      |   0.0107    |          *        |
           3     0.0725    |          |*     |   0.0552    |          |*       |
           4    -0.0149    |          *      |   0.0107    |          *        |
           5     0.0426    |          |*     |  -0.1015    |        * |        |
```

Output 3.17 *Continued*

```
              BLACKD   Dfbeta                   CULP      Dfbeta

 Case                  (1 unit = 0.06)                    (1 unit = 0.06)
Number    Value      -8  -4  0 2 4 6 8         Value    -8  -4  0 2 4 6 8

    1    -0.00144    |          *        |     0.0467    |          |*       |
    2     0.0118     |          *        |     0.0102    |          *        |
    3    -0.1303     |       *  |        |    -0.0118    |          *        |
    4     0.0118     |          *        |     0.0102    |          *        |
    5    -0.0640     |         *|        |     0.0666    |          |*       |
                          C                              CBAR
 Case                 (1 unit = 0.03)                    (1 unit = 0.03)
Number    Value      0 2 4 6 8  12  16        Value     0 2 4 6 8  12  16

    1     0.00433    |*                  |     0.00420   |*                  |
    2     0.000227   |*                  |     0.000224  |*                  |
    3     0.0599     |  *                |     0.0580    |  *                |
    4     0.000227   |*                  |     0.000224  |*                  |
    5     0.0275     | *                 |     0.0255    | *                 |


                    DIFDEV                            DIFCHISQ

 Case                 (1 unit = 0.38)                    (1 unit = 1.03)
Number    Value      0 2 4 6 8  12  16        Value     0 2 4 6 8  12  16

    1     0.2619     | *                 |     0.1417    |*                  |
    2     0.0385     |*                  |     0.0195    |*                  |
    3     2.0789     |       *           |     1.8049    |  *                |
    4     0.0385     |*                  |     0.0195    |*                  |
    5     0.5823     |  *                |     0.3465    |*                  |
```

You get slightly less output if you use the IPLOTS option, which produces horizontal (rather than vertical) plots for the residual and influence statistics. For more control, you must use the OUTPUT statement, which allows you to pick precisely those statistics you want and write them into a SAS data set. Then, if you want plots, you can use the PLOT or GPLOT procedure. For example, to get predicted values and residuals, I used this program:

```
PROC LOGISTIC DES DATA=my.penalty;
   MODEL death = culp blackd whitvic;
   OUTPUT OUT=a(KEEP= death pred up lo chi dev) P=pred U=up L=lo
       RESCHI=chi RESDEV=dev;
```

I used the KEEP option in the data set specification, otherwise LOGISTIC writes *all* the variables that are in the input data set. The first 10 observations in data set A are shown in Output 3.18.

Output 3.18   *First 10 Cases in Data Set A from LOGISTIC*

OBS	DEATH	PRED	LO	UP	CHI	DEV
1	1	0.87910	0.72097	0.95341	0.37085	0.50765
2	0	0.01894	0.00412	0.08264	-0.13895	-0.19556
3	1	0.36405	0.21621	0.54295	1.32170	1.42160
4	0	0.01894	0.00412	0.08264	-0.13895	-0.19556
5	1	0.75699	0.47426	0.91495	0.56659	0.74619
6	0	0.04312	0.01499	0.11775	-0.21229	-0.29692
7	0	0.04312	0.01499	0.11775	-0.21229	-0.29692
8	0	0.04312	0.01499	0.11775	-0.21229	-0.29692
9	0	0.87910	0.72097	0.95341	-2.69654	-2.05562
10	0	0.04312	0.01499	0.11775	-0.21229	-0.29692

To examine some of the influence statistics, I included the statement

```
OUTPUT OUT=b(KEEP= dculp dblack dwhitvic dev)
     DFBETAS=int dculp dblack dwhitvic DIFDEV=dev;
```

The DFBETAS option must be followed by a list of names of variables that will contain the influence statistics—one for the intercept and one for each of the independent variables in the model. The first 10 cases in data set B are shown in Output 3.19. The DEV column is an estimate of how much the deviance would change if that particular observation were deleted from the model. The value of 4.44 for case 9 is fairly large; the largest in the data set is 6.08 for case 86, the same case that had the largest residual. That won't be true in general—cases with large residuals aren't always the most influential. The first three columns give estimates of how much each of the coefficients would change with the removal of that case, divided by the standard error of the coefficient.

Output 3.19 *First 10 Cases in Data Set B from LOGISTIC*

OBS	DCULP	DBLACK	DWHITVIC	DEV
1	0.04666	-0.00144	0.02109	0.26191
2	0.01018	0.01183	0.01068	0.03847
3	-0.01180	-0.13034	0.05525	2.07892
4	0.01018	0.01183	0.01068	0.03847
5	0.06655	-0.06397	-0.10152	0.58229
6	0.01793	0.01682	0.00005	0.08874
7	0.01793	0.01682	0.00005	0.08874
8	0.01793	0.01682	0.00005	0.08874
9	-0.33928	0.01049	-0.15336	4.44753
10	0.01793	0.01682	0.00005	0.08874

Hosmer and Lemeshow (1989) recommend plotting the deviance influence statistics against the predicted values. This can be accomplished with the program:

```
PROC GPLOT DATA=b;
  PLOT dev*pred / VAXIS=AXIS1 HAXIS=AXIS1;
  SYMBOL V=DOT HEIGHT=.35;
  AXIS1 MINOR=NONE WIDTH=2 MAJOR=(WIDTH=2);
RUN;
```

The results shown in Figure 3.1 are fairly typical of this kind of diagnostic plot. The curve sloping upward to the right corresponds to observations that have the dependent variable equal to 0. The curve sloping downward from the left corresponds to observations with the dependent variable equal to 1. According to Hosmer and Lemeshow, you should watch out for points on the graph with high values of the influence statistic that are also well separated from other points. Perhaps the two points in the upper right hand corner might satisfy that criterion.

Figure 3.1 *Plot of DIFDEV Statistics Versus Predicted Values*

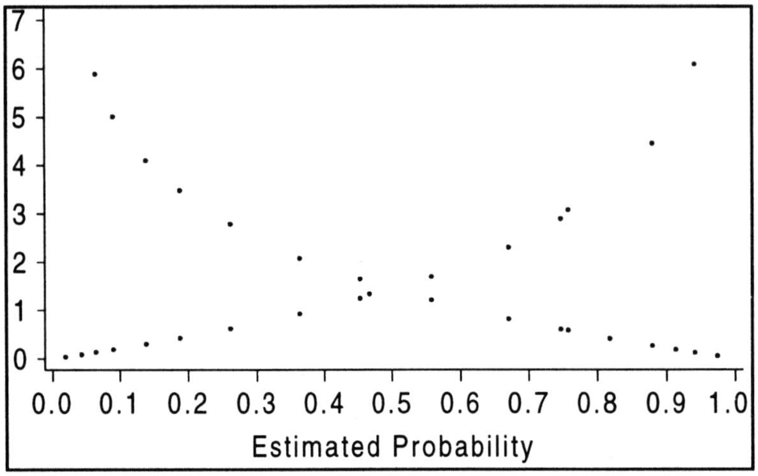

3.9 Latent Variables and Standardized Coefficients

The logit model can be derived by assuming an underlying model for a continuous variable which is then dichotomized. While this rationale is not essential, it can be helpful in understanding several aspects of the model:

- How the model might have arisen in the real world.
- Where standardized coefficients come from.
- How the logit model is related to the probit and complementary log-log models.
- How the model can be generalized to ordinal dependent variables.
- How unobserved heterogeneity can affect logit coefficients.

In this section, we'll examine the first two points, leaving the other three for later.

Here's the idea. Suppose we have a dependent variable z that is measured on a continuous scale. And suppose further that z is related to a set of explanatory variables $x_1, x_2, \ldots, x_k$ by a linear model,

$$z = \alpha_0 + \alpha_1 x_1 + \alpha_2 x_2 + \ldots + \alpha_k x_k + \sigma \varepsilon \qquad (3.11)$$

where ε is a random disturbance term, independent of the x's, and σ is a constant. Now suppose that we can't directly observe z. Instead, we observe y which is equal to 1 if z is greater than some constant μ and is equal to 0 if $z \le \mu$. We then ask, how is y related to the x's? The answer depends on the probability distribution of ε.

Suppose ε has something called a *standard logistic distribution*. That is, ε has a probability density function given by

$$f(\varepsilon) = \frac{e^{\varepsilon}}{\left(1 + e^{\varepsilon}\right)^2} \tag{3.12}$$

which is graphed in Figure 3.2. This graph looks a lot like a normal distribution. In fact, I doubt that anyone could distinguish a logistic distribution from a normal distribution that has the same mean and variance just by examining plots of their density functions.

Figure 3.2   *Density Function for Logistic Distribution*

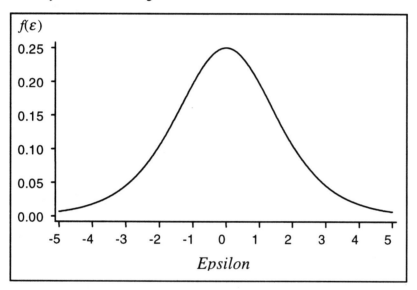

If ε has a logistic distribution, it follows that the dependence of y on the x's is given by the logit model:

$$\log\left[\frac{\Pr(y=1)}{\Pr(y=0)}\right] = \beta_0 + \beta_1 x_1 + \beta_2 x_2 + \dots + \beta_k x_k \ . \tag{3.13}$$

Furthermore, there is a simple relationship between the α's in equation (3.11) and the β's in equation (3.13):

$$\beta_0 = \frac{\alpha_0 - \mu}{\sigma}$$
$$\beta_j = \frac{\alpha_j}{\sigma}, \qquad j = 1, \dots, k. \tag{3.14}$$

Because we don't know what σ is and have no way of estimating it, we can't directly estimate the α's. But since $\beta_j = 0$ implies $\alpha_j = 0$ (except for the intercept), testing whether the

β coefficients are 0 is equivalent to testing whether the α coefficients are 0. So the usual chi-square tests apply equally to the manifest (3.13) and latent versions (3.11) of the model.

That brings us to the standardized coefficients that always appear in LOGISTIC output. Standardized coefficients are designed to measure the relative importance of the explanatory variables in a regression model. In both linear and logistic regression, ordinary coefficients cannot generally be compared across different variables because the coefficients depend directly on the metrics in which the variables are measured. If x is measured in years, for example, its coefficient will be 12 times as large as if it were measured in months.

In linear models, one solution to this comparability problem is to convert all coefficients to standard deviation units. These standardized coefficients tell you how many standard deviations the dependent variable y changes for a 1-standard deviation increase in each of the x variables. The original coefficients are transformed to standardized coefficients by the simple formula

$$\beta_j^* = \frac{\beta_j \sigma_j}{\sigma_d}, \qquad j = 1,...,k, \tag{3.15}$$

where β_j^* is a standardized coefficient, σ_d is the standard deviation of the *dependent* variable, and σ_j is the standard deviation of x_j.

Will this formula work for the logit model? There's no problem multiplying each coefficient by the standard deviation of the corresponding x variable. But what should we use for σ_d? Because the observed y is dichotomous, it doesn't make a lot of sense to talk about changes in standard deviation units for this variable. Actually, the choice isn't crucial because every coefficient is divided by the same σ_d. That implies that the relative magnitudes of the standardized coefficients are the same for any choice of denominator. The choice in LOGISTIC is to take σ_d to be the standard deviation of the disturbance term ε in the latent model for the continuous variable z (equation 3.11). If ε has a standard logistic distribution, its standard deviation is $\pi/\sqrt{3}=1.8138$. This is the value used for σ_d in equation (3.15). (An implicit assumption is that the scale factor σ in equation (3.11) is equal to 1).

Output 3.20 shows the usual LOGISTIC printout, including the standardized coefficients, for a model we've already examined with GENMOD. Let's work through the calculation of the standardized coefficient for CULP in case you ever want to do it for coefficients estimated in GENMOD. The standard deviation for CULP is 1.541 (obtained with PROC MEANS). We multiply this by its coefficient (1.2709) and divide by 1.8138 to get the standardized coefficient 1.0799. As in ordinary linear regression, standardized coefficients *can* be greater than 1 or less than –1. Clearly CULP has by far the strongest effect on the outcome, followed by BLACKD and WHITVIC. Notice that this is the same rank order as the chi-square statistics. That's often the case, but not always.

Output 3.20 *LOGISTIC Output for a Death Penalty Model*

Variable	Parameter Estimate	Standard Error	Wald Chi-Square	Pr > Chi-Square	Standardized Estimate	Odds Ratio
INTERCPT	-5.2182	0.9298	31.4934	0.0001	.	.
CULP	1.2709	0.1962	41.9447	0.0001	1.079943	3.564
BLACKD	1.6360	0.5954	7.5489	0.0060	0.452521	5.135
WHITVIC	0.8477	0.5563	2.3216	0.1276	0.229867	2.334

While the standardized coefficients produced by LOGISTIC may be helpful in evaluating the relative importance of the explanatory variables, caution should be exercised in interpreting the magnitudes of these numbers. As we've just seen, the coefficients depend on a rather arbitrary choice for the denominator in equation (3.15). In my experience, they tend to be quite a bit larger than standardized coefficients in conventional linear models. They are also rather idiosyncratic to PROC LOGISTIC. If you include them in your research reports, don't expect others to understand them without explanation.

In addition, well-known cautions about standardized coefficients in *linear* models apply here as well. Because standardized coefficients depend heavily on the degree of variability in the explanatory variables, they can vary substantially from one population to another even when the underlying coefficients are the same. For that reason, it's dangerous to compare standardized coefficients across different groups or subgroups (Kim and Feree 1981).

3.10 Probit and Complementary Log-Log Models

The logit model is not the only model appropriate for binary dependent variables. The LOGISTIC and GENMOD procedures can also estimate two other widely-used models, the probit model and the complementary log-log model. In this section, I'll briefly discuss each of these models, with an emphasis on how they compare with the logit model.

The latent variable model we examined in the last section should help to motivate these models. The equation for the continuous latent variable z was

$$z = \alpha_0 + \alpha_1 x_1 + \alpha_2 x_2 + \ldots + \alpha_k x_k + \sigma \varepsilon$$

The observed variable y was equal to 1 or 0 depending on whether z was above or below some threshold value μ. We saw that if ε has a standard logistic distribution, the dependence of y on the x's is given by a logit model. Now suppose that ε has a standard *normal* distribution. That implies that y depends on the x's by way of a probit model. And if ε has a standard *extreme-value distribution* (also known as a Gumbel or double-exponential distribution), we get the complementary log-log model.

Now for the details. Both models can be seen as ways of transforming a probability into something that has no upper or lower bound. The probit model is often written as

$$\Phi^{-1}(p_i) = \beta_0 + \beta_1 x_{i1} + \beta_2 x_{i2} + \ldots + \beta_k x_{ik} \, , \tag{3.16}$$

where p_i is the probability that $y_i = 1$ and $\Phi^{-1}(p_i)$ is the inverse of the cumulative distribution function of a standard normal variable. This function is called the *probit function*.

Obviously, the probit function needs a little explanation. Recall that a standard normal variable has a normal distribution with a mean of 0 and a standard deviation of 1. Like every random variable, a standard normal variable has a cumulative distribution function (c.d.f.). For every possible value of the variable, the c.d.f. gives the probability that the variable is less than that value. For example, the probability that a standard normal variable is less than 1.96 is .975. You've certainly encountered the standard normal c.d.f. before—the "normal table" in the back of every introductory statistics text is either the standard normal c.d.f. or some simple variation on that function.

The *inverse* of the c.d.f. simply reverses this function. For a given probability of .90, the inverse of the c.d.f. tells you which number corresponds to a probability of .90 that the random variable falls below that number. In this case, the value is 1.65. We say, then, that 1.65 is the probit transformation of .90. Table 3.2 shows probit values for selected probabilities. As probabilities range between 0 and 1, the probit function ranges between $-\infty$ and $+\infty$. For comparison, I've also included the logit and complementary log-log functions.

Table 3.2   *Probit, Logit and Complementary Log-Log Functions*

Probability	Probit	Logit	C-log-log
.1	−1.65	−2.20	−2.25
.2	−.84	−1.39	−1.49
.3	−.52	−.85	−1.03
.4	−.25	−.41	−.67
.5	.00	.00	−.37
.6	.25	.41	−.09
.7	.52	.85	.19
.8	.84	1.39	.48
.9	1.65	2.20	.83

Like the logit model, the probit model is usually estimated by maximum likelihood. In both LOGISTIC and GENMOD, the way to specify a probit model is to put LINK=PROBIT as an option in the MODEL statement. (There's also a LINK=LOGIT option, but that's the default for binary data).

Here's the PROC LOGISTIC code for a probit model corresponding to the logit model in Output 3.20:

```
PROC LOGISTIC DES DATA=my.penalty;
   MODEL death = culp blackd whitvic / LINK=PROBIT;
RUN;
```

The results are shown in Output 3.21. The first thing to notice is that the last three columns of numbers are very similar to those shown in Output 3.20 for the corresponding logit model. In general, chi-squares, *p*-values, and standardized coefficients will usually be quite close for logit and probit models, although never identical. On the other hand, parameter estimates and standard errors are quite a bit lower for the probit model than for the logit model. Typically, logit coefficients are about 80% larger than probit coefficients. This difference has no substantive meaning and merely reflects the wider range covered by the logit transformation for a given change in the probabilities, as shown in Table 3.2.

Output 3.21 *LOGISTIC Output for a Probit Model*

```
            Analysis of Maximum Likelihood Estimates

            Parameter  Standard    Wald       Pr >     Standardized
Variable  DF  Estimate   Error   Chi-Square  Chi-Square   Estimate

INTERCPT   1   -2.9932   0.4745    39.7910     0.0001          .
CULP       1    0.7357   0.1011    52.9409     0.0001     1.133983
BLACKD     1    0.9179   0.3200     8.2266     0.0041     0.460494
WHITVIC    1    0.4483   0.3061     2.1450     0.1430     0.220494
```

The standardized estimates are again calculated from the formula

$$\beta_j^* = \beta_j \left(\frac{\sigma_j}{\sigma_d} \right), \qquad j = 1,...,k,$$

but now $\sigma_d = 1$, the standard deviation of a standard normal distribution. So the standardized estimates are just the original coefficients multiplied by the standard deviations of the independent variables.

Output 3.22 shows the GENMOD output for the same model. I wouldn't have bothered with this except for one thing. Even though the coefficient estimates are identical to those produced by LOGISTIC, the standard errors (and therefore the chi-squares and *p*-values) are a little different from those in Output 3.21. The reason is that GENMOD uses the Newton-Raphson algorithm to get the ML estimates, and LOGISTIC uses iteratively reweighted least squares (also called Fisher scoring). These two algorithms are equivalent for logit models but diverge for any other model. (That's because logit is the unique "canonical" link function). For the probit and complementary log-log models, they produce the same coefficients but different standard errors. In both procedures, you can switch to the other algorithm (by using the TECHNIQUE= option in LOGISTIC and the SCORING= option in GENMOD), but there's rarely a serious need for that. Likelihood-ratio chi-squares are invariant to the algorithm, which is another reason to prefer them.

Output 3.22 *GENMOD Output for a Probit Model*

```
            Analysis Of Parameter Estimates

Parameter   DF   Estimate   Std Err   ChiSquare   Pr>Chi

INTERCEPT    1    -2.9932    0.4734    39.9716    0.0001
CULP         1     0.7357    0.1008    53.2434    0.0001
BLACKD       1     0.9179    0.3201     8.2235    0.0041
WHITVIC      1     0.4483    0.3024     2.1983    0.1382
```

Is there any reason to choose a probit model over a logit model? Not really, as long as the goal is to estimate a model for a single binary dependent variable. The two models are very close and rarely lead to different qualitative conclusions. It would take extremely large samples to reliably discriminate between them. On the other hand, the probit model is more easily generalized to applications that have multiple dichotomous outcome variables. Good examples include factor analysis with dichotomous observed variables (Muthén 1984) or simultaneous equation models for dichotomous endogenous variables (Heckman 1978). Probit is superior in these settings because the models can be based on the multivariate normal distribution, for which there is a well-developed theory and efficient computational algorithms. Multivariate logistic distributions have received much less attention.

The third model for binary data is the complementary log-log. Although not so widely known, the complementary log-log model has an important application in the area of event history (survival) analysis. The model says that

$$\log[-\log(1-p_i)] = \beta_0 + \beta_1 x_{i1} + \beta_2 x_{i2} + ... + \beta_k x_{ik} \qquad (3.17)$$

The expression on the left-hand side is called the complementary log-log transformation. Like the logit and the probit transformation, the complementary log-log transformation takes a number restricted to the (0, 1) interval and converts it into something with no upper or lower bound. Note that the log of 1–*p* is always a negative number. This is changed to a positive number before taking the log a second time. Solving for *p*, we can also write the model as:

$$p_i = 1 - \exp\{-\exp[\beta_0 + \beta_1 x_{i1} + \beta_2 x_{i2} + ... + \beta_k x_{ik}]\} . \qquad (3.18)$$

The complementary log-log model has one major difference from the logit and probit models. As shown in Table 3.2, while the logit and probit transformations are symmetrical around *p*=.50, the complementary log-log transformation is *asymmetrical*. This is also apparent from Figure 3.3 which graphs the function in equation (3.18) for a single x variable with $\beta_0=0$ and $\beta_1=1$. It's an S-shaped curve all right, but it approaches 1 much more rapidly than it approaches 0.

Figure 3.3   *Plot of Complementary Log-Log Model*

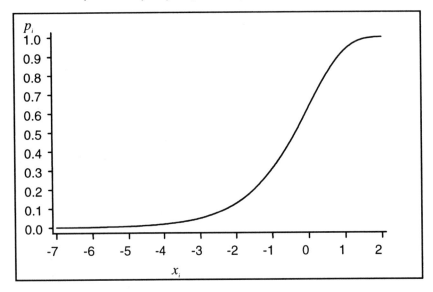

Why would you ever want an asymmetrical model? Because the complementary log-log model is closely related to continuous-time models for the occurrence of events. The most popular method of event history analysis is the *Cox regression* method, which is based on a model called the *proportional hazards model* (Cox 1972). Special cases of this model include the Weibull regression model and the exponential regression model. The proportional hazards model can be written as

$$\log h(t) = \alpha(t) + \beta_1 x_{i1} + \beta_2 x_{i2} + ... + \beta_k x_{ik} \tag{3.19}$$

where $h(t)$ is something called the *hazard* of an event at time t and $\alpha(t)$ is an unspecified function of time. While this is not the place to discuss hazards in any detail, you can think of the hazard as the instantaneous propensity for the occurrence of events.

If you have data that contains the exact times at which events occur, you can estimate this model by a method known as *partial likelihood*. But suppose the only information you have about an event (say, a death) is whether or not it occurred in a particular year. In that case, what model should you use for the dichotomous outcome? It turns out that if events are generated by an underlying proportional hazards model (equation 3.19), then the probability of an event in some well-defined interval of time is given by the complementary log-log model (equation 3.18). Furthermore, the β coefficients in these models are identical. That doesn't mean you'll get the same results regardless of whether you use Cox regression for continuous data or complementary log-log analysis for discrete data. It does mean that both methods are estimating the same underlying coefficients and, therefore, have the same interpretation. For more detailed information, see Chapter 7 of my 1995 book, *Survival Analysis Using the SAS System.*

To estimate a complementary log-log model in the GENMOD or LOGISTIC procedure, you put LINK=CLOGLOG as an option in the MODEL statement. Output 3.23 shows the results of doing this in LOGISTIC for a model comparable to the one in Output 3.22. With regard to qualitative conclusions, the results are quite similar to those for the logit and probit models. Moreover, all the coefficients are bracketed by the logit and the probit coefficients. In most applications I've seen, results from the complementary log-log model are not very different from logit or probit. But occasionally you'll find results that suggest qualitatively different conclusions. The standardized estimates are again calculated from the formula (equation 3.15), but now $\sigma_d = \pi/\sqrt{6} = 1.28$, the standard deviation of the standard extreme value distribution.

Output 3.23 *LOGISTIC Output for a Complementary Log-Log Model*

```
               Analysis of Maximum Likelihood Estimates

                Parameter  Standard     Wald        Pr >    Standardized
Variable   DF    Estimate    Error   Chi-Square  Chi-Square   Estimate

INTERCPT    1     -4.1453    0.6713    38.1315      0.0001         .
CULP        1      0.8374    0.1181    50.2734      0.0001      1.006279
BLACKD      1      1.0975    0.4030     7.4170      0.0065      0.429324
WHITVIC     1      0.7040    0.3954     3.1697      0.0750      0.269984
```

For the death-penalty data, the interpretation of the complementary log-log model in terms of an underlying proportional hazards model is really not plausible. The model isn't predicting whether an event occurs in some interval of time. Rather, given that a penalty trial takes place, it's predicting which of two kinds of outcomes occur. In cases where the model *is* plausible, we can calculate exp(β) for each coefficient to get an adjusted *hazard ratio*. For example, if we take the coefficient for BLACKD and exponentiate it, we get exp(1.0975)= 3.00. We could then say that the estimated hazard of a death sentence for a black defendant was three times the hazard for a white defendant.

One final point about the complementary log-log model. Because logit and probit models are symmetrical, reversing the coding of the dependent variable (from 0,1 to 1,0) only changes the signs of the coefficients. For the complementary log-log model, on the other hand, reversing the coding can give you completely different results. It's crucial, then, to set up the model to predict the probability of an *event*, not the absence of the event.

3.11 Unobserved Heterogeneity

In Section 3.9, I explained how the logit model could be derived from a dichotomized linear model with a disturbance term that has a logistic distribution. There we saw that the logit coefficients were related to the coefficients in the underlying linear model by the formula $\beta_j = \alpha_j/\sigma$, where β_j is the logit coefficient for x_j, α_j is the corresponding coefficient in the linear model, and σ is the coefficient of the disturbance term ε. This random disturbance term can be seen as representing all omitted explanatory variables that are independent of the measured x variables, commonly referred to as *unobserved heterogeneity*. Because σ controls the variance of the disturbance, we conclude that greater unobserved heterogeneity leads to logit coefficients that are attenuated toward 0. I'll refer to this attenuation as *heterogeneity shrinkage*.

This assessment doesn't depend on the plausibility of the latent variable model. Suppose we take an ordinary logit model and put a disturbance term in the equation:

$$\log\left[\frac{\Pr(y=1|\varepsilon)}{\Pr(y=0|\varepsilon)}\right] = \beta_0 + \beta_1 x_1 + \beta_2 x_2 + \ldots + \beta_k x_k + \sigma\varepsilon. \tag{3.20}$$

We assume that ε is independent of the x's and has a standard logistic distribution, as in equation (3.12). Notice that the probabilities on the left-hand side are expressed conditionally on ε. If we then express the model unconditionally, it can be shown (Allison 1987) that the result is closely approximated by

$$\log\left[\frac{\Pr(y=1)}{\Pr(y=0)}\right] = \beta_0^* + \beta_1^* x_1 + \beta_2^* x_2 + \ldots + \beta_k^* x_k \tag{3.21}$$

where

$$\beta_j^* = \frac{\beta_j}{\sqrt{1 + \sigma^2}}.$$

If we start with a probit model (and a standard normal disturbance) instead of a logit model, this result is exact rather than approximate. Again, we see that as the disturbance variance gets larger, the logit (or probit) coefficients get smaller.

Obviously, we can never measure and include all the variables that affect the dependent variable, so there will always be some heterogeneity shrinkage. What are the practical implications? First, in interpreting the results of a logit regression, we should keep in mind that the magnitudes of the coefficients and the corresponding odds ratios are likely to be conservative to some degree. Second, to keep such shrinkage to a minimum, it's always desirable to include important explanatory variables in the model—even if we think those variables are uncorrelated with the variables already in the model. This advice is especially relevant to randomized experiments where there is a tendency to ignore covariates and look only at the effect of the treatment on the response. That may be OK for linear models, but logit models yield superior estimates of the treatment effect when all relevant covariates are included.

A third problem is that differential heterogeneity can confound comparisons of logit coefficients across different groups. If, for example, you want to compare logit coefficients estimated separately for men and women, you must implicitly assume that the degree of unobserved heterogeneity is the same in both groups. Elsewhere, I have proposed a method of adjusting for differential heterogeneity (Allison 1999).

Heterogeneity shrinkage is characteristic of a wide variety of non-linear regression models (Gail et al. 1984). The phenomenon is closely related to a distinction that is commonly made between *population-averaged models* and *subject-specific* models. The model that explicitly includes the disturbance term (equation 3.20) is called a subject-specific model, because its coefficients describe how the log-odds changes if the explanatory variables are changed for that particular individual. On the other hand, equation (3.21)— which integrates out the disturbance term—is called a population-averaged model because its coefficients describe what happens to a whole population when the explanatory variables are changed for all individuals. If our interest is in understanding the underlying causal mechanism, then subject-specific coefficients are of primary interest. If the aim is to determine the aggregate consequences of some policy change that affects everyone, then population-averaged coefficients may be more appropriate. Keep in mind, however, that there is only one true subject-specific model, but the population-averaged model may change with the population and the degree of unobserved heterogeneity.

Can we ever estimate the subject-specific model or can we only approximate it by including more and more explanatory variables? If we have only one observation per individual, the subject-specific model cannot be directly estimated. But if there are two or more observations per individual, the parameter σ is identified, which means that the subject-specific coefficients can be recovered. We'll discuss methods for accomplishing that in Chapter 8. Unobserved heterogeneity is closely related to a phenomenon known as *overdispersion*, which arises when estimating a logit model that has grouped data. We'll discuss overdispersion in the next chapter.

3.12 Sampling on the Dependent Variable

The logit model has a unique sampling property that is extremely useful in a variety of situations. In the analysis of linear models, sampling on the dependent variable is widely known to be potentially dangerous. In fact, much of the literature on selection bias in linear models has to do with fixing the problems that arise from such sampling (Heckman 1979). That's not true for the logit model, however. You can do disproportionate stratified random sampling on the dependent variable without biasing the coefficient estimates.

Here's a simple example. Table 3.3 shows a hypothetical table for employment status by high school graduation. The odds ratio for this table is 570×52/(360×22)=3.74. If we estimated a logit model predicting employment status from high school graduation, the coefficient would be log(3.74)=1.32. (If we reversed the independent and dependent variables, the logit coefficient would still be 1.32.) Now suppose we take a 10% random sample from the employed column and delete the other 90% of employed persons from the table. Ignoring sampling variability, the numbers in the employed column would change to 57 and 36. The new odds ratio is 57×52/(36×22)=3.74 and, of course, the logit coefficient is still 1.32. We see, then, that sampling on the dependent variable doesn't change odds ratios.

Table 3.3   *Employment Status by High School Graduation*

High School Graduate	Employment Status	
	Employed	Unemployed
Yes	570	22
No	360	52

This property of contingency tables has been known for decades. More recently, it's been extended to logit models with continuous independent variables (Prentice and Pyke 1979); the slope coefficients are not biased by disproportionate random sampling on the dependent variable. The intercept does change under such sampling schemes, but ordinarily we don't care about the intercept anyway.

This property has a couple of important practical implications. Suppose you have a census tape with a million observations. You want to analyze the determinants of employment status, but you don't want to stare at your computer screen while LOGISTIC chugs through a million cases. So you take a 1% simple random sample, giving you 10,000 cases. If the unemployment rate is 5%, you would expect to get about 9500 employed cases and 500 unemployed cases. Not bad, but you can do better. For a given sample size, the standard errors of the coefficients depend heavily on the split on the dependent variable. As a general rule, you're much better off with a 50-50 split than with a 95-5 split. The solution is to take a 10% sample of the unemployed cases and a 0.5% sample of the employed cases. That way you end up with about 5,000 cases of each, which will give you much smaller standard errors for the coefficients.

After you've estimated the logit model from the disproportionately stratified sample, you can easily correct the intercept to reflect the true population proportions (Hosmer and Lemeshow 1989, p. 180). For example, suppose you estimated a model predicting the probability of unemployment and you get an intercept of b_o, Suppose, further, that the sampling fraction for unemployed persons was p_u, and the sampling fraction for employed persons was p_e. Then, the corrected intercept is $b_o-\log(p_u/p_e)$.

The other application of sampling on the dependent variable is the case-control study, widely used in the biomedical sciences (Breslow and Day 1980) but occasionally found in the social sciences as well. Here's how it works. You want to study the determinants of some rare disease. By surveying doctors and hospitals, you manage to identify all 75 persons diagnosed with that disease (the cases) in your metropolitan area. To get a comparison group, you recruit a random sample of healthy persons in the general population of the metropolitan area (the controls). You pool the cases and the controls into a single sample and do a logit regression predicting case vs. control, based on various background characteristics. Often the controls are matched to the cases on one or more criteria, but that's not an essential feature of the design. In Chapter 8, we'll see how to analyze matched case-control data.

Chapter 4

Logit Analysis of Contingency Tables

4.1 Introduction

To many people, categorical data analysis means the analysis of contingency tables, also known as cross tabulations. For decades, the mainstay of contingency table analysis was the chi-square test introduced by Karl Pearson in 1900. However, things changed dramatically with the development of the loglinear model in the late 1960s and early 1970s. Loglinear analysis made it possible to analyze multi-way contingency tables, testing both simple and complex hypotheses in an elegant statistical framework. In Chapter 10, we'll see how to estimate loglinear models by using the GENMOD procedure.

Although loglinear analysis is still a popular approach to the analysis of contingency tables, logit analysis can often do a better job. In fact, there is an intimate relationship between the two approaches. For a contingency table, every logit model has a loglinear model that is its exact equivalent. The converse doesn't hold—there are loglinear models that don't correspond to any logit models—but in most cases, such models have little substantive interest.

If logit and loglinear models are equivalent, why use the logit model? Here are three reasons:

- The logit model makes a clear distinction between the dependent variable and the independent variables. The loglinear model makes no such distinction—all the conceptual variables are on the right-hand side of the equation.

- The loglinear model has many more parameters than the corresponding logit model. Most of these are nuisance parameters that have no substantive interest, and their inclusion in the model can be confusing (and potentially misleading).
- With larger tables, loglinear models are much more prone to convergence failure because of cell frequencies of 0.

In short, logit analysis can be much simpler than loglinear analysis even when estimating equivalent models. As we shall see, logit analysis of contingency tables has more in common with ordinary multiple regression than it does with traditional chi-square tests. In the remainder of this chapter, we'll see how to analyze contingency tables by using either the LOGISTIC or the GENMOD procedure. The emphasis will be on GENMOD, however, because its CLASS statement and more flexible MODEL statement are particularly handy for contingency table analysis. In this chapter, we'll look only at tables where the dependent variable is dichotomous, but later chapters will consider tabular data with dependent variables having more than two categories. Much of what we do in this chapter will involve the application of tools already developed in preceding chapters.

4.2 A Logit Model for a 2 × 2 Table

Let's begin with the simplest case—a dichotomous dependent variable and a single dichotomous independent variable. That leads to a 2 × 2 table like the one in Table 2.2, reproduced here as Table 4.1.

Table 4.1   *Death Sentence by Race of Defendant*

	Blacks	Nonblacks	Total
Death	28	22	50
Life	45	52	97
Total	73	74	147

If we have access to the individual-level data, we can simply estimate a logit model directly, as with the following GENMOD program:

```
PROC GENMOD DATA=my.penalty;
   MODEL death = blackd / D=B;
RUN;
```

Results are shown in Output 4.1. Exponentiating the BLACKD coefficient yields 1.47, which is the odds ratio we calculated earlier, directly from the table. It is not statistically significant.

Output 4.1 *GENMOD Output for a Logit Model*

```
                Criteria For Assessing Goodness Of Fit

     Criterion             DF        Value       Value/DF

     Deviance             145      187.2704        1.2915
     Scaled Deviance      145      187.2704        1.2915
     Pearson Chi-Square   145      147.0000        1.0138
     Scaled Pearson X2    145      147.0000        1.0138
     Log Likelihood         .      -93.6352           .



                Analysis Of Parameter Estimates

   Parameter    DF    Estimate    Std Err   ChiSquare  Pr>Chi

   INTERCEPT     1     -0.8602     0.2543    11.4392    0.0007
   BLACKD        1      0.3857     0.3502     1.2135    0.2706
```

Now, suppose we don't have the individual-level data. All we have is Table 4.1. There are two different ways to get the tabular data into either GENMOD or LOGISTIC. The first method is to create a data set that has one record for each of the four cell frequencies in the table, together with appropriately coded variables that represent race and sentence:

```
DATA tab4_1a;
   INPUT f blackd death;
   DATALINES;
22 0 1
28 1 1
52 0 0
45 1 0
;
```

Then we use the FREQ statement in GENMOD or LOGISTIC to specify that each of these data lines is to be replicated using the number of replications given by the variable F. In GENMOD we have

```
PROC GENMOD DATA=tab4_1a;
  FREQ f;
  MODEL death = blackd / D=B;
RUN;
```

Results are *identical* to those in Output 4.1.

The other way to handle tabular data is to use the *events/trials* syntax, which is available in both GENMOD and LOGISTIC. Instead of inputting all four internal cell counts in the table, we input the cell frequencies for death sentences along with the column totals:

```
DATA tab4_1b;
  INPUT death total blackd;
  DATALINES;
22 74 0
28 73 1
;
```

Then we specify a dependent variable that has two parts, separated by a slash:

```
PROC GENMOD DATA=tab4_1b;
  MODEL death/total = blackd / D=B;
RUN;
```

Instead of replicating the observations, GENMOD treats the variable DEATH as having a binomial distribution with the number of trials (an apt term for this data) given by the variable TOTAL. Results are shown in Output 4.2. Comparing Output 4.2 with Output 4.1, you see that everything is the same except for the deviance and Pearson chi-square, both of which are 0 with the event/trials syntax. This illustrates two points:

- Maximum likelihood estimates, their standard errors, and the log-likelihood are invariant to grouping (as long as the cases grouped together are identical with respect to the variables in the model).
- The deviance and Pearson chi-square are *not* invariant to grouping.

Output 4.2   *GENMOD Output Using Events/Trials Syntax*

```
                 Criteria For Assessing Goodness Of Fit

            Criterion          DF        Value      Value/DF

            Deviance            0        0.0000         .
            Scaled Deviance     0        0.0000         .
            Pearson Chi-Square  0        0.0000         .
            Scaled Pearson X2   0        0.0000         .
            Log Likelihood      .      -93.6352         .


                     Analysis Of Parameter Estimates

         Parameter   DF    Estimate    Std Err   ChiSquare   Pr>Chi

         INTERCEPT    1     -0.8602     0.2543    11.4392     0.0007
         BLACKD       1      0.3857     0.3502     1.2135     0.2706
```

Why does the deviance change? Recall that the deviance is a likelihood ratio test that compares the fitted model with a saturated model. The problem is that the saturated model changes with the grouping. In Output 4.2, the saturated model is also the fitted model, with two parameters for the two data lines. That's why the deviance is 0. For Output 4.1, the saturated model implicitly has a parameter for each of the 147 observations, and its log-likelihood is 0. This is also the saturated model for a tabular analysis that uses the FREQ statement because GENMOD is actually operating on 147 observations rather than just two. For the remainder of this chapter, I'll use the *event/trials* syntax because the grouped deviance is generally more useful as a goodness-of-fit measure. As explained in Section 2.8, the deviance based on individual-level data does *not* have a chi-square distribution.

The events/trials syntax also works in PROC LOGISTIC:

```
PROC LOGISTIC DATA=tab4_1b;
  MODEL death/total = blackd / AGGREGATE SCALE=N;
RUN;
```

Note that with this syntax, you do *not* need the DESCENDING option in the MODEL statement. The AGGREGATE and SCALE options are included so that we also get the deviance and Pearson chi-square, as shown in Output 4.3. Of course, both are 0 in this case because we've fitted a saturated model.

Output 4.3 *LOGISTIC Output Using Events/Trials Syntax*

```
             Deviance and Pearson Goodness-of-Fit Statistics
                                                            Pr >
            Criterion       DF        Value    Value/DF   Chi-Square

            Deviance         0       2.8E-14       .          .
            Pearson          0      4.02E-21       .          .


      Model Fitting Information and Testing Global Null Hypothesis BETA=0

                                     Intercept
                       Intercept        and
      Criterion          Only        Covariates    Chi-Square for Covariates

      AIC               190.491       191.270           .
      SC                193.481       197.251           .
      -2 LOG L          188.491       187.270       1.221 with 1 DF (p=0.2693)
      Score                .             .          1.218 with 1 DF (p=0.2697)


                   Analysis of Maximum Likelihood Estimates

                  Parameter Standard    Wald       Pr >     Standardized   Odds
      Variable DF Estimate   Error   Chi-Square Chi-Square    Estimate    Ratio

      INTERCPT  1  -0.8602   0.2543   11.4392     0.0007          .          .
      BLACKD    1   0.3857   0.3502    1.2135     0.2706      0.106697    1.471
```

For a 2×2 table, we can also produce many of these results by using PROC FREQ:

```
PROC FREQ DATA=tab4_1a;
   WEIGHT f;
   TABLES blackd*death / CHISQ CMH;
RUN;
```

Selected results are shown in Output 4.4.

Output 4.4   *PROC FREQ Results*

```
              STATISTICS FOR TABLE OF BLACKD BY DEATH

    Statistic                        DF    Value      Prob
    ----------------------------------------------------------
    Chi-Square                        1    1.218      0.270
    Likelihood Ratio Chi-Square       1    1.221      0.269
    Continuity Adj. Chi-Square        1    0.864      0.353
    Mantel-Haenszel Chi-Square        1    1.210      0.271
    Fisher's Exact Test (Left)                        0.899
                        (Right)                       0.176
                        (2-Tail)                      0.299


       Estimates of the Common Relative Risk (Row1/Row2)
                                            95%
    Type of Study    Method          Value  Confidence Bounds
    ----------------------------------------------------------
    Case-Control     Mantel-Haenszel  1.471   0.740    2.924
     (Odds Ratio)    Logit            1.471   0.740    2.921
```

The CHISQ option gives us several statistics for testing the null hypothesis that the two variables are independent, which is equivalent to the hypothesis that the slope is 0 in the logit model. Notice that Pearson's chi-square (labeled simply chi-square in the output) is identical to the score statistic in the LOGISTIC Output 4.3. The likelihood ratio chi-square in Output 4.4 is identical to the chi-square labeled –2LOG L in Output 4.3. The CMH option gives us the odds ratio, which is identical to the odds ratio in the LOGISTIC output.

4.3   A Three-Way Table

As we've just seen, using GENMOD to estimate a logit model for a 2 × 2 table doesn't tell you much more than you would get with PROC FREQ. But with a 3-way table, things get more interesting.

Consider Table 4.2, which shows the cross classification of race, gender, and occurrence of sexual intercourse for a national sample of 15- and 16-year-olds, reported by Morgan and Teachman (1988).

Table 4.2   *Race by Gender by Sexual Intercourse*

		Intercourse	
Race	Gender	Yes	No
White	Male	43	134
	Female	26	149
Black	Male	29	23
	Female	22	36

Let's analyze Table 4.2 as a logit model, with intercourse as the dependent variable and race and sex as independent variables. Using the events/trials syntax in GENMOD, we have:

```
DATA interco;
  INPUT white male yes no;
  total=yes+no;
  DATALINES;
1 1 43 134
1 0 26 149
0 1 29 23
0 0 22 36
;
PROC GENMOD DATA=interco;
  MODEL yes/total=white male / D=B;
RUN;
```

Output 4.5   *GENMOD Output for Analysis of Three-Way Table*

```
          Criteria For Assessing Goodness Of Fit

       Criterion          DF      Value      Value/DF

       Deviance            1      0.0583      0.0583
       Scaled Deviance     1      0.0583      0.0583
       Pearson Chi-Square  1      0.0583      0.0583
       Scaled Pearson X2   1      0.0583      0.0583
       Log Likelihood      .    -245.8974        .

             Analysis Of Parameter Estimates

   Parameter   DF   Estimate   Std Err   ChiSquare  Pr>Chi

   INTERCEPT    1    -0.4555    0.2221     4.2045    0.0403
   WHITE        1    -1.3135    0.2378    30.5132    0.0001
   MALE         1     0.6478    0.2250     8.2873    0.0040
```

Results are shown in Output 4.5. The first thing to notice is that the deviance is only
.058 with 1 degree of freedom. Because we're working with grouped data, we can treat this as
a chi-square statistic and calculate a *p*-value. A chi-square of .058 is so low that it's hardly
necessary to do the calculation. But for the sake of illustration, here's a little program that
will compute the *p*-value in SAS:

```
DATA;
  CHI=1-PROBCHI(.0583,1);
  PUT CHI;
RUN;
```

The PUT statement writes the *p*-value of 0.8092033193 in the LOG file. Because this is a
goodness-of-fit test, a high *p*-value means that the model fits well. Clearly this model fits the
data extremely well.

But what is the deviance testing? Remember that the deviance always compares the
fitted model with a saturated model. For a $2 \times 2 \times 2$ table, the saturated logit model includes
an interaction between the two explanatory variables in their effects on the dependent
variable. There's one coefficient for this interaction, corresponding to the single degree of
freedom for the deviance. So, in this case, the deviance is testing the null hypothesis that the
interaction coefficient is 0. We conclude that there's no evidence for an interaction.

To see this more explicitly, let's actually fit the model with the interaction:

```
PROC GENMOD DATA=interco;
   MODEL yes/total=white male white*male/ D=B;
RUN;
```

In Output 4.6 we see that the deviance is 0, as it should be for a saturated model. The interaction term has a chi-square of .0583 with a *p*-value of .8092, identical to what we got for the deviance in the "main effects" model. The absence of an interaction means that race has the same effect for both boys and girls. And gender has the same effect for both blacks and whites.

Output 4.6   *GENMOD Output for a Saturated Model*

```
        Criteria For Assessing Goodness Of Fit

        Criterion              DF        Value       Value/DF

        Deviance                0        0.0000          .
        Scaled Deviance         0        0.0000          .
        Pearson Chi-Square      0        0.0000          .
        Scaled Pearson X2       0        0.0000          .
        Log Likelihood          .     -245.8682          .

              Analysis Of Parameter Estimates

    Parameter    DF    Estimate    Std Err    ChiSquare   Pr>Chi

    INTERCEPT     1     -0.4925     0.2706      3.3118     0.0688
    WHITE         1     -1.2534     0.3441     13.2675     0.0003
    MALE          1      0.7243     0.3888      3.4696     0.0625
    WHITE*MALE    1     -0.1151     0.4765      0.0583     0.809
```

What exactly are those effects? In Output 4.5, the coefficient for MALE is .6478 with a *p*-value of .004. Exponentiating the coefficient yields 1.91. We can say, then, that the estimated odds of having had sexual intercourse by age 15 are nearly twice as large for males as for females, after adjusting for racial differences. It would probably be a mistake to put too much faith in the exact value 1.91, however. A 95% confidence interval—which I calculated by hand using exp{.6478±2(.225)}—is between 1.21 and 3.00.

For WHITE, the highly significant, adjusted odds ratio is exp{−1.3135} = .269, indicating that the odds of intercourse for whites is a little more than one-fourth the odds for blacks. It may be easier to interpret the reciprocal 1/.269 = 3.72, which says that the odds for blacks are nearly four times the odds for whites, controlling for gender differences. This has a 95% confidence interval of exp{1.3135±2(.2378)}, or 2.3 to 6. That's about all we can usefully do with this table. We could examine residuals but because the model fits so well, there's little point.

4.4 A Four-Way Table

Things are only a little more complicated with four-way tables except that more interactions are possible. Consider Table 4.3, reported by Seeman (1977) based on surveys conducted in France and the United States. In each country, the respondent was asked about his own occupation, his father's occupation, and whether he considered himself a member of the working class. Occupations were classified into manual and non-manual. Our goal is to estimate a logit model for the dependence of working class identification on the other three variables.

Table 4.3   *Identification with the Working Class by Country and Occupation*

Country	Occupation	Father's Occupation	Identifies with the Working Class		Total
			Yes	No	
France	Manual	Manual	85	22	107
		Non-manual	44	21	65
	Non-manual	Manual	24	42	66
		Non-manual	17	154	171
U.S.	Manual	Manual	24	63	87
		Non-manual	22	43	65
	Non-manual	Manual	1	84	85
		Non-manual	6	142	148

Here's a DATA step for reading in the table data:

```
DATA working;
   INPUT france manual famanual total working;
   DATALINES;
1   1   1   107   85
1   1   0    65   44
1   0   1    66   24
1   0   0   171   17
0   1   1    87   24
0   1   0    65   22
0   0   1    85    1
0   0   0   148    6
;
```

Let's first consider a model with no interactions:

```
PROC GENMOD DATA=working;
   MODEL working/total = france manual famanual / D=B;
RUN;
```

I could have specified the explanatory variables as CLASS variables, but there's no advantage in doing that for dichotomous variables coded 1 and 0. In fact, there's an advantage in *not* putting them in a CLASS statement because the output would then be cluttered with extra lines for the omitted category of each variable.

The results in Output 4.7 show highly significant effects of all three variables. Not surprisingly, higher probabilities of working class identification are found in France, among men who work in manual occupations and among men whose fathers worked in manual occupations. But the model doesn't fit the data very well. With a deviance of 18.98 on 4 degrees of freedom, the *p*-value is only .0008. Clearly something's missing from the model.

Output 4.7   *GENMOD Output for Working Class Identification*

```
           Criteria For Assessing Goodness Of Fit

    Criterion              DF        Value      Value/DF

    Deviance                4       18.9759       4.7440
    Scaled Deviance         4       18.9759       4.7440
    Pearson Chi-Square      4       18.9803       4.7451
    Scaled Pearson X2       4       18.9803       4.7451
    Log Likelihood          .     -326.7692          .


             Analysis Of Parameter Estimates

    Parameter    DF    Estimate   Std Err   ChiSquare   Pr>Chi

    INTERCEPT     1     -3.6902    0.2547    209.9408    0.0001
    FRANCE        1      1.9474    0.2162     81.1509    0.0001
    MANUAL        1      2.5199    0.2168    135.1497    0.0001
    FAMANUAL      1      0.5522    0.2017      7.4965    0.0062
```

What's missing are the interaction terms: three 2-way interactions and one 3-way interaction. Each has 1 degree of freedom, giving us the 4 degrees of freedom for the deviance. Because 3-way interactions are a pain to interpret, let's see if we can get by with just the 2-way interactions:

```
PROC GENMOD DATA=working;
  MODEL working/total = france manual famanual
     france*manual france*famanual manual*famanual / D=B;
RUN;
```

Output 4.8   *Model with All 2-Way Interactions*

```
            Criteria For Assessing Goodness Of Fit

        Criterion           DF        Value      Value/DF

        Deviance             1        3.1512       3.1512
        Scaled Deviance      1        3.1512       3.1512
        Pearson Chi-Square   1        2.8836       2.8836
        Scaled Pearson X2    1        2.8836       2.8836
        Log Likelihood       .     -318.8568          .

               Analysis Of Parameter Estimates

    Parameter          DF    Estimate    Std Err    ChiSquare   Pr>Chi

    INTERCEPT           1     -3.5075     0.4269     67.4944     0.0001
    FRANCE              1      1.4098     0.4585      9.4564     0.0021
    MANUAL              1      2.9517     0.4612     40.9590     0.0001
    FAMANUAL            1      0.0879     0.4869      0.0326     0.8568
    FRANCE*MANUAL       1     -0.2311     0.4966      0.2166     0.6416
    FRANCE*FAMANUAL     1      1.3375     0.4364      9.3945     0.0022
    MANUAL*FAMANUAL     1     -0.5968     0.4370      1.8655     0.1720
```

In Output 4.8 we see that the model with all three 2-way interactions fits reasonably well. The *p*-value for a chi-square of 3.15 with 1 degree of freedom is .08—not great but still acceptable. The 1 degree of freedom corresponds to the excluded 3-way interaction. In essence, the deviance is testing whether or not this interaction is 0. Examining the Wald chi-squares for the three 2-way interactions, we find that country × father's occupation is highly significant but the other two are far from significant. (Not shown are likelihood ratio chi-squares which are virtually identical). That suggests a model with just one 2-way interaction, for which results are shown in Output 4.9.

Output 4.9   *Model with One 2-Way Interaction*

```
              Criteria For Assessing Goodness Of Fit

      Criterion              DF       Value       Value/DF

      Deviance                3       5.3744       1.7915
      Scaled Deviance         3       5.3744       1.7915
      Pearson Chi-Square      3       5.2649       1.7550
      Scaled Pearson X2       3       5.2649       1.7550
      Log Likelihood          .     -319.9684         .

              Analysis Of Parameter Estimates

   Parameter         DF    Estimate   Std Err   ChiSquare  Pr>Chi

   INTERCEPT          1     -3.1796    0.2713   137.3772   0.0001
   FRANCE            1      1.1772    0.2876    16.7549   0.0001
   MANUAL            1      2.5155    0.2162   135.3432   0.0001
   FAMANUAL          1     -0.3802    0.3211     1.4020   0.2364
   FRANCE*FAMANUAL   1      1.5061    0.4098    13.5067   0.0002
```

When the two nonsignificant interactions are deleted, the deviance goes up but the degrees of freedom goes up even faster, giving us an improved *p*-value of .15. Moreover, the difference in deviance between the models in Output 4.9 and Output 4.8 is only 2.22 with 2 degrees of freedom, far from significant. So deleting the two interactions does not significantly worsen the fit.

Let's interpret the parameter estimates in Output 4.9. The coefficient for MANUAL is the most straightforward because it's not involved in the interaction. Calculating exp(2.5155) = 12.4, we can say that manual workers have an odds of identification with the working class that is more than 12 times the odds for non-manual workers.

To interpret the effects of the other variables, we must keep in mind a general principle regarding interactions: the main effect for a variable that's also in a 2-way interaction can be interpreted as the effect of that variable when the *other* variable is 0. For example, the FAMANUAL coefficient of –.38 represents the effect of FAMANUAL when FRANCE=0, that is, when the respondent lives in the U.S. Thus, having a father with a manual occupation has a negative (but not significant) effect on working class identification among men in the U.S. To get the effect of father's occupation in France, we *add* the interaction coefficient to the main effect, 1.5061 + (–.3802) = 1.13. Exponentiating gives us an adjusted odds ratio of 3.1. In France, then, men whose fathers had a manual occupation have an odds of identification that is more than three times the odds for men whose fathers did not have a manual occupation.

Similarly, the main effect of FRANCE is the effect of country among those men whose fathers did *not* have a manual occupation. Calculating exp(1.1772) = 3.2, we find that in this group, Frenchmen had an odds of identification three times the odds for Americans. Among men whose fathers had a manual occupation, the adjusted odds ratio for France vs. U.S. is exp(1.1772+1.5061)=14.6, nearly 15 times as large.

Suppose you want a confidence interval for the odds ratio of 14.6. To do this, you first get a confidence interval for the sum 1.1772+1.5061=2.6833. Then you exponentiate the upper and lower limits. But how do you get the confidence interval for the sum? There are two ways to do it. One is to recode the father's occupation so that the 0s and 1s are reversed, then rerun the model. In the new model, the main effect of FRANCE will be 2.6833—the effect when a father's occupation is manual. You get confidence intervals for that coefficient in the usual way, by adding and subtracting two standard errors.

The other method of getting a confidence interval makes use of the fact that for any two coefficients b_1 and b_2, the variance of their sum is given by

$$\text{var}(b_1 + b_2) = \text{var}(b_1) + \text{var}(b_2) + 2\text{cov}(b_1, b_2) \tag{4.1}$$

These variances and covariances can be obtained from the covariance matrix of the coefficients, produced by the COVB option in the MODEL statement. For the model in Output 4.9, the covariance matrix reported by GENMOD is:

Parameter Number	PRM1	PRM2	PRM3	PRM4	PRM5
PRM1	0.07359	-0.05813	-0.03366	-0.04398	0.04586
PRM2	-0.05813	0.08271	0.01218	0.04741	-0.07827
PRM3	-0.03366	0.01218	0.04675	-0.007484	0.004862
PRM4	-0.04398	0.04741	-0.007484	0.10309	-0.10267
PRM5	0.04586	-0.07827	0.004862	-0.10267	0.16794

The two coefficients we're interested in correspond to PRM2 and PRM5. Applying equation (4.1) we have

$$\text{var}(b_2 + b_5) = .08271 + .16794 + 2(-.07827) = .09411$$

The standard error of the sum is just the square root of the variance, that is, .3068. The desired 95% confidence interval is then exp{2.6833±1.96(.3068)} or 8.0 to 26.7.

To sum up our analysis, manual workers and Frenchmen are more likely to identify with the working class. In France, men whose fathers had a manual occupation are also more likely to identify with the working class, an effect that is independent of one's own occupation. In the U.S., however, a father's occupation makes little, if any, difference.

4.5   A Four-Way Table with Ordinal Explanatory Variables

Next we consider a $2 \times 2 \times 4 \times 4$ table, reported by Sewell and Shah (1968), for a sample of 4,991 high school seniors in Wisconsin. The dependent variable was whether or not they planned to attend college in the following year. The three independent variables were coded as follows:

IQ	1=low, 2=lower middle, 3=upper middle, 4=high
SES	1=low, 2=lower middle, 3=upper middle, 4=high
PARENT	1=low parental encouragement, 2=high encouragement.

Below is a DATA step to read in the table. There is one record for each combination of the independent variables. The fourth variable TOTAL is the number of students who had each set of values for the independent variables, and the last variable COLL is the number of students who planned to attend college. Thus, on the first line, we see that there were 353 students who were low on all three independent variables; of those, only four planned to attend college.

```
DATA wisc;
  INPUT iq parent ses total coll;
  DATALINES;
1   1   1   353     4
1   1   2   234     2
1   1   3   174     8
1   1   4    52     4
1   2   1    77    13
1   2   2   111    27
1   2   3   138    47
1   2   4    96    39
2   1   1   216     9
2   1   2   208     7
2   1   3   126     6
2   1   4    52     5
2   2   1   105    33
2   2   2   159    64
2   2   3   184    74
2   2   4   213   123
3   1   1   138    12
```

```
3   1   2   127    12
3   1   3   109    17
3   1   4    50     9
3   2   1    92    38
3   2   2   185    93
3   2   3   248   148
3   2   4   289   224
4   1   1    77    10
4   1   2    96    17
4   1   3    48     6
4   1   4    25     8
4   2   1    92    49
4   2   2   178   119
4   2   3   271   198
4   2   4   468   414
;
```

Now we're ready for GENMOD:

```
PROC GENMOD DATA=wisc;
   CLASS iq ses;
   MODEL coll/total=iq ses parent / D=B TYPE3;
RUN;
```

IQ and SES are listed as CLASS variables so that they will be treated as categorical rather than quantitative variables. The TYPE3 option is needed to produce test statistics for sets of dummy variables created by the CLASS statement; otherwise GENMOD only prints a chi-square for each constructed dummy variable.

Output 4.10 *GENMOD Output for a Four-Way Table*

```
            Criteria For Assessing Goodness Of Fit

Criterion             DF        Value       Value/DF

Deviance              24       25.2358       1.0515
Scaled Deviance       24       25.2358       1.0515
Pearson Chi-Square    24       24.4398       1.0183
Scaled Pearson X2     24       24.4398       1.0183
Log Likelihood         .     -2166.0549         .
```

Output 4.10 *Continued*

```
            Analysis Of Parameter Estimates

Parameter         DF    Estimate    Std Err    ChiSquare   Pr>Chi

INTERCEPT          1     -3.1005     0.2123     213.3353    0.0001
IQ          1      1     -1.9663     0.1210     264.2400    0.0001
IQ          2      1     -1.3722     0.1024     179.7284    0.0001
IQ          3      1     -0.6331     0.0976      42.0830    0.0001
IQ          4      0      0.0000     0.0000        .           .
SES         1      1     -1.4140     0.1210     136.6657    0.0001
SES         2      1     -1.0580     0.1029     105.7894    0.0001
SES         3      1     -0.7516     0.0976      59.3364    0.0001
SES         4      0      0.0000     0.0000        .           .
PARENT             1      2.4554     0.1014     586.3859    0.0001
SCALE              0      1.0000     0.0000        .           .

NOTE:  The scale parameter was held fixed.

   LR Statistics For Type 3 Analysis

Source        DF    ChiSquare   Pr>Chi

IQ             3    361.5648    0.0001
SES            3    179.8467    0.0001
PARENT         1    795.6139    0.0001
```

In Output 4.10, we see that a model with main effects and no interactions fits the data well. Even though GENMOD doesn't compute a *p*-value for the deviance, whenever the deviance is close to the degrees of freedom, you can be sure that the *p*-value is well above .05. (In this case, the *p*-value is .39.) As with the previous table, the deviance is a test statistic for the null hypothesis that all the omitted terms (three 2-way interactions and one 3-way interaction) are 0.

Despite the fact that the overall deviance is not significant, I also checked to see if any of the two-way interactions might be significant. This could happen if most of the deviance was attributable to a single interaction. The GENMOD code for fitting all the two-way interactions is:

```
PROC GENMOD DATA=wisc;
   CLASS iq ses;
   MODEL coll/total=iq|ses|parent @2/ D=B TYPE3;
RUN;
```

The syntax IQ|SES|PARENT is shorthand for all possible interactions and lower-order terms among the three variables. Because I wasn't interested in the three-way interaction, I included the @2 option, which restricts the model to 2-way interactions and main effects. In Output 4.11 (produced by the TYPE3 option), we see that none of the 2-way interactions is statistically significant.

Output 4.11   *Likelihood Ratio Tests for a Model with 2-Way Interactions*

```
LR Statistics For Type 3 Analysis

Source        DF    ChiSquare   Pr>Chi

IQ             3      25.2021    0.0001
SES            3       2.5691    0.4629
SES*IQ         9      12.4052    0.1914
PARENT         1     724.5295    0.0001
PARENT*IQ      3       2.9357    0.4017
PARENT*SES     3       2.2237    0.5273
```

Now we can feel confident that the main-effects model in Output 4.10 is a reasonably good fit to the data. From the likelihood ratio statistics at the bottom of the output, we see that each of the three variables is highly significant, with parental encouragement having the strongest effect, followed by IQ and then SES.

Turning to the parameter estimates, the easiest one to interpret is the coefficient of 2.4554 for PARENT. Although PARENT has values of 1 for low encouragement and 2 for high encouragement, the coefficient would be identical if the values were 0 for low and 1 for high. Calculating $\exp(2.4554) = 11.65$, we can say that students whose parents gave high levels of encouragement are nearly 12 times as likely to plan to attend college as students whose parents gave low levels of encouragement. Because the sample size is large, this adjusted odds ratio is estimated with good precision: the 95% confidence interval is 9.5 to 14.3 (calculated by hand using the Wald method).

To interpret the IQ and SES coefficients, it's essential to remember that by default GENMOD uses the highest value of a CLASS variable as the reference category. Each of the coefficients is a comparison between a particular category and the reference category. For example, the coefficient of -1.9663 for IQ 1 is a comparison between the low IQ and the high IQ group. Exponentiating this coefficient yields .14, indicating that the odds of college plans among the low IQ group are about one seventh the odds in the high IQ group. For IQ 2, we have $\exp(-1.3722) = .25$. This tell us that students in the lower-middle IQ group have odds that are only about one-fourth the odds for the high group. Finally, comparing upper-middle and high groups, we have exp(–.6331) = .53. Thus, the highest group has about double the odds of college plans as the upper-middle group. From the chi-square column, we see that each of these contrasts with the reference category is statistically significant at well beyond the .001 level.

Again, each of the SES coefficients is a contrast with the high SES category. Each SES level is significantly different from the highest category and, as you might expect, the odds of college plans goes up with each increase in SES. But what about comparisons between other categories? Suppose we want to know if there's a significant difference between lower-middle (SES 2) and upper-middle (SES 3) groups with respect to college plans. The magnitude of the difference is found by taking the difference in coefficients: –.7516 – (–1.058) = .3064. Exponentiating yields 1.36, indicating that the odds of college plans are about 36% higher in the upper-middle than in the lower-middle group. To test for significance of the difference, we can use a CONTRAST statement after the MODEL statement:

```
CONTRAST 'UM vs. LM' ses 0 1 -1 0;
```

The text within the single quotes is a label; a label is mandatory but it can be any text you want. The four numbers after SES tell GENMOD to multiply the SES 1 coefficient by 0, SES 2 by 1, SES 3 by –1, and SES 4 by 0. GENMOD then sums the results and does a likelihood ratio test of the null hypothesis that the sum is equal to 0. Of course, this is equivalent to testing whether the difference between SES 2 and SES 3 is 0. The output clearly indicates that the difference is significant:

```
CONTRAST Statement Results

Contrast      DF    ChiSquare  Pr>Chi  Type

UM vs. LM      1      9.1318    0.0025  LR
```

The pattern of coefficients for IQ and SES suggests that SES and IQ might be treated as quantitative variables, thereby obtaining a more parsimonious representation of the data. This is easily accomplished by removing those variables from the CLASS statement. I estimated two models, one removing IQ from the CLASS statement and the other removing SES from the CLASS statement. When IQ is treated as a quantitative variable, the deviance is 25.84 with 26 degrees of freedom and a *p*-value of .47. When SES is treated as quantitative, the deviance is 35.24 with 26 degrees of freedom and a *p*-value of .11. While this is still an acceptable fit, it suggests that perhaps the effect of SES is not quite linear. To get a more sensitive test, we can take the difference in deviances between the model with SES as categorical (25.24) and the model with SES as quantitative (35.24), yielding a chi-square of 10 with 2 degrees of freedom (the difference in degrees of freedom for the two models). This test has a *p*-value of .0067, telling us that the model with SES as categorical fits significantly better than the model with SES as quantitative.

Output 4.12 gives the results for the model with SES as categorical and IQ as quantitative. By removing IQ from the CLASS statement, we impose the restriction that each one-level jump in IQ has the same effect on the odds of planning to go to college. Exponentiating the IQ coefficient of .6682, we get 1.95. We can then say that each one-level increase in IQ approximately doubles the odds (controlling for SES and parental encouragement). Consequently, moving three steps (from IQ 1 to IQ 4) multiplies the odds by $1.95^3 = 7.4$.

Output 4.12   *Model with Quantitative Effect of IQ*

```
             Analysis Of Parameter Estimates

 Parameter        DF    Estimate    Std Err   ChiSquare   Pr>Chi

 INTERCEPT        1     -5.7635     0.2265    647.7589    0.0001
 IQ               1      0.6682     0.0367    332.0319    0.0001
 SES       1      1     -1.4131     0.1209    136.5537    0.0001
 SES       2      1     -1.0566     0.1028    105.5986    0.0001
 SES       3      1     -0.7486     0.0975     58.9692    0.0001
 SES       4      0      0.0000     0.0000        .          .
 PARENT           1      2.4532     0.1013    586.0945    0.0001
```

The coefficients for SES and PARENT are about the same as they were in Output 4.10. Examination of the SES coefficients yields some insight into why couldn't we impose a linear effect of SES. If the effect of SES were linear, the difference between adjacent coefficients should be the same at every level. Yet, while the difference between SES 4 and SES 3 is .75, the difference between SES 3 and SES 2 is only .31. With a sample size of nearly 5,000, even small differences like this may show up as statistically significant.

Although GENMOD doesn't compute an R^2, it's easy enough to calculate one yourself. First, you must fit a null model—a model with no explanatory variables. For the data at hand, this can be done with the statement:

```
MODEL coll/tot= / D=B;
```

The deviance for the null model is 2262.61. For the model in Output 4.12, the deviance is 25.85. The difference of 2236.76 is the chi-square for the testing of the null hypothesis that all the coefficients are 0. Applying the formula in equation (3.10) yields a generalized R^2 of .36.

Before leaving the four-way table, let's consider one more model. It's reasonable to argue that parental encouragement is an intervening variable in the production of college plans. Students with high IQ and high SES are more likely to get parental encouragement for attending college. As a result, controlling for parental encouragement may obscure the overall impact of these two variables. To check this possibility, Output 4.13 displays a model that excludes PARENT. The coefficient for IQ increases slightly—on the odds scale, it's about 14% larger. For SES the change is more dramatic. The coefficient for SES 1 has a magnitude of 2.13 in Output 4.13 compared with 1.41 in Output 4.12, corresponding to odds ratios of 8.41 vs. 4.10. So the effect of going from the lowest to highest category of SES more than doubles when PARENT is removed from the model. It appears, then, that parental encouragement mediates a substantial portion of the overall effect of SES on college plans.

Output 4.13 *Model without PARENT*

```
              Analysis Of Parameter Estimates

Parameter        DF    Estimate    Std Err   ChiSquare  Pr>Chi

INTERCEPT         1     -1.5724    0.1123    196.1821   0.0001
IQ                1      0.7953    0.0335    565.1182   0.0001
SES        1      1     -2.1340    0.1091    382.5562   0.0001
SES        2      1     -1.5361    0.0935    269.6874   0.0001
SES        3      1     -0.9776    0.0894    119.4661   0.0001
SES        4      0      0.0000    0.0000         .         .
```

4.6   Overdispersion

When estimating logit models with grouped data, it often happens that the model doesn't fit—the deviance and Pearson chi-square are large, relative to the degrees of freedom. Lack of fit is sometimes described as *overdispersion*. Overdispersion has two possible causes:

■   An incorrectly specified model: more interactions and/or nonlinearities are needed in the model.

- ■ Lack of independence of the observations: this can arise from unobserved heterogeneity that operates at the level of groups rather than individuals.

We've already seen examples of the first cause. Now let's look at an example where overdispersion may arise from dependence among the observations. The sample consists of 40 U.S. biochemistry departments in the late 1950s and early 1960s (McGinnis, Allison and Long 1982). Three variables are measured:

NIH Total NIH obligations to the university in 1964, in millions of dollars
DOCS Number of biochemistry doctorates awarded during the period
PDOC Number of doctorates who got postdoctoral training

The aim is to estimate a logit model predicting the probability that a doctorate will receive postdoctoral training.

Here's the SAS code to read in the data:

```
DATA my.nihdoc;
  INPUT nih docs pdoc;
  DATALINES;
.5 8 1
.5 9 3
.835 16 1
.998 13 6
1.027 8 2
2.036 9 2
2.106 29 10
2.329 5 2
2.523 7 5
2.524 8 4
2.874 7 4
3.898 7 5
4.118 10 4
4.130 5 1
4.145 6 3
4.242 7 2
4.280 9 4
4.524 6 1
4.858 5 2
4.893 7 2
4.944 5 4
5.279 5 1
5.548 6 3
5.974 5 4
6.733 6 5
```

```
7 12 5
9.115 6 2
9.684 5 3
12.154 8 5
13.059 5 3
13.111 10 8
13.197 7 4
13.433 86 33
13.749 12 7
14.367 29 21
14.698 19 5
15.440 10 6
17.417 10 8
18.635 14 9
21.524 18 16
;
```

We then specify a logit model by using GENMOD with the *event/trials* syntax:

```
PROC GENMOD DATA=my.nihdoc;
   MODEL pdoc/docs=nih / D=B;
RUN;
```

In Output 4.14, we see that there is a highly significant effect of NIH obligations. Each one-million dollar increase is associated with a 100[1−exp(.0729)])=7.6% increase in the odds that a graduate will pursue postdoctoral training. But the model doesn't fit well. The deviance is nearly 70% larger than the degrees of freedom, with a *p*-value less than .01.

Output 4.14 *GENMOD Results for Doctorate Data*

```
      Criteria For Assessing Goodness Of Fit

   Criterion           DF        Value      Value/DF

   Deviance            38      64.1642       1.6885
   Scaled Deviance     38      64.1642       1.6885
   Pearson Chi-Square  38      61.0211       1.6058
   Scaled Pearson X2   38      61.0211       1.6058
   Log Likelihood       .    -306.2974          .


         Analysis Of Parameter Estimates

Parameter   DF    Estimate    Std Err   ChiSquare  Pr>Chi

INTERCEPT   1      -0.7871     0.1748    20.2746    0.0001
NIH         1       0.0729     0.0158    21.2405    0.0001
```

What can we do about this? Well, we can get a saturated model by deleting NIH and putting in dummy variables for 39 of the 40 universities. That wouldn't be very informative, however—we might just as well look at the percentages receiving postdoctoral training across the 40 universities. Because there's only one independent variable, we don't have the option of including interactions, but we can allow for nonlinearities by including powers of NIH in the model. I tried a squared term but that didn't help at all. The addition of a cubed term got the *p*-value up to .032, but further powers didn't bring any improvement (I tried up to the 7th power). In short, any polynomial model with enough terms to fit would be so complicated that it would have little appeal over the saturated model.

However, it's quite possible that the lack of fit is due not to departures from linearity in the effect NIH funding but to a lack of independence in the observations. There are many characteristics of biochemistry departments besides NIH funding that may have some impact on whether their graduates seek and get postdoctoral training. Possibilities include the prestige of the department, whether the department is in an agricultural school or a medical school, and the age of the department. Omitting these variables from the model could induce a residual correlation among the observations: people from the same department tend to have the same outcome because they share a common environment. This lack of independence will produce what is called *extra-binomial variation*—the variance of the dependent variable will be greater than what is expected under the assumption of a binomial distribution. Besides producing a large deviance, extra-binomial variation can result in underestimates of the standard errors and overestimates of the chi-square statistics.

One approach to this problem is to adjust the chi-squares and test statistics, leaving the coefficient estimates unchanged. The adjustment is quite simple: Take the ratio of the goodness-of-fit chi-square to its degrees of freedom, and then divide all the individual chi-squares by that ratio. Equivalently, take the square root of the ratio and multiply all the standard errors by that number. This adjustment can be based either on the Pearson chi-square or the deviance, but most authorities prefer the Pearson statistic.

The adjustment is easily implemented in GENMOD. In the MODEL statement, the option DSCALE makes the adjustment with the deviance chi-square and the option PSCALE uses the Pearson chi-square. In LOGISTIC, the corresponding options are SCALE=D and SCALE=P. You must also include the AGGREGATE option or LOGISTIC won't know how to compute the goodness-of-fit statistics.

Output 4.15 shows the results for GENMOD with the PSCALE option. For the first time, we see something besides 1.0 for the SCALE parameter. As noted at the bottom of the output, this is just the square root of the Pearson's chi-square divided by the degrees of freedom. The standard errors were obtained by multiplying the original standard errors by this scale factor. The chi-squares were obtained by dividing the chi-squares in Output 4.14 by 1.6058, resulting in a decline from 21.2 to 13.2 for NIH. Because the deviance and the Pearson chi-square are pretty close for this data, switching to the DSCALE option wouldn't make much difference.

Output 4.15   *Doctorate Model with Overdispersion Adjustment*

```
                  Criteria For Assessing Goodness Of Fit

           Criterion            DF        Value      Value/DF

           Deviance             38       64.1642       1.6885
           Scaled Deviance      38       39.9573       1.0515
           Pearson Chi-Square   38       61.0211       1.6058
           Scaled Pearson X2    38       38.0000       1.0000
           Log Likelihood        .     -190.7424          .


                       Analysis Of Parameter Estimates

      Parameter    DF    Estimate    Std Err    ChiSquare   Pr>Chi

      INTERCEPT     1     -0.7871     0.2215     12.6257     0.0004
      NIH           1      0.0729     0.0200     13.2272     0.0003
      SCALE         0      1.2672     0.0000        .           .


 NOTE: The scale parameter was estimated by the square root of
 Pearson's Chi-Squared/DOF.
```

Note that the coefficients in Output 4.15 with the PSCALE option are exactly the same as those in Output 4.14 without the overdispersion correction. PROC LOGISTIC offers an additional overdispersion correction proposed by Williams (1982) that modifies the coefficients as well as the standard errors. Based on the method of quasi-likelihood, these coefficients may be more statistically efficient than the conventional estimates. The SAS code for implemeting this correction is

```
PROC LOGISTIC DATA=my.nihdoc;
  MODEL pdoc/docs=nih / D=B AGGREGATE SCALE=WILLIAMS;
RUN;
```

Results are shown in Output 4.16. Williams' method uses iterative reweighting of the observations, and this is reflected in much of the reported output. In the preliminary output, we see the weight function used at the final iteration, along with the sum of the weights. This sum can be thought of as the effective sample size after correction for overdispersion. Although both Pearson and deviance chi-squares are reported, there is a warning that they are not to be used to assess the fit of the model. Both the coefficient and the chi-square for NIH are a little larger than they were under the simpler PSCALE correction in Output 4.15. (For other approaches to analyzing this data see Allison (1987)). Note that when the group size variable (DOCS in this example) has the same value for all groups, Williams' method does not alter the conventional coefficient estimates, and the standard error correction is the same as the simpler adjustment using Pearson's chi-square.

Output 4.16 *Doctorate Model with Williams' Adjustment for Overdispersion*

```
Weight Variable: 1 / ( 1 + 0.042183 * (DOCS - 1) )
Sum of Weights: 276.89669094
Link Function: Logit


                         Response Profile

              Ordered  Binary                    Total
              Value    Outcome       Count        Weight

                  1    EVENT           216       133.24419
                  2    NO EVENT        243       143.65250


           Deviance and Pearson Goodness-of-Fit Statistics
                                                        Pr >
           Criterion      DF      Value    Value/DF   Chi-Square

           Deviance       38     39.8872    1.0497      0.3862
           Pearson        38     38.0000    1.0000      0.4695


              Number of events/trials observations: 40

WARNING: Because the Williams method was used to accommodate
         overdispersion, the Pearson chi-squared statistic and the
         deviance can no longer be used to assess the goodness of fit
         of the model.

   Model Fitting Information and Testing Global Null Hypothesis BETA=0

                              Intercept
                 Intercept      and
     Criterion     Only      Covariates    Chi-Square for Covariates

     AIC          385.469      370.396           .
     SC           389.598      378.654           .
     -2 LOG L     383.469      366.396      17.073 with 1 DF (p=0.0001)
     Score           .            .        16.788 with 1 DF (p=0.0001)
```

Output 4.16 *Continued*

		Analysis of Maximum Likelihood Estimates				
Variable	DF	Parameter Estimate	Standard Error	Wald Chi-Square	Pr > Chi-Square	Standardized Estimate	Odds Ratio
INTERCPT	1	-0.7522	0.2084	13.0333	0.0003	.	.
NIH	1	0.0829	0.0206	16.1428	0.0001	0.218879	1.086

What makes the doctorate example different from the earlier examples in this chapter is that the individuals are grouped into naturally occurring clusters, in this case, university departments. It's reasonable to suppose that individuals in the same department are *not* independent—not only can they influence each other, but they are also exposed to many common factors that may produce the same outcome. In most contingency table analyses, on the other hand, individuals are grouped together merely because they have the same values on some discrete variable. In such cases, there is usually no reason to think that the observations within groups are anything other than independent. When independence is presumed, the correct strategy for dealing with overdispersion is to elaborate the model until you find a version that does fit the data, not to casually invoke the overdispersion options. If, after diligent investigation, you cannot come up with a reasonably parsimonious model with an acceptable fit to the data, then there may be some value in correcting the standard errors and test statistics for any remaining overdispersion. But be aware that the correction for overdispersion always produces chi-square tests that are lower than they would be without the correction. Note also that overdispersion does *not* arise from heterogeneity *within* groups. The problem stems from differences *between* groups, which are not fully described by the measured variables. In Chapter 8, we'll see how to analyze individual-level data when there is clustering and a lack of independence. The problem is the same—standard errors that are biased downward—but the solution is rather different.

It's also worth noting that the "badness of fit" for the NIH data comes primarily from a small number of observations. When I used the OBSTATS option in the MODEL statement of GENMOD, I found that two departments had deviance residuals (see Section 2.8) greater than 2.5. In particular, the largest department—with 86 doctorates and 33 postdocs—had a predicted value of 47 postdocs. The department with 19 doctorates had a predicted value of 11 postdocs, but only 5 observed postdocs. When the model is fit after deleting these two observations, the deviance falls to 37.9 with 36 degreees of freedom, for a *p*-value of .38.

While this result is not inconsistent with the hypothesis of overdispersion, it does suggest that special attention be paid to these two departments to determine how they differ from others.

One way they differ is size. Both departments graduated many more doctorates than the median number of 8. Perhaps we can improve the fit by including DOCS as an independent variable in the model:

```
PROC GENMOD DATA=my.nihdoc;
  MODEL pdoc/docs=nih docs/ D=B;
RUN;
```

As shown in Output 4.17, this change does produce a much better fitting model, with a *p*-value of .07. Departmental size has a highly significant, negative effect on the probability that a new doctorate will get a postdoctoral fellowship. In general, the most desirable way to deal with overdispersion is to incorporate covariates that account for differences among the groups. But that may not always be possible.

Output 4.17 *Doctorate Model with DOCS as a Covariate*

```
           Criteria For Assessing Goodness Of Fit

     Criterion            DF        Value      Value/DF

     Deviance             37       50.3161      1.3599
     Scaled Deviance      37       50.3161      1.3599
     Pearson Chi-Square   37       47.8917      1.2944
     Scaled Pearson X2    37       47.8917      1.2944
     Log Likelihood        .     -299.3734         .


              Analysis Of Parameter Estimates

   Parameter   DF   Estimate   Std Err   ChiSquare   Pr>Chi

   INTERCEPT    1    -0.6662    0.1786    13.9102    0.0002
   NIH          1     0.0988    0.0178    30.6586    0.0001
   DOCS         1    -0.0131    0.0036    13.3971    0.0003
```

Chapter 5

Multinomial Logit Analysis

5.1   Introduction

Binary logit analysis is ideal when your dependent variable has two categories, but what if it has three or more? In some cases, it may be reasonable to collapse categories so that you have only two, but that strategy inevitably involves some loss of information. In other cases, collapsing categories could seriously obscure what you're trying to study. Suppose you want to estimate a model predicting whether newly registered voters choose to register as Democrats, Republicans, or Independents. Combining any two of these outcomes could lead to seriously misleading conclusions.

How you deal with such situations depends somewhat on the nature of the outcome variable and the goal of the analysis. If the categories of the dependent variable have an inherent ordering, the methods in the next chapter should do the job. If there's no inherent ordering and the goal is a model in which *characteristics of the outcome categories* predict choice of category, then the discrete-choice model of Chapter 7 is probably what you need. In this chapter we consider models for unordered categories where the predictor variables are characteristics of the individual, and possibly the individual's environment. For example, we could estimate a model predicting party choice of newly registered voters based on information about the voter's age, income, and years of schooling. We might also include information about the precinct in which the voter is registering.

The model is called the multinomial logit model because the probability distribution for the outcome variable is assumed to be a multinomial rather than a binomial distribution. Because the multinomial logit model can be rather complicated to interpret when the outcome variable has many categories, I'll begin with the relatively simple case of a three-category outcome.

5.2   Example

As in the binomial case, let's start with a real example. Several years ago, I did a survey of 195 undergraduates at the University of Pennsylvania in order to study the effects of parenting styles on altruistic behavior. One of the questions was "If you found a wallet on the street, would you (1) keep the wallet and the money, (2) keep the money and return the wallet, or (3) return both the wallet and the money." The distribution of responses for the WALLET variable was:

Value   Frequency

1	24	keep both
2	50	keep money
3	121	return both

Possible explanatory variables are

MALE   1= male, 0 = female

BUSINESS   1=enrolled in business school, 0=otherwise

PUNISH   A variable describing whether student was physically punished by parents at various ages:

   1 = punished in elementary school but not middle or high school
   2 = punished in elementary and middle school but not high school
   3 = punished at all three levels.

EXPLAIN   "When you were punished, did your parents generally explain why what you did was wrong?"

   1 = almost always, 0 = sometimes or never.

In the next section we construct a multinomial logit model for the dependence of WALLET on the explanatory variables.

5.3   A Model for Three Categories

First, some notation. Define

p_{i1} = the probability that WALLET=1 for person i,

p_{i2} = the probability that WALLET=2 for person i,

p_{i3} = the probability that WALLET=3 for person i.

Let $\mathbf{x}_i$ be a column vector of explanatory variables for person i:

$$\mathbf{x}_i = [1 \quad x_{i1} \quad x_{i2} \quad x_{i3} \quad x_{i4}]'$$

If this is unfamiliar, you can just think of $\mathbf{x}_i$ as a single explanatory variable. In order to generalize the logit model to this three-category case, it's tempting to consider writing three binary logit models, one for each outcome:

$$\log\left(\frac{p_{i1}}{1-p_{i1}}\right) = \boldsymbol{\beta}_1 \mathbf{x}_i$$

$$\log\left(\frac{p_{i2}}{1-p_{i2}}\right) = \boldsymbol{\beta}_2 \mathbf{x}_i$$

$$\log\left(\frac{p_{i3}}{1-p_{i3}}\right) = \boldsymbol{\beta}_3 \mathbf{x}_i$$

where the $\boldsymbol{\beta}$'s are row vectors of coefficients. This turns out to be an unworkable approach, however. Because $p_{i1}+p_{i2}+p_{i3}=1$, these three equations are inconsistent. If the first two equations are true, for example, the third cannot be true. Instead, we formulate the model as follows:

$$\log\left(\frac{p_{i1}}{p_{i3}}\right) = \boldsymbol{\beta}_1 \mathbf{x}_i$$

$$\log\left(\frac{p_{i2}}{p_{i3}}\right) = \boldsymbol{\beta}_2 \mathbf{x}_i$$

$$\log\left(\frac{p_{i1}}{p_{i2}}\right) = \boldsymbol{\beta}_3 \mathbf{x}_i$$

These equations are mutually consistent and one is redundant. For example, the third equation can be obtained from the first two. Using properties of logarithms, we have

$$\log\left(\frac{p_{i1}}{p_{i2}}\right) = \log\left(\frac{p_{i1}}{p_{i3}}\right) - \log\left(\frac{p_{i2}}{p_{i3}}\right)$$

$$= \boldsymbol{\beta}_1 \mathbf{x}_i - \boldsymbol{\beta}_2 \mathbf{x}_i$$

$$= (\boldsymbol{\beta}_1 - \boldsymbol{\beta}_2)\mathbf{x}_i$$

which implies that $\boldsymbol{\beta}_3 = \boldsymbol{\beta}_1 - \boldsymbol{\beta}_2$. Solving for the three probabilities, we get

$$p_{i1} = \frac{e^{\boldsymbol{\beta}_1 \mathbf{x}_i}}{1 + e^{\boldsymbol{\beta}_1 \mathbf{x}_i} + e^{\boldsymbol{\beta}_2 \mathbf{x}_i}}$$

$$p_{i2} = \frac{e^{\boldsymbol{\beta}_2 \mathbf{x}_i}}{1 + e^{\boldsymbol{\beta}_1 \mathbf{x}_i} + e^{\boldsymbol{\beta}_2 \mathbf{x}_i}}$$

$$p_{i3} = \frac{1}{1 + e^{\boldsymbol{\beta}_1 \mathbf{x}_i} + e^{\boldsymbol{\beta}_2 \mathbf{x}_i}} \ .$$

Because the three numerators sum to the common denominator, we immediately verify that the three probabilities sum to 1.

As with the binary logit model, the most general approach to estimation is maximum likelihood. I won't go through the derivation, but it's very similar to the binary case. Again, the Newton-Raphson algorithm is widely used to get the maximum likelihood estimates. The only SAS procedure that will do this is CATMOD.

5.4   Estimation with CATMOD

CATMOD is a very general procedure for categorical data analysis. In addition to the multinomial logit model, it does loglinear analysis and a variety of specialized models by using either maximum likelihood (ML) or weighted least squares estimation. Although the weighted least squares algorithm only works for grouped data, it can estimate a somewhat wider class of models than maximum likelihood. I consider only ML here, however.

ML estimation of the multinomial logit model is the default in CATMOD so the syntax is relatively simple. One thing to remember, however, is that CATMOD (by default) treats all variables as categorical. If you want to treat an explanatory variable as quantitative, you must put it in a DIRECT statement. For reasons that I'll explain in Section 5.8, I routinely put *all* variables in a DIRECT statement. If any dummy variables are needed in the model, I create them in a DATA step.

Here's the code to estimate a model for the wallet data:

```
PROC CATMOD DATA=my.wallet;
  DIRECT male business punish explain;
  MODEL wallet = male business punish explain / NOITER;
RUN;
```

For now, I'm treating PUNISH as a quantitative variable, but later I'll explore a categorical coding. The NOITER option suppresses the printing of details of the iterations.

Before doing the analysis, CATMOD always groups the data into a contingency table. If some of the explanatory variables are continuous, the grouping process may produce only one observation per cell. For the wallet data, however, three of the explanatory variables are dichotomous, and PUNISH has only three values. Consequently, CATMOD was able to group the 195 cases into 23 different *population profiles*, each profile having exactly the same values on the explanatory variables. The profiles shown in Output 5.1 are printed by default, but you can suppress this listing with the NOPROFILE option in the MODEL statement.

Output 5.1   *Grouping Produced by CATMOD*

```
                    POPULATION PROFILES
                                          Sample
    Sample  MALE BUSINESS  PUNISH  EXPLAIN  Size
    -------------------------------------------------
       1     0     0         1       0      12
       2     0     0         1       1      50
       3     0     0         2       0       7
       4     0     0         2       1       7
       5     0     0         3       0       5
       6     0     0         3       1       3
       7     0     1         1       0       1
       8     0     1         1       1       5
       9     0     1         2       0       1
      10     0     1         2       1       3
      11     0     1         3       0       3
      12     1     0         1       0       9
      13     1     0         1       1      40
      14     1     0         2       0       8
      15     1     0         2       1       3
      16     1     0         3       0       3
      17     1     0         3       1       3
      18     1     1         1       0       5
      19     1     1         1       1      16
      20     1     1         2       0       2
      21     1     1         2       1       4
      22     1     1         3       0       2
      23     1     1         3       1       3
```

The grouping feature has two significant implications. First, if the sample is large and if each independent variable has only a few values, estimation on the grouped data can be *much* faster than estimation on the individual-level data. Second, grouping affects the deviance statistic (likelihood ratio chi-square) in ways that can invalidate comparisons between models unless special care is taken. More on this later.

Output 5.2   *CATMOD Output for Wallet Data*

```
          MAXIMUM-LIKELIHOOD ANALYSIS-OF-VARIANCE TABLE

       Source                 DF   Chi-Square      Prob
       -----------------------------------------------------
       INTERCEPT               2       17.79      0.0001
       MALE                    2       12.28      0.0022
       BUSINESS                2        4.69      0.0960
       PUNISH                  2       10.92      0.0043
       EXPLAIN                 2        9.77      0.0076


       LIKELIHOOD RATIO       36       31.95      0.6619



          ANALYSIS OF MAXIMUM-LIKELIHOOD ESTIMATES

                                       Standard   Chi-
    Effect          Parameter  Estimate  Error   Square   Prob
    ----------------------------------------------------------------
    INTERCEPT            1     -3.4712   0.8439   16.92  0.0000
                         2     -1.2917   0.6073    4.52  0.0334
    MALE                 3      1.2673   0.5546    5.22  0.0223
                         4      1.1699   0.3715    9.92  0.0016
    BUSINESS             5      1.1804   0.5486    4.63  0.0314
                         6      0.4179   0.4233    0.97  0.3235
    PUNISH               7      1.0817   0.3335   10.52  0.0012
                         8      0.1957   0.2889    0.46  0.4981
    EXPLAIN              9     -1.6006   0.5455    8.61  0.0033
                        10     -0.8040   0.4034    3.97  0.0463
```

The main results are shown in Output 5.2. In the first panel of the output, we get global tests for the effect of each variable on the outcome variable, controlling for the other variables in the model. The label—Maximum-Likelihood Analysis-of-Variance Table—is a little misleading. Except for the last line, all the chi-square statistics are Wald statistics, not likelihood ratio statistics. Each chi-square is a test of the null hypothesis that the explanatory variable has no effect on the outcome variable. In this example, there are two degrees of freedom for each chi-square because each variable has two coefficients. So the null hypothesis is that both coefficients are 0. BUSINESS has a *p*-value of .10, but the other three variables are all significant at beyond the .01 level.

The last line in this panel, labeled "Likelihood Ratio," is equivalent to the deviance statistic produced by PROC GENMOD. It's equal to twice the positive difference between the log-likelihoods for the fitted model and the saturated model, and high *p*-values suggest a good fit. The *p*-value of .66 is reassuring, but you should be cautious when interpreting this statistic. As I've repeatedly stressed, deviance statistics calculated from individual-level data do not have chi-square distributions. Because of the grouping, this isn't exactly individual-level data. Nevertheless, we see in Output 5.1 that many of the groups are quite small, and this could lead to inaccurate *p*-values.

The lower panel of Output 5.2 reports the coefficient estimates and associated statistics. As with PROC LOGISTIC, the chi-squares are Wald chi-squares. PROC CATMOD is somewhat weak in labeling this part of the output, but if you keep in mind a few general principles, you can usually make sense of things. The first thing to know is that CATMOD always estimates $K-1$ equations for K categories on the dependent variable. So with a 3-category outcome there are implicitly two equations. For each variable, the first coefficient listed is for the first equation, the second coefficient is for the second equation, and so on. In this example, all the odd-numbered coefficients are for equation 1 and all the even-numbered coefficients are for equation 2. The next thing to remember is that each equation is a contrast between a given category and a reference category. Like CLASS variables in GENMOD, the reference category is always the highest value of the dependent variable. In this case, it's WALLET=3, return the wallet and money. So the first equation is a model for 1 vs. 3, keeping both vs. returning both. The second equation is a model for category 2 vs. category 3, keeping the money and returning the wallet vs. returning both.

To make this clearer, I usually find it helpful to reorganize the CATMOD output into separate equations, as shown in Table 5.1. The first column corresponds to equation 1, the second column to equation 2. The third column, an equation predicting category 1 vs. category 2, can be obtained by simply subtracting the numbers in column 2 from those in column 1. Alternatively, you can get these numbers by recoding the WALLET variable so that "keep the money" is the reference category, instead of "return both" (that is, by changing 2's to 4's) and then rerunning the model. With the recoded data, all the even-numbered parameters correspond to those in the third column of Table 5.1. By doing it this way, you also get *p*-values for all the coefficients.

Table 5.1   *Reorganized Output from PROC CATMOD*

	Keep both vs. return both	Keep one vs. return both	Keep both vs. keep one
INTERCEPT	–3.47**	–1.29*	–2.18*
MALE	1.27*	1.17*	.10
BUSINESS	1.18*	.42	.76
PUNISH	1.08**	.20	.89*
EXPLAIN	–1.60**	–.80*	–.80

$*p<.05, **p<.01$

Examining the first column, we see that all the variables have significant effects on keeping both vs. returning both. Because all the variables were included in the DIRECT statement, the coefficients may be interpreted just like coefficients in a binary logit model. Exponentiating the coefficient for MALE, we get $\exp(1.27) = 3.56$. We can then say that the odds that a male will keep both rather than return both are about 3.5 times the odds for females. Similarly, the odds for students in the business school are about $\exp(1.18) = 3.25$ times the odds for those in other schools. For PUNISH we have $\exp(1.08) = 2.94$, implying that each 1-level increase in that variable multiplies the odds of keeping both vs. returning both by about 3. Finally, students whose parents explained their punishments had odds that were only one-fifth=$\exp(-1.60)$ the odds for those parents who did not explain.

The coefficients in the second column have the same sign as those in the first but are generally much smaller. That's not surprising because the behaviors being compared are less extreme. We still see a big effect of gender. The odds that a male will keep the money vs. returning both are more than three times the odds for females. While the coefficient for EXPLAIN has been cut in half, the odds for those whose parents did *not* explain are still more than double the odds for those whose parents did explain.

The third column has a dual interpretation. The coefficients represent the effect of the explanatory variables on being in category 1 vs. category 2. But they also represent the difference between the coefficients in the first two columns. PUNISH is the only variable whose coefficient declined significantly from column 1 to column 2. Equivalently, PUNISH is the only variable having a significant effect on keeping both vs. keeping the money only.

Each one-level increase of PUNISH more than doubles the odds of keeping both vs. keeping the money only.

It's also possible to test the null hypothesis that *all* the coefficients in the first column are identical to the corresponding coefficients in the second column. The easy way to do it is to include the keyword _RESPONSE_ as a variable in the MODEL statement:

```
MODEL wallet = _RESPONSE_ male business punish explain /
        NOITER;
```

Without going into details, the effect of this statement is to estimate a single set of coefficients rather than separate sets of coefficients for each contrast on the dependent variable. The likelihood ratio (deviance) for this model can then be compared with the likelihood ratio for the model without _RESPONSE_ . In this case, the difference is 14.22 with 4 degrees of freedom for a *p*-value of .007. The low *p*-value tells us to reject the null hypothesis and conclude that at least one pair of coefficients differs across the two equations.

A more general—but more complicated—method is to use a CONTRAST statement after the MODEL statement:

```
CONTRAST 'all'  @1 male 1     @2 male -1,
                @1 business 1 @2 business -1,
                @1 punish 1   @2 punish -1,
                @1 explain 1  @2 explain -1;
```

The CONTRAST statement in CATMOD is very similar to the CONTRAST statement in GENMOD, except for the @ notation. @1 refers to parameters in the first equation and @2 refers to parameters in the second equation. (The CATMOD documentation calls these equations *response functions*.) The first line of the statement says to take the coefficient for MALE in the first equation and multiply it by 1. Then take the coefficient for MALE in the second equation and multiply it by –1. The sum of these products is equal to the difference between the two coefficients. The CONTRAST statement produces a test of the null hypothesis that all the differences are 0. For this example, we get the output:

```
CONTRASTS OF MAXIMUM-LIKELIHOOD ESTIMATES

Contrast                    DF   Chi-Square    Prob
---------------------------------------------------
all                          4       12.29    0.0153
```

This differs slightly from the _RESPONSE_ method because the chi-square is a Wald test rather than a likelihood ratio test.

Although the low value of the likelihood ratio (deviance) statistic in Output 5.2 suggests that the "main effects" model provides an adequate fit to that data, that could be misleading because of the somewhat sparse grouping of the data. A better approach is to directly test for the presence of interactions by including them in the model. Like GENMOD, CATMOD allows multiplicative terms to be included in the MODEL statement. Here's a model with all six 2-way interactions:

```
MODEL wallet = male business punish explain male*business
    male*punish male*explain business*punish business*explain
    punish*explain / NOITER;
```

Results in Output 5.3 give little evidence for interactions—the smallest *p*-value is .22. To test the hypothesis that *all* the 2-way interactions are 0, we can take the difference in likelihood ratio statistics for this model and the one in Output 5.2. That yields a chi-square of 9.17 with 12 degrees of freedom, which is far from statistically significant.

Output 5.3   *ANOVA Table for 2-Way Interaction Model*

```
MAXIMUM-LIKELIHOOD ANALYSIS-OF-VARIANCE TABLE

Source                DF   Chi-Square      Prob
------------------------------------------------
INTERCEPT              2         6.93     0.0313
MALE                  2         0.76     0.6830
BUSINESS              2         0.91     0.6340
PUNISH                2         3.36     0.1865
EXPLAIN               2         0.18     0.9132
MALE*BUSINESS         2         2.49     0.2873
MALE*PUNISH           2         0.34     0.8440
MALE*EXPLAIN          2         1.27     0.5299
BUSINESS*PUNISH       2         0.98     0.6118
BUSINESS*EXPLAIN      2         0.88     0.6453
PUNISH*EXPLAIN        2         3.00     0.2235

LIKELIHOOD RATIO     24        22.78     0.5330
```

5.5 Estimation with a Binary Logit Procedure

As we've just seen, the multinomial logit model can be interpreted as a set of binary logit equations, each equation corresponding to a comparison between two of the categories of the dependent variable. It turns out that you can legitimately estimate the multinomial logit model by running a set of binary logit models (Begg and Gray 1984). For each two-category contrast, observations that fall into other categories are excluded. Here's how to do it for the three columns of Table 5.1:

```
PROC LOGISTIC DATA=my.wallet;
  WHERE wallet NE 2;
  MODEL wallet=male business punish explain;
RUN;
PROC LOGISTIC DATA=my.wallet;
  WHERE wallet NE 1;
  MODEL wallet=male business punish explain;
RUN;
PROC LOGISTIC DATA=my.wallet;
  WHERE wallet NE 3;
  MODEL wallet=male business punish explain;
RUN;
```

In the WHERE statements, NE means "not equal to." Because WALLET has only three categories, removing any one of them reduces the model to a binary logit model. Results are shown in Table 5.2. Comparing this with Table 5.1, we see that the coefficients are very similar but not identical. The significance levels are also pretty much the same, although the *p*-value for BUSINESS is slightly below .05 in Table 5.1 and slightly above in Table 5.2.

Table 5.2   *Multinomial Estimates by Using Binary Logits*

	Keep both vs. return both	Keep one vs. return both	Keep both vs. keep one
INTERCEPT	–3.53**	–1.33*	–2.28*
MALE	1.42*	1.14*	.18
BUSINESS	1.07	.38	.79
PUNISH	1.09**	.23	.87*
EXPLAIN	–1.63**	–.77*	–.68

*p<.05, **p<.01

The coefficients in Table 5.2 are no more biased than the ones in Table 5.1 (in technical terms, they have the same probability limit). But the binary estimates in Table 5.2 are less efficient—they have somewhat larger standard errors. Furthermore, unlike Table 5.1, the third column of Table 5.2 is *not* exactly equal to the difference between the first two columns. Finally, estimation by binary logits won't give you a global test of whether *all* the coefficients for a particular variable are equal to 0, as do the tests in the Analysis of Variance section of Output 5.2.

What's the point of this exercise? Well, occasionally you may find yourself in a situation where it's more convenient to do binary estimation than multinomial estimation. One possible advantage in doing it this way is that you can have different sets of variables in different equations. But I think the main payoff is conceptual. When I first learned this equivalence, it really helped me understand that the multinomial model is built up of binomial models. The simultaneous estimation procedure is just a technical refinement.

5.6   General Form of the Model

To this point, we've been dealing with just three categories for the dependent variable. Now let's generalize the model to J categories, with the running index $j=1, ..., J$. Let p_{ij} be the probability that individual i falls into category j. The model is then

$$\log\left(\frac{p_{ij}}{p_{iJ}}\right) = \boldsymbol{\beta}_j \mathbf{x}_i \qquad j = 1,...,J-1 \qquad (5.1)$$

where $\mathbf{x}_i$ is a column vector of variables describing individual i and $\boldsymbol{\beta}_j$ is a row vector of coefficients for category j. Note that each category is compared with the highest category J. These equations can be solved to yield

$$p_{ij} = \frac{e^{\boldsymbol{\beta}_j \mathbf{x}_i}}{1 + \sum_{k=1}^{J-1} e^{\boldsymbol{\beta}_k \mathbf{x}_i}} \qquad j = 1,...,J-1 \qquad (5.2)$$

Because the probabilities for all J categories must sum to 1, we have

$$p_{iJ} = \frac{1}{1 + \sum_{k=1}^{J-1} e^{\boldsymbol{\beta}_k \mathbf{x}_i}}$$

After the coefficients are estimated, the logit equation for comparing any two categories j and k of the dependent variable can be obtained from

$$\log\left(\frac{p_{ij}}{p_{ik}}\right) = \left(\boldsymbol{\beta}_j - \boldsymbol{\beta}_k\right)\mathbf{x}_i \; .$$

5.7   Contingency Table Analysis

As with binary logit analysis, the multinomial logit model can be easily applied to the analysis of contingency tables. Consider Table 5.3, which was tabulated from the 1991 General Social Survey (Agresti 1996).

Table 5.3   *Belief in an Afterlife, by Gender and Race*

		Belief in Afterlife		
		Yes	Undecided	No
White	Female	371	49	74
	Male	250	45	71
Black	Female	64	9	15
	Male	25	5	13

The dependent variable—belief in an afterlife—has three categories, which we'll treat as unordered. Here's how to fit the multinomial logit model with CATMOD:

```
DATA my.afterlif;
  INPUT white female belief freq;
  DATALINES;
1 1 1 371
1 1 2  49
1 1 3  74
1 0 1 250
1 0 2  45
1 0 3  71
0 1 1  64
0 1 2   9
0 1 3  15
0 0 1  25
```

```
0 0 2   5
0 0 3  13
;
PROC CATMOD DATA=my.afterlif;
  WEIGHT freq;
  DIRECT white female;
  MODEL belief=white female / NOITER PRED;
RUN;
```

Note that belief is coded: 1=Yes, 2=Undecided, and 3=No. Because "No" has the highest value, it becomes the reference category parameterizing the model.

Results are shown in Output 5.4. From the ANOVA table, we see evidence for a gender effect but no indication of a race effect. The likelihood ratio (deviance) indicates that the model fits very well. In this case, that simply means that there's no evidence of an interaction between race and gender in their effects on belief in an afterlife.

Output 5.4 *CATMOD Results for Afterlife Data*

```
        MAXIMUM-LIKELIHOOD ANALYSIS-OF-VARIANCE TABLE

    Source                DF   Chi-Square    Prob
    -------------------------------------------------
    INTERCEPT              2       34.14     0.0000
    WHITE                 2        2.08     0.3534
    FEMALE                2        7.21     0.0272

    LIKELIHOOD RATIO      2        0.85     0.6525



        ANALYSIS OF MAXIMUM-LIKELIHOOD ESTIMATES

                                  Standard   Chi-
Effect          Parameter  Estimate   Error   Square   Prob
-----------------------------------------------------------
INTERCEPT           1       0.8831   0.2426   13.25   0.0003
                    2      -0.7580   0.3614    4.40   0.0359
WHITE               3       0.3418   0.2370    2.08   0.1493
                    4       0.2710   0.3541    0.59   0.4442
FEMALE              5       0.4186   0.1713    5.97   0.0145
                    6       0.1051   0.2465    0.18   0.6700
```

In the lower portion of the output, the odd-numbered parameters pertain to the equation for yes vs. no (1 vs. 3): the even-numbered parameters pertain to the equation for undecided vs. no (2 vs. 3). The gender effect seems to be entirely concentrated in the yes/no contrast. Taking exp(.4186)=1.52, we can say that women are about 50% more likely than men to say that they believe in an afterlife.

Now, suppose we wanted to test the null hypothesis that *all* the coefficients are 0. In GENMOD, we would estimate a null model by removing both variables, and then taking the difference in the deviances for the fitted and null models. Unfortunately, that doesn't work with CATMOD. Whenever you delete variables from the model (main effects, not interactions), CATMOD collapses the table across levels of the excluded variables. Deleting both WHITE and FEMALE results in a one-way table for BELIEF only. The likelihood ratio statistic is 0, so it appears that deleting the variables produces a *better* fit.

There are two ways to fix this problem. One is to compare log-likelihoods rather than deviances, because these are invariant to the level of grouping on the independent variables. To see the log-likelihoods, you have to remove the NOITER option from the MODEL statement. For the fitted model, CATMOD reports 1547.45 for $-2 \times$ log-likelihood. For the null model, the figure is 1556.20. The difference is 8.75 with 4 degrees of freedom (the number of coefficients deleted), for a *p*-value of .07.

The alternative method is to use the POPULATION statement. This statement forces CATMOD to use a specified level of grouping so that likelihood ratio statistics can be compared across different models. For this example, the SAS code for fitting the null model is

```
PROC CATMOD DATA=my.afterlif;
  WEIGHT freq;
  DIRECT white female;
  POPULATION white female;
  MODEL belief= / NOITER PRED;
RUN;
```

Here the POPULATION statement ensures that the original table will not be collapsed when variables are removed from the MODEL. The likelihood ratio statistic for this model is 9.60 with 6 degrees of freedom. From that we subtract .85 with 2 degrees of freedom for the fitted model, giving us 8.75 with 4 degrees of freedom—the same as we got from the log-likelihood comparison.

In the program code, I included the option PRED. While not essential, this option produces a table of observed and predicted probabilities, as shown in Output 5.5. The "Samples" correspond to the four configurations of the independent variables, previously referred to as population profiles. For each sample, the lines labeled as function numbers 1 and 2 are the observed and predicted logits for the two logit equations. The lines labeled P1, P2, and P3 include the observed proportions and predicted probabilities for each sample. The residual column is the difference between the observed and predicted value on each line (with no division by standard error or other standardization). Examining the residuals for the P lines, we see that none of them are very large. If you want to see predicted and observed *frequencies* instead of probabilities, you can change the option to PRED=FREQ. Unfortunately, you can't get both on the same run. You can also write this output (including values of the independent variables) onto a SAS data set by using the RESPONSE statement with an OUT= option, which makes it possible to do any additional analysis on the saved table rather than on the original data set. This is convenient if you're working with a large data set that collapses into a much smaller table.

Output 5.5   *Observed and Predicted Values Produced by CATMOD*

```
MAXIMUM-LIKELIHOOD PREDICTED VALUES FOR RESPONSE FUNCTIONS AND PROBABILITIES

                -------Observed-------   -------Predicted------
        Function               Standard               Standard
Sample  Number   Function       Error     Function     Error      Residual
--------------------------------------------------------------------------
   1       1     0.65392647   0.34194017  0.88305212  0.24263714  -0.2291257
           2     -0.9555114   0.52623481  -0.7580088  0.36135435  -0.1975026

          P1     0.58139535   0.07523217  0.62216401  0.04920983  -0.0407687
          P2     0.11627907   0.04888483  0.12055943  0.03305449  -0.0042804
          P3     0.30232558   0.07003734  0.25727656  0.04555334   0.04504902

   2       1     1.45083288   0.28686524  1.30160255  0.22648903   0.14923033
           2     -0.5108256   0.42163702  -0.652945   0.3404589    0.14211937

          P1     0.72727273   0.04747572  0.70735168  0.04031377   0.01992105
          P2     0.10227273   0.03230062  0.10018119  0.02639193   0.00209154
          P3     0.17045455   0.04008511  0.19246714  0.0346491   -0.0220126

   3       1     1.25878104   0.13447865  1.22482647  0.12810449   0.03395457
           2     -0.4560174   0.19054325  -0.4870336  0.18314551   0.03101617

          P1     0.68306011   0.02432077  0.67827035  0.02354119   0.00478976
          P2     0.12295082   0.01716474  0.12244794  0.01657235   0.00050288
          P3     0.19398907   0.02066896  0.19928172  0.02008154  -0.0052926

   4       1     1.61213697   0.1273143   1.6433769   0.12408349  -0.0312399
           2     -0.4122448   0.18417838  -0.3819697  0.17875053  -0.030275

          P1     0.75101215   0.0194558   0.75456083  0.01875676  -0.0035487
          P2     0.09919028   0.01344893  0.09956287  0.01307961  -0.0003726
          P3     0.14979757   0.01605647  0.1458763   0.01530558   0.00392127
```

5.8   CATMOD Coding of Categorical Variables

In the analysis of the wallet data, we treated PUNISH—which has values of 1, 2, and 3—as a quantitative variable. This assumes that the effect of changing from 1 to 2 is the same as the effect of changing from 2 to 3. How can we test this assumption? The simplest way is to remove PUNISH from the DIRECT statement, thereby telling SAS to treat it as a categorical variable. When I did that, I got a likelihood ratio statistic of 31.92 with 34 degrees of freedom. Subtracting that result from the likelihood ratio in Output 5.2 yields a chi-square of .03 with 2 degrees of freedom. In other words, the fit hardly improved at all when the linearity constraint was relaxed. We conclude that treating PUNISH as a quantitative variable is fully consistent with the data.

Removing PUNISH from the DIRECT statement is fine for testing linearity, but if linearity is rejected it's not so easy to interpret the coefficients. In Output 5.6 we see that CATMOD reports four coefficients for PUNISH. When I explain what they mean, you'll see why I generally prefer to create dummy variables in the DATA step rather than let CATMOD manage them.

Output 5.6   *CATMOD Model with Categorical Version of PUNISH*

```
           ANALYSIS OF MAXIMUM-LIKELIHOOD ESTIMATES

                                     Standard    Chi-
Effect          Parameter  Estimate    Error    Square    Prob
-----------------------------------------------------------------
INTERCEPT           1       -1.3108    0.4836     7.35    0.0067
                    2       -0.9060    0.3918     5.35    0.0207
MALE                3        1.2672    0.5541     5.23    0.0222
                    4        1.1716    0.3717     9.93    0.0016
BUSINESS            5        1.1791    0.5486     4.62    0.0316
                    6        0.4156    0.4234     0.96    0.3264
PUNISH              7       -1.0954    0.3661     8.95    0.0028
                    8       -0.2008    0.2915     0.47    0.4909
                    9        0.0497    0.3920     0.02    0.8992
                   10        0.0484    0.3488     0.02    0.8897
EXPLAIN            11       -1.5935    0.5490     8.43    0.0037
                   12       -0.7978    0.4060     3.86    0.0494
```

As before, the odd-numbered coefficients correspond to keep both vs. keep none and the even-numbered coefficients correspond to keep one vs. keep none. Things become a little clearer if we rearrange and label the PUNISH coefficients, as in Table 5.4. I'll explain the derived coefficients in the third row in a moment.

Table 5.4   *Rearrangement of PUNISH Coefficients from Output 5.6*

	Keep both vs. keep none	Keep one vs. keep none
PUNISH 1	−1.0954	−.2008
PUNISH 2	.0497	.0484
PUNISH 3	(1.0457)	(.1524)

The crucial thing to remember about categorical variables in CATMOD is that even though there is an omitted category (PUNISH=3), the coefficients are *not* contrasts with this category. Instead of setting one of the three coefficients equal to 0, CATMOD constrains their *sum* to be 0. This is sometimes called analysis of variance coding or effect coding, as opposed to the dummy variable coding used by GENMOD. I wouldn't mind this so much if CATMOD reported all three coefficients for PUNISH but, in fact, it only reports two of the three. To get the third coefficient, you must sum the ones that *are* reported and change the sign of the result. That's how I got the numbers in parenthesis in Table 5.4. You can verify that the three numbers in each column add up to 0.

Each coefficient in Table 5.4 can be thought of as a deviation from the "average" outcome rather than as a contrast with some specific category. In the first column, we see that PUNISH=2 is right in the middle, while 1 and 3 are at the extremes. The pattern is the same in the second column but the extremes are much smaller. The differences between any two coefficients in a column are identical to the differences obtained under dummy variable coding. That implies that subtracting the last coefficient in each column from the two above it produces the coefficients that would be obtained with dummy variable coding. These are shown in Table 5.5.

Table 5.5   *Dummy Variable Coefficients for PUNISH*

	Keep both vs. keep none	Keep one vs. keep none
PUNISH 1	− 2.1411	−.3532
PUNISH 2	−.9960	−.1040
PUNISH 3	.0000	.0000

So if you're willing to do a little work, you can make the CATMOD output for CLASS variables speak clearly. Personally, I would rather put in the work up front, creating appropriate dummy variables in a DATA step and putting all variables in the DIRECT statement. That way I know exactly what I'm getting.

5.9   Problems of Interpretation

When the dependent variable has only three categories, the multinomial logit model is reasonably easy to interpret. But as the number of categories increases, it becomes more and more difficult to tell a simple story about the results. As we've seen, the model is most naturally interpreted in terms of effects on contrasts between pairs of categories for the dependent variable. But with a five-category dependent variable, there are 10 different possible pairs of categories. With a 10-category dependent variable, the number of pairs shoots up to 45. There's no simple solution to this problem, but Long (1997) has proposed a graphical method of interpreting the coefficients that can be very helpful for a moderate number of categories.

There's still another interpretational problem that even experienced users of multinomial logit analysis may overlook. In binary logit analysis, if a variable x has a positive coefficient, you know that every increase in x results in an increase in the probability of the designated outcome. That's not always true in the multinomial model.

Consider the following hypothetical example. Suppose the dependent variable has three categories (1, 2, and 3) and there is a single independent variable x. When we estimate a multinomial logit model, we get the following two equations:

$$\log\left(\frac{p_1}{p_3}\right) = 1.0 - 2.0x$$

$$\log\left(\frac{p_2}{p_3}\right) = 1.0 - 1.0x.$$

How can we describe the effect of x on p_2? Because the coefficient of x in the second equation is negative, it's tempting to say that increases in x produce decreases in the probability of being in category 2. But if we solve the equations for p_2, we get

$$p_2 = \frac{e^{1-x}}{1 + e^{1-x} + e^{1-2x}}$$

A graph of this equation is shown in Figure 5.1. We see that when p_2 is below .5, increases in x produce increases in p_2. When p_2 is above .5, increases in x produce decreases in p_2.

Figure 5.1   *Effect of x on the Probability of Being in Category 2*

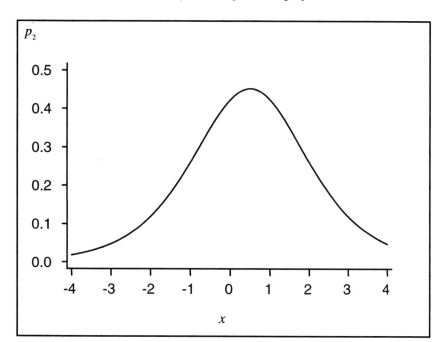

What's going on here? The diagram in Figure 5.2 might help make sense of the situation. The structure of the model is such that increases in x tend to move individuals from category 2 to category 3. But increases in x also tend to move individuals from category 1 to category 2. When x is very low, most of the cases are in category 1, so most of the movement is from 1 to 2 and the proportion of cases in 2 goes up. Eventually, however, there are few cases left in 1 so most of the movement is from 2 to 3, and the proportion remaining in 2 declines.

Figure 5.2   *Movement of Individuals as x Increases*

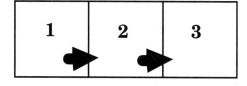

The upshot of this phenomenon is that multinomial logit coefficients must always be interpreted as effects on contrasts between pairs of categories, never on the probability of being in a particular category.

Chapter 6

Logit Analysis for Ordered Categories

6.1   Introduction

In the last chapter we studied the multinomial logit model for dependent variables with three or more _unordered_ categories. When the categories are ordered, it would not be incorrect to simply ignore the ordering and estimate a multinomial model. However, there are two reasons for preferring models that take the ordering into account:

- They are much easier to interpret.
- Hypothesis tests are more powerful.

The disadvantage of ordered models is that they impose restrictions on the data that may be inappropriate. So whenever you use an ordered model, it's important to test whether its restrictions are valid.

Unlike the unordered case, there are several different ways of generalizing the logit model to handle ordered categories. In this chapter, we'll examine three:

- The cumulative logit model
- The adjacent categories model
- The continuation ratio model.

When the dependent variable has only two categories, all three models reduce to the usual binary logit model.

Of the three, the cumulative logit model—also known as the ordered logit or ordinal logit model—is the most widely applicable, and the one that is most easily used in SAS. The adjacent categories model is also an attractive general approach, but SAS can only estimate the model when the data is grouped. The continuation ratio model is more specialized. It's designed for situations in which the ordered categories represent a progression through stages.

6.2   Cumulative Logit Model: Example

The cumulative logit model (McCullagh 1980) could hardly be easier to implement in SAS. Whenever PROC LOGISTIC encounters more than two categories on the dependent variable, it automatically estimates a cumulative logit model. Let's try it and see what we get. Then we'll step back and discuss the underlying model.

In Chapter 5, we analyzed data in which the dependent variable was the response to the question, "If you found a wallet on the street, would you (1) keep the wallet and the money, (2) keep the money and return the wallet, or (3) return both the wallet and the money." Although we treated these response categories as unordered, there's also an obvious ordering: 1 is the most unethical response, 3 is the most ethical, and 2 is in the middle. To fit a cumulative logit model to this data, we submit the program:

```
PROC LOGISTIC DATA=my.wallet;
  MODEL wallet = male business punish explain;
RUN;
```

(In case you've forgotten, the explanatory variables are defined in Section 5.2.) Results are shown in Output 6.1.

The output looks virtually identical to output for a binary logit model, except for something new in the middle: the "Score Test for the Proportional Odds Assumption." I'll explain this in more detail later. For now, it's sufficient to say that this statistic tests whether the ordinal restrictions are valid, and high *p*-values are desirable. In this case, we find no reason to reject the model. Another difference in the output is that there are two intercepts instead of just one. In general, the number of intercepts for *all* the ordinal models in this chapter is one less than the number of categories on the dependent variable. But like the usual intercept, these rarely have any substantive interest.

Output 6.1 *LOGISTIC Output for Cumulative Logit Model, Wallet Data*

```
Data Set: MY.WALLET
Response Variable: WALLET
Response Levels: 3
Number of Observations: 195
Link Function: Logit


                          Response Profile

                    Ordered
                    Value   WALLET     Count

                      1       1          24
                      2       2          50
                      3       3         121



         Score Test for the Proportional Odds Assumption

            Chi-Square = 5.1515 with 4 DF (p=0.2721)

   Model Fitting Information and Testing Global Null Hypothesis BETA=0

                              Intercept
                 Intercept       and
   Criterion       Only       Covariates   Chi-Square for Covariates

   AIC            356.140      319.367              .
   SC             362.686      339.005              .
   -2 LOG L       352.140      307.367       44.773 with 4 DF (p=0.0001)
   Score             .            .         40.875 with 4 DF (p=0.0001)

               Analysis of Maximum Likelihood Estimates

             Parameter Standard    Wald       Pr >    Standardized   Odds
   Variable DF Estimate  Error  Chi-Square Chi-Square   Estimate     Ratio

   INTERCP1 1   -3.2691  0.5612   33.9325    0.0001         .          .
   INTERCP2 1   -1.4913  0.5085    8.6008    0.0034         .          .
   MALE     1    1.0636  0.3255   10.6768    0.0011      0.293955    2.897
   BUSINESS 1    0.7370  0.3515    4.3971    0.0360      0.171635    2.090
   PUNISH   1    0.6874  0.2246    9.3646    0.0022      0.259567    1.989
   EXPLAIN  1   -1.0453  0.3392    9.4979    0.0021     -0.264113    0.352
```

Turning to the more familiar portions of the output, we see from the global tests that there is strong evidence that at least one of the coefficients is not 0. This is further confirmed by the lower portion of the output which shows that all the coefficients have *p*-values below .05. In the next section, we'll see how the parameter estimates and odds ratios can be interpreted in a fashion that is nearly identical to interpretation in a binary logit model.

Comparing Output 6.1 with the multinomial logit results for the same data (Output 5.2), we find a few major differences. The most obvious is that the multinomial model has two coefficients for every explanatory variable while the cumulative model has only one. This makes the cumulative model much simpler to present and interpret. A less apparent difference is that the *p*-values for the tests of whether each variable has an effect on the dependent variable are all lower in the cumulative model. This is crucial for BUSINESS, which has a *p*-value of .10 in the multinomial model (with the 2 degrees of freedom ANOVA test) but .036 in the cumulative model. The differences in *p*-values illustrate the claim I made earlier, that hypothesis tests in the cumulative logit model are more powerful.

6.3   Cumulative Logit Model: Explanation

I'll explain the cumulative logit model in three different ways. I begin with an intuitive, nonmathematical description. Then I present a formal definition of the model in terms of cumulative probabilities. Finally, I explain how the model can be derived from a latent variable model.

Here's the nonmathematical explanation. Suppose you wanted to analyze the wallet data but all you had was a binary logit program. One solution to that dilemma is to group two of the three categories together so that you have a dichotomy. To get as even a split as possible on the dependent variable, the best grouping is to combine categories 1 and 2 together and leave 3 by itself. That way, there are 74 cases in the (1, 2) category and 121 cases in category 3. Here's the SAS code for doing that:

```
DATA a;
  SET my.wallet;
  IF wallet=1 THEN wallet=2;
RUN;
PROC LOGISTIC DATA=a;
  MODEL wallet = male business punish explain;
RUN;
```

The results are shown in Output 6.2

Output 6.2   *Logistic Results for Dichotomized Wallet Data*

Variable	DF	Parameter Estimate	Standard Error	Wald Chi-Square	Pr > Chi-Square	Standardized Estimate	Odds Ratio
INTERCPT	1	-1.3189	0.5465	5.8246	0.0158	.	.
MALE	1	1.1846	0.3408	12.0833	0.0005	0.327379	3.269
BUSINESS	1	0.6357	0.3812	2.7809	0.0954	0.148040	1.888
PUNISH	1	0.5072	0.2474	4.2032	0.0403	0.191498	1.661
EXPLAIN	1	-1.0201	0.3662	7.7610	0.0053	-0.257747	0.361

There's nothing sacred about the first grouping, however. We could also group 2 and 3 together (for 171 cases) and leave 1 by itself (with 24 cases). The alternative code is:

```
DATA a;
  SET my.wallet;
  IF wallet=3 THEN wallet=2;
RUN;
PROC LOGISTIC DATA=a;
  MODEL wallet = male business punish explain;
RUN;
```

The results are shown in Output 6.3.

Output 6.3   *Results for Alternative Dichotomization of Wallet Data*

Variable	DF	Parameter Estimate	Standard Error	Wald Chi-Square	Pr > Chi-Square	Standardized Estimate	Odds Ratio
INTERCPT	1	-3.7154	0.8017	21.4797	0.0001	.	.
MALE	1	0.8268	0.5290	2.4427	0.1181	0.228503	2.286
BUSINESS	1	1.0130	0.5142	3.8811	0.0488	0.235905	2.754
PUNISH	1	1.0108	0.3075	10.8034	0.0010	0.381684	2.748
EXPLAIN	1	-1.2760	0.5112	6.2313	0.0126	-0.322422	0.279

What does this have to do with the cumulative logit model? Just this: the cumulative model constrains the coefficients in these two binary logit models to be the same but allows the intercepts to differ. Comparing Output 6.2 and Output 6.3, it appears that the coefficients are *not* identical. But the cumulative logit model just chalks the differences up to random error and estimates a weighted average of the corresponding coefficients. Comparing Output

6.1 with 6.2 and 6.3, we see that in every case the cumulative logit coefficient is in between the two binary coefficients. Moreover, the two intercepts in Output 6.1 are quite close to the intercepts in Output 6.2 and 6.3.

In short, the cumulative logit model says that it doesn't make any difference how you dichotomize the dependent variable—the effects of the explanatory variables are always the same. However, as we see in Output 6.1, we do get a test of whether this is a reasonable constraint. The score test of the proportional odds assumption is a test of the null hypothesis that the corresponding coefficients in Output 6.2 and 6.3 are equal. The 4 degrees of freedom correspond to the four pairs of coefficients. With a *p*-value of .27, there's clearly insufficient evidence to reject the null hypothesis. In other words, the differences between Output 6.2 and Output 6.3 could easily be due to chance.

Now let's formalize the model in a way that will apply to an indefinite number of categories on the dependent variable. As in the multinomial model, let p_{ij} be the probability that individual *i* falls into category *j* of the dependent variable. We assume that the categories are ordered in the sequence *j*=1, ..., *J*. Next we define *cumulative probabilities*

$$F_{ij} = \sum_{m=1}^{j} p_{im}$$

In words, F_{ij} is the probability that individual *i* is in the *j*th category *or lower*. Each F_{ij} corresponds to a different dichotomization of the dependent variable. We then specify the model as a set of *J*–1 equations,

$$\log\left(\frac{F_{ij}}{1 - F_{ij}}\right) = \alpha_j + \boldsymbol{\beta}\mathbf{x}_i \qquad j = 1,...,J - 1 \tag{6.1}$$

where $\boldsymbol{\beta}\mathbf{x}_i = \beta_1 x_{i1} + ... + \beta_k x_{ik}$. Although there is a single set of coefficients, there is a different intercept for each of the equations.

The way the model is usually set up, the explanatory variables predict the probability of being in a *lower* category rather than in a higher category. That's the default in LOGISTIC. But we could have just as easily defined the cumulative probabilities as

$$F_{ij} = \sum_{m=j}^{J} p_{im}$$

the probability of being in the *j*th category or *higher*. Then the model predicts the probability of being in a *higher* category. That's what you get if you use the DESCENDING option in the PROC statement. If you use this option, the intercepts will be different and all the coefficients will have the opposite sign.

That's all there is to the model. As usual, we'll estimate it by maximum likelihood methods, although weighted least squares is a reasonable alternative when the data is grouped.

Like the binary logit model, the cumulative logit model can be viewed as arising from a continuous variable that's been chopped up into categories. Let z_i be a continuous random variable that depends on a set of explanatory variables $\mathbf{x}_i$ according to a linear model:

$$z_i = \alpha^* + \boldsymbol{\beta}^* \mathbf{x}_i + \sigma \varepsilon_i \; . \tag{6.2}$$

We don't observe z directly, however. Instead, there is a set of cut points or *thresholds*, $\tau_1, \ldots, \tau_{J-1}$, that are used to transform z into the observed variable y according to the following rules:

$$
\begin{aligned}
y &= 1 \text{ if } \tau_1 < z \\
y &= 2 \text{ if } \tau_2 < z \le \tau_1
\end{aligned}
\tag{6.3}
$$

.

.

.

$$y = J \text{ if } z \le \tau_{J-1}$$

If we assume that ε_i has a standard logistic distribution, it follows that the dependence of y on $\mathbf{x}$ is given by the cumulative logit model in equation (6.1). The coefficients in equation (6.1) are related to the coefficients in equation (6.2) by

$$\alpha_j = \frac{\alpha^* - \tau_j}{\sigma}$$

$$\boldsymbol{\beta} = \boldsymbol{\beta}^* / \sigma. \tag{6.4}$$

Although we can't recover the underlying coefficients, if we test the null hypothesis that an observed coefficient is 0, this is equivalent to testing whether the underlying coefficient is 0.

The remarkable thing about this model is that the $\boldsymbol{\beta}$ coefficients don't depend on the placement of the thresholds. That means that some of the τ's may be close together while others may be far apart, but the effects of the explanatory variables stay the same. The position of the τ's does, of course, affect the intercepts and the relative numbers of cases that fall into the different categories. But there is a sense in which the cumulative logit model makes no assumptions about the distances between observed categories.

In the latent variable interpretation of the *binary* logit model, we saw that if ε had a standard normal distribution, we got a probit model. And if ε had a standard extreme-value distribution, we got a complementary log-log model. The same results generalize to the cumulative model, although I won't discuss these models further. As in the binary case, you can invoke these models in LOGISTIC with the LINK=PROBIT or LINK=CLOGLOG options in the MODEL statement.

6.4 Cumulative Logit Model: Practical Considerations

Now we're ready to interpret the coefficients in Output 6.1. Because I didn't use the DESCENDING option, the model predicts the probability of being in a lower category and, in this case, that means less ethical behavior. Each reported odds ratio can be interpreted as the effect of the variable on the odds of being in a lower rather than in a higher category, *without regard to how you dichotomize the outcome*. For example, the adjusted odds ratio for males is 2.897. We can say, then, that the odds of males being in a lower category (rather than a higher category) is nearly three times the odds for females. Among those in the business school, the odds of being in a lower category are a little more than twice the odds for those in other schools. For PUNISH, the adjusted odds ratio of 1.99 tells us that each one-level increase in PUNISH doubles the odds of being in a lower rather than a higher category. Finally, those students whose parents explained their punishments have odds of being in a lower category that's only about 35% of the odds for those parents who did not explain.

How should the intercepts be interpreted? My preferred answer is "Don't bother." But if you really must know, the first intercept, –3.2691 in Output 6.1, is the predicted log-odds of being in category 1 rather than in categories 2 or 3, when all the explanatory variables have values of 0. (Actually, it's impossible for PUNISH to be 0 because it only has values of 1, 2, or 3.) Exponentiating gives us .038. So the predicted odds of being in category 1 versus the other two is .038. Similarly, the second intercept, –1.4913, is the log-odds of being in categories 1 or 2 rather than in category 3, when all the *x* variables are 0. Exponentiating gives us odds of .225. So people are more than four times as likely to be in category 3 than in the other two categories if they have values of 0 on all the independent variables.

A word of caution about the score test for the "proportional odds assumption": the *SAS/STAT User's Guide* warns that the test may tend to reject the null hypothesis more often than is warranted. In my own experience, if there are many independent variables and if the sample size is large, this test will usually produce *p*-values below .05. I don't think that means that the cumulative logit model should always be rejected in such cases. For one thing, changing the specification of the model can often markedly change the *p*-value for this test; for example, adding or deleting variables, adding or deleting interactions, or adding or deleting polynomial terms. If you're really concerned about low *p*-values for this test, you may find it useful to estimate separate models for different dichotomizations of the dependent variable. That way, you can get a better sense of which variables have coefficients that are not invariant across dichotomizations. In any case, you can always go back to the unordered multinomial model.

How many categories can the dependent variable have in a cumulative logit model? Unlike the multinomial logit model, the cumulative model does *not* get more difficult to interpret as you add more categories. On the other hand, each additional category does add an intercept to the model. That means that the model won't work for rank-ordered data in which no two individuals have the same rank—there would be more parameters to estimate than observations in the sample. As a very rough rule of thumb, I would say that it's reasonable to estimate a cumulative logit model if there are at least 10 observations for each category on the dependent variable. Of course, you also need enough observations overall to get decent estimates of the coefficients. As the number of categories on the dependent variable gets larger, ordinary linear regression becomes an attractive alternative, especially if the distribution of cases is not highly skewed.

Many of the issues and options discussed in Chapters 2 and 3 for the binary logit model also apply to the cumulative logit model. For example, everything I said about confidence intervals is true for the cumulative logit model. Multicollinearity is a comparable problem in the cumulative model, and the approach to diagnosis is the same. Problems of non-convergence and infinite parameters can occur in the cumulative model, although perhaps with somewhat reduced frequency. As the number of categories on the dependent variable increases, it's harder to find explanatory variables that perfectly predict the dependent variable. The generalized R^2 is available for the cumulative logit model and its formula is identical to equation (3.10).

One difference between binary and cumulative models in LOGISTIC is that many regression diagnostics are not available for the cumulative model. The INFLUENCE and IPLOTS options have no effect at all for the cumulative model. Using the OUTPUT statement, you can't get any of the residuals or influence statistics. However, you can produce predicted probabilities for each individual and each category, together with upper and lower confidence limits if you wish.

You can get predicted values for the model in Output 6.1, by including the statement

```
OUTPUT OUT=a PRED=p;
```

after the MODEL statement. For each observation in the original data set, there are two records in the OUTPUT data set, one for each of the first two categories on the dependent variable. (With *J* categories on the dependent variable, there will be *J*–1 predicted values for each observation.) The first 10 records in data set A (corresponding to the first five cases in the original data set) are shown in Output 6.4. The first two records are for the first person in the original data set. The first line gives a predicted probability of .13076 that WALLET has a value of 1. The second line gives the predicted probability that WALLET will have a value *less than or equal to* 2. To get the predicted probability that WALLET is actually equal to 2, we must subtract the preceding probability, i.e., .47092–.13076=.34016. To get the predicted probability that WALLET=3, we must subtract the predicted probability that WALLET=2 from 1, that is, 1–.47092=.52908. For the next two lines, the predicted probabilities are .05024, .18812, and .76164 for levels 1, 2, and 3, respectively. Keep in mind that when you use the DESCENDING option, the predicted probabilities are the probabilities that the dependent variable has values *greater than or equal to* the specified level.

Output 6.4 *Predicted Values for Wallet Data (First Five Cases)*

OBS	PUNISH	EXPLAIN	WALLET	MALE	BUSINESS	_LEVEL_	P
1	2	0	2	0	0	1	0.13076
2	2	0	2	0	0	2	0.47092
3	2	1	2	0	0	1	0.05024
4	2	1	2	0	0	2	0.23836
5	1	1	3	0	0	1	0.02591
6	1	1	3	0	0	2	0.13597
7	2	0	3	0	0	1	0.13076
8	2	0	3	0	0	2	0.47092
9	1	1	1	1	0	1	0.07154
10	1	1	1	1	0	2	0.31313

6.5 Cumulative Logit Model: Contingency Tables

The cumulative logit model can be very useful in analyzing contingency tables. Consider Table 6.1, which was tabulated by Sloane and Morgan (1996) from the General Social Survey. Our goal is to estimate a model for the dependence of happiness on year and marital status.

Table 6.1 *General Happiness by Marital Status and Year*

		Very happy	Pretty happy	Not too happy
1974	Married	473	493	93
	Unmarried	84	231	99
1984	Married	332	387	62
	Unmarried	150	347	117
1994	Married	571	793	112
	Unmarried	257	889	234

Here's the SAS program to read the table:

```
DATA happy;
  INPUT year married happy count;
  y84 = year EQ 2;
  y94 = year EQ 3;
```

```
    DATALINES;
1 1 1 473
1 1 2 493
1 1 3  93
1 0 1  84
1 0 2 231
1 0 3  99
2 1 1 332
2 1 2 387
2 1 3  62
2 0 1 150
2 0 2 347
2 0 3 117
3 1 1 571
3 1 2 793
3 1 3 112
3 0 1 257
3 0 2 889
3 0 3 234
;
```

The two lines after the INPUT statement define dummy variables. For example, Y84 =1 when YEAR is equal to 2, otherwise 0. Note that unlike GENMOD, it's necessary to define the dummy variables for YEAR in the DATA statement. Notice also that I've coded HAPPY so that 1 is very happy and 3 is not too happy.

To fit the cumulative logit model, we run the following program, with results shown in Output 6.5:

```
PROC LOGISTIC DATA=happy;
   FREQ count;
   MODEL happy = married y84 y94 / AGGREGATE SCALE=N;
   TEST y84, y94;
RUN;
```

Output 6.5   *Cumulative Logit Results for Happiness Table*

```
                  Score Test for the Proportional Odds Assumption

                   Chi-Square = 26.5204 with 3 DF (p=0.0001)

                  Deviance and Pearson Goodness-of-Fit Statistics


                                                          Pr >
              Criterion        DF       Value   Value/DF   Chi-Square

              Deviance          7      30.9709   4.4244      0.0001
              Pearson           7      31.4060   4.4866      0.0001


                         Number of unique profiles: 6

             Model Fitting Information and Testing Global Null Hypothesis BETA=0

                                       Intercept
                           Intercept      and
           Criterion         Only      Covariates    Chi-Square for Covariates


           AIC             10937.042    10586.698           .
           SC              10950.347    10619.961           .
           -2 LOG L        10933.042    10576.698       356.343 with 3 DF (p=0.0001)
           Score               .            .           348.447 with 3 DF (p=0.0001)


                        Analysis of Maximum Likelihood Estimates

                    Parameter Standard    Wald       Pr >     Standardized    Odds
           Variable DF Estimate  Error  Chi-Square Chi-Square    Estimate    Ratio


           INTERCP1 1   -1.3203  0.0674  383.2575    0.0001         .           .
           INTERCP2 1    1.4876  0.0684  473.6764    0.0001         .           .
           MARRIED  1    0.9931  0.0553  322.9216    0.0001      0.270315     2.700
           Y84      1    0.0479  0.0735    0.4250    0.5145      0.011342     1.049
           Y94      1   -0.0716  0.0636    1.2673    0.2603     -0.019737     0.931


                         Linear Hypotheses Testing

                        Wald                     Pr >
           Label     Chi-Square        DF      Chi-Square

                       3.7619           2        0.1524
```

The first thing we see in Output 6.5 is that the score test for the proportional odds assumption indicates fairly decisive rejection of the model. This is corroborated by the overall goodness-of-fit tests (obtained with the AGGREGATE option), which have *p*-values less than .0001. The score test has 3 degrees of freedom corresponding to the constraints imposed on the three coefficients in the model. Roughly speaking, the score test can be thought of as one component of the overall deviance. So we can say that approximately 85% of the deviance stems from the constraints imposed by the cumulative logit model. The remaining 15% (and 4 degrees of freedom) comes from possible interactions between year and marital status.

Should we reject the model? Keep in mind that the sample size is quite large (5,724 cases), so it may be hard to find any parsimonious model with a *p*-value above .05. But let's postpone a decision until we examine more evidence. Turning to the lower part of the output, we see strong evidence that married people report greater happiness than the unmarried but little evidence for change over time. Neither of the individual year coefficients is statistically significant. A simultaneous test that both coefficients are 0 (produced by the TEST statement and reported under "Linear Hypothesis Testing") is also nonsignificant. So let's try deleting the year variables and see what happens (Output 6.6).

Output 6.6 *Happiness Model with Year Variables Deleted*

```
            Score Test for the Proportional Odds Assumption

            Chi-Square = 0.3513 with 1 DF (p=0.5534)

         Deviance and Pearson Goodness-of-Fit Statistics

                                                    Pr >
         Criterion      DF      Value    Value/DF   Chi-Square

         Deviance        1      0.3508    0.3508     0.5537
         Pearson         1      0.3513    0.3513     0.5534

                   Number of unique profiles: 2

              Analysis of Maximum Likelihood Estimates

             Parameter Standard    Wald       Pr >    Standardized  Odds
  Variable DF Estimate   Error  Chi-Square Chi-Square   Estimate    Ratio

  INTERCP1 1   -1.3497  0.0459  865.8084    0.0001         .          .
  INTERCP2 1    1.4569  0.0468  968.1489    0.0001         .          .
  MARRIED  1    1.0017  0.0545  337.2309    0.0001      0.272655    2.723
```

Now the model fits great. Of course, there's only 1 degree of freedom in the score test because only one coefficient is constrained across the two implicit equations. The deviance and Pearson chi-squares also have only 1 degree of freedom because LOGISTIC has regrouped the data after the elimination of the year variables. Interpreting the marital status effect, we find that married people have odds of higher happiness that are nearly three times the odds for unmarried people.

It's tempting to leave it at this, but the fact that the score statistic declined so dramatically with the deletion of the year variables suggests that something else is going on. To see what it might be, let's fit separate models for the two ways of dichotomizing the happiness variable.

```
DATA a;
 SET happy;
 lesshap=happy GE 2;
 nottoo=happy EQ 3;
RUN;
PROC LOGISTIC DATA=a;
   FREQ count;
   MODEL lesshap=married y84 y94;
RUN;
PROC LOGISTIC DATA=a;
   FREQ count;
   MODEL nottoo=married y84 y94;
RUN;
```

Results are in Output 6.7. If the cumulative logit model is correct, the coefficients for the three variables should be the same in the two models. That's nearly true for MARRIED. But Y94 has a negative coefficient in the first model and a positive coefficient in the second. Both are significant at beyond the .01 level. This is surely the cause of the difficulty with the cumulative logit model. What seems to be happening is that 1994 *is* different from the other two years, but not in a way that could be described as a uniform increase or decrease in happiness. Rather, in that year there were relatively more cases in the middle category and fewer in the two extreme categories.

It's possible to generalize the cumulative logit model to accommodate patterns like this. Specifically, one can model the parameter σ in equation (6.2) as a function of explanatory variables. In this example, the year variables would show up in the equation for σ but not in the linear equation for z. Although some commercial packages have this feature (for example, LIMDEP), LOGISTIC does not. In Chapter 10, we'll see how this pattern can be modeled as a log-linear model.

Output 6.7   *Results from Alternative Dichotomizations of General Happiness*

```
1 vs. (2,3)

              Parameter Standard    Wald       Pr >     Standardized   Odds
   Variable DF Estimate   Error  Chi-Square Chi-Square    Estimate     Ratio

   INTERCPT 1   -1.2411   0.0735   285.4516   0.0001                    .
   MARRIED  1    0.9931   0.0624   253.2457   0.0001     0.270311     2.700
   Y84      1    0.00668  0.0801     0.0070   0.9335     0.001582     1.007
   Y94      1   -0.2204   0.0699     9.9348   0.0016    -0.060762     0.802

(1,2) vs. 3

              Parameter Standard    Wald       Pr >     Standardized   Odds
   Variable DF Estimate   Error  Chi-Square Chi-Square    Estimate     Ratio

   INTERCPT 1    1.2511   0.0915   186.8473   0.0001                    .
   MARRIED  1    1.0109   0.0842   144.1700   0.0001     0.275159     2.748
   Y84      1    0.1928   0.1140     2.8603   0.0908     0.045643     1.213
   Y94      1    0.3037   0.0996     9.3083   0.0023     0.083737     1.355
```

6.6   Adjacent Categories Model

Another general model for ordered categorical data is the adjacent categories model. As before, we let p_{ij} be the probability that individual i falls into category j of the dependent variable, and we assume that the categories are ordered in the sequence $j=1, ..., J$. Now take any pair of categories that are adjacent, such as j and $j+1$. We can write a logit model for the contrast between these two categories as a function of explanatory variables:

$$\log\left(\frac{p_{ij}}{p_{i,j+1}}\right) = \alpha_j + \boldsymbol{\beta}_j \mathbf{x}_i \qquad j = 1,..., J-1, \qquad (6.5)$$

where $\boldsymbol{\beta}_j \mathbf{x}_i = \beta_{j1} x_{i1} + ... + \beta_{jk} x_{ik}$. There are $J-1$ of these paired contrasts. It turns out that this is just another way of writing the multinomial logit model for unordered categories. In other words, equation (6.5) is equivalent to equation (5.1). To get the adjacent categories model for ordered data, we impose a constraint on this set of equations. Specifically, we assume that $\boldsymbol{\beta}_j = \boldsymbol{\beta}$ for all j. In other words, instead of having a different set of coefficients for every adjacent pair, there is only one set for the lot of them. So our adjacent category model becomes

$$\log\left(\frac{p_{ij}}{p_{i,j+1}}\right) = \alpha_j + \boldsymbol{\beta}\mathbf{x}_i \qquad j = 1,...,J-1 \tag{6.6}$$

Notice that the right-hand side is identical to equation (6.1), which defines the cumulative model, but the left-hand side compares individual categories rather than grouped, cumulative categories.

Although the adjacent category model is a special case of the multinomial logit model, CATMOD doesn't allow the imposition of the appropriate constraints, at least not with maximum likelihood estimation. If the data is grouped, however, as in a contingency table, CATMOD can estimate the model by weighted least squares. Here's how to do it with the happiness data:

```
PROC CATMOD DATA=happy;
  WEIGHT count;
  DIRECT married y84 y94;
  RESPONSE ALOGIT;
  MODEL happy = _RESPONSE_ married y84 y94 / WLS;
RUN;
```

The RESPONSE statement with the ALOGIT option invokes the adjacent categories function for the dependent variable, as in equation (6.5). Putting _RESPONSE_ in the MODEL statement tells CATMOD to estimate a single set of coefficients rather than a different set for each pair of categories, as in equation (6.6). Results are shown in Output 6.8.

The first thing to notice is that the residual chi-square test indicates that the model doesn't fit. In fact, the value is fairly close to the deviance and Pearson chi-squares we got for the cumulative logit model in Output 6.5. As in that output, we also find a strong effect of marital status but little evidence for an effect of calendar year. The signs are reversed from Output 6.5, but that's just a consequence of the way CATMOD parameterizes the model. (On the left-hand side of equation (6.6), it puts the $j+1$ on top and the j on the bottom). The adjusted odds ratio for MARRIED is exp(.8035)=2.23. This tells us that, whenever we compare adjacent happiness categories, married people have more than double the odds of being in the happier category than unmarried people have.

Output 6.8   *CATMOD Output for Adjacent Categories Model, Happiness Data*

```
                     ANALYSIS-OF-VARIANCE TABLE

   Source                  DF    Chi-Square      Prob
   -------------------------------------------------------

   RESIDUAL                 7        35.74      0.0000

            ANALYSIS OF WEIGHTED-LEAST-SQUARES ESTIMATES

                                       Standard    Chi-
   Effect          Parameter  Estimate   Error    Square   Prob
   -------------------------------------------------------------
   INTERCEPT            1      -0.0437   0.0507      0.74   0.3885
   _RESPONSE_           2       1.0737   0.0295   1323.91   0.0000
   MARRIED              3      -0.8035   0.0453    314.22   0.0000
   Y84                  4      -0.0563   0.0588      0.92   0.3386
   Y94                  5       0.0353   0.0516      0.47   0.4945
```

Because the model doesn't fit, we can do what we did with the cumulative logit model: fit separate equations for each of the two adjacent pairs. In this case, we can easily accomplish that by removing _RESPONSE_ from the MODEL statement. The results are shown in Output 6.9.

Output 6.9   *Adjacent Categories Model with Two Sets of Coefficients*

```
                    ANALYSIS-OF-VARIANCE TABLE

   Source                  DF    Chi-Square      Prob
   -------------------------------------------------------

   RESIDUAL                 4         4.16      0.3845

            ANALYSIS OF WEIGHTED-LEAST-SQUARES ESTIMATES

                                       Standard    Chi-
   Effect          Parameter  Estimate   Error    Square   Prob
   -------------------------------------------------------------
   INTERCEPT            1       0.9211   0.0770    143.03   0.0000
                        2      -0.8998   0.0939     91.90   0.0000
   MARRIED              3      -0.8619   0.0646    178.10   0.0000
                        4      -0.7087   0.0863     67.46   0.0000
   Y84                  5       0.0295   0.0831      0.13   0.7230
                        6      -0.2105   0.1181      3.18   0.0747
   Y94                  7       0.2900   0.0726     15.94   0.0001
                        8      -0.4036   0.1024     15.53   0.0001
```

These results are quite similar to what is shown in Output 6.7. The MARRIED coefficient is quite stable across the two equations, while the Y94 coefficients differ dramatically: they have opposite signs and both are highly significant. Again, the message is that in 1994, the middle category was more strongly favored over the two extremes.

Despite clear-cut differences in the formulation and interpretation of the cumulative logit model and the adjacent categories model, the two models tend to yield very similar conclusions in practice. I prefer the cumulative model, both for its appealing latent variable interpretation and for its ready availability in software. But the adjacent categories model has one advantage, at least in principle: it's easy to formulate a model with selective constraints on coefficients (although such models can't be estimated in CATMOD). For example, we could force the MARRIED coefficient to be the same for all category pairs, but allow the year coefficients to be different. In fact, we'll see how to do that in Chapter 10, when we estimate the adjacent categories model by using the equivalent loglinear model.

6.7   Continuation Ratio Model

The cumulative logit and adjacent categories models are reasonable candidates for almost any ordered categorical variable. Our third model—the continuation ratio model—is more specialized. It's only appropriate when the ordered categories represent a progression of stages, so that individuals must pass through each lower stage before they go on to higher stages. In those situations, the continuation ratio model is more attractive than the other two.

Because the model is most often applied to educational attainment, let's use that as our example here. Table 6.2 gives frequency counts for three categories of education for 2,294 males who failed to pass the Armed Forces Qualification Test, cross classified by race, age, and father's education (Fienberg 1980). The fact that they failed to pass the test is irrelevant to our purposes.

Table 6.2   *Educational Attainment by Race, Age, and Father's Education*

			Educational Attainment		
Race	Age	Father's Education*	Grammar School	Some HS	HS Graduate
White	<22	1	39	29	8
		2	4	8	1
		3	11	9	6
		4	48	17	8
	≥ 22	1	231	115	51
		2	17	21	13
		3	18	28	45
		4	197	111	35
Black	<22	1	19	40	19
		2	5	17	7
		3	2	14	3
	≥ 22	4	49	79	24
		1	110	133	103
		2	18	38	25
		3	11	25	18
		4	178	206	81

*1=grammar school, 2=some high school, 3=high school graduate, 4=not available.

We could, of course, estimate a cumulative logit or an adjacent category model for this table. We could also ignore the ordinality altogether and estimate a multinomial logit model. But let's think about how the attainment process works in this case. The first step is to get past grammar school. We could estimate a binary logit model with the dependent variable equal to 1 if the person went past grammar school and 0 if he didn't, essentially collapsing the two higher categories. The next step is to graduate from high school, *given that you started high school*. For this step, we could eliminate all the men who never started high school (those in the first column of frequency counts) and estimate a logit model with the dependent variable equal to 1 if the person graduated and 0 if he didn't.

Now, suppose we believe that the effects of the explanatory variables are the same at each step. It would make sense, then, to constrain the coefficients to be equal across steps so that we only get a single set of coefficients. That's the essential idea of the continuation ratio model.

Let's formalize the model for *J* categories on the dependent variable. As usual we assume that the categories are ordered in the sequence $j=1, ..., J$. Let y_i be the dependent variable that can take on one of these J values. Define A_{ij} as the probability that individual i advances to stage $j+1$, given that he made it to stage j. More formally,

$$A_{ij} = \Pr(y_i > j \mid y_i \geq j).$$

We then specify $J{-}1$ logit equations,

$$\log\left(\frac{A_{ij}}{1-A_{ij}}\right) = \alpha_j + \boldsymbol{\beta}\mathbf{x}_i \qquad j = 1,...,J-1 \tag{6.7}$$

where $\boldsymbol{\beta}\mathbf{x}_i = \beta_1 x_{i1} + ... + \beta_k x_{ik}$. Again the right-hand side of equation (6.7) is just like the cumulative logit model and the adjacent categories model, with a separate intercept for each stage but a single set of coefficients. The left-hand side can also be rewritten in terms of the original probabilities, p_{ij}:

$$\log\left(\frac{A_{ij}}{1-A_{ij}}\right) = \log\left[\frac{\sum_{m=j+1}^{J} p_{im}}{p_{ij}}\right]$$

How can this model be estimated? Surprisingly, we can do it with an ordinary binary logit procedure. The trick is in the way the data set is constructed. Again, imagine doing a sequence of binary logit analyses. For each stage, you construct a data set that excludes all individuals who didn't make it to that stage, with a dummy dependent variable indicating whether or not the individual advanced to the next stage. Now, instead of doing separate analyses, we combine these data sets into a single set, including a variable indicating which stage the data came from. Finally, we estimate a single binary logit model on the combined data.

Here's how do it for the data in Table 6.2. First, we read in the data in the usual way. (To save space, two records are placed on each data line, which is accommodated by the @@ in the INPUT statement).

```
DATA my.afqt;
  INPUT white old faed ed count @@;
  DATALINES;
1  0  1  1   39   0  0  1  1   19
1  0  1  2   29   0  0  1  2   40
1  0  1  3    8   0  0  1  3   19
1  0  2  1    4   0  0  2  1    5
1  0  2  2    8   0  0  2  2   17
```

```
1  0  2  3    1    0  0  2  3     7
1  0  3  1   11    0  0  3  1     2
1  0  3  2    9    0  0  3  2    14
1  0  3  3    6    0  0  3  3     3
1  0  4  1   48    0  0  4  1    49
1  0  4  2   17    0  0  4  2    79
1  0  4  3    8    0  0  4  3    24
1  1  1  1  231    0  1  1  1   110
1  1  1  2  115    0  1  1  2   133
1  1  1  3   51    0  1  1  3   103
1  1  2  1   17    0  1  2  1    18
1  1  2  2   21    0  1  2  2    38
1  1  2  3   13    0  1  2  3    25
1  1  3  1   18    0  1  3  1    11
1  1  3  2   28    0  1  3  2    25
1  1  3  3   45    0  1  3  3    18
1  1  4  1  197    0  1  4  1   178
1  1  4  2  111    0  1  4  2   206
1  1  4  3   35    0  1  4  3    81
;
```

The data set for the first stage is then constructed as follows:

```
DATA first;
  SET my.afqt;
  stage=1;
  advance = ed GE 2;
RUN;
```

For the second stage, we have:

```
DATA second;
  SET my.afqt;
  stage=2;
  IF ed=1 THEN DELETE;
  advance = ed EQ 3;
RUN;
```

The two data sets are concatenated into a single set by

```
DATA concat;
  SET first second;
RUN;
```

Alternatively, we can create the combined data set in a single DATA step:

```
DATA combined;
  SET my.afqt;
   stage=1;
   advance = ed GE 2;
  OUTPUT;
   stage=2;
   IF ed=1 THEN DELETE;
   advance = ed EQ 3;
  OUTPUT;
RUN;
```

Now we're ready to do the logit analysis with PROC GENMOD:

```
PROC GENMOD DATA=combined;
  FREQ count;
  CLASS faed;
  MODEL advance=stage white old faed / D=B TYPE3;
RUN;
```

The results in Output 6.10 show strong effects of race, father's education, and stage, but little or no effect of age (at the time of the AFQT examination). White soldiers are only about half as likely to advance to the next stage as blacks. As you might expect, with increasing education of the father, the odds of advancing go up substantially, with the lowest probability of advancement among soldiers whose father's education was "unavailable."

Output 6.10　*GENMOD Results for Continuation Ratio Model*

```
Parameter          DF    Estimate    Std Err   ChiSquare   Pr>Chi

INTERCEPT           1      1.5268     0.1352    127.4325    0.0001
STAGE               1     -1.1785     0.0753    244.9955    0.0001
WHITE               1     -0.6918     0.0731     89.5733    0.0001
OLD                 1      0.0919     0.0867      1.1228    0.2893
FAED       1        1      0.2678     0.0776     11.9123    0.0006
FAED       2        1      0.6771     0.1336     25.7059    0.0001
FAED       3        1      1.2031     0.1339     80.7282    0.0001
FAED       4        0      0.0000     0.0000        .          .
SCALE               0      1.0000     0.0000        .          .

NOTE:   The scale parameter was held fixed.


 LR Statistics For Type 3 Analysis

Source        DF    ChiSquare   Pr>Chi

STAGE          1     261.2403    0.0001
WHITE          1      91.9243    0.0001
OLD            1       1.1235    0.2892
FAED           3      98.8242    0.0001
```

Like the other ordinal models, this one imposes some restrictions, namely that the effects of the explanatory variables are the same at each stage. We can test this by including interactions between STAGE and the other three variables:

```
MODEL advance=stage white old faed stage*white stage*old
        stage*faed / D=B TYPE3;
```

This produced the likelihood ratio statistics shown in Output 6.11. Clearly there are interactions with all three variables, which means that each variable has different effects on advancement into high school and advancement to high school graduation.

Output 6.11 *Tests for Interaction between STAGE and Other Variables*

```
LR Statistics For Type 3 Analysis

Source        DF    ChiSquare   Pr>Chi

STAGE          1     134.9623   0.0001
WHITE          1      54.3564   0.0001
OLD            1       3.2099   0.0732
FAED           3      90.3155   0.0001
WHITE*STAGE    1      24.0652   0.0001
OLD*STAGE      1       8.8908   0.0029
FAED*STAGE     3      11.1189   0.0111
```

When none of the variables has an invariant effect, you're better off estimating separate models for each stage rather than attempting to interpret the interactions in the combined data set. We can do that with the program

```
PROC GENMOD DATA=first;
   FREQ count;
   CLASS faed;
   MODEL advance= white old faed / D=B TYPE3;
RUN;
PROC GENMOD DATA=second;
   FREQ count;
   CLASS faed;
   MODEL advance= white old faed / D=B TYPE3;
RUN;
```

The results in Output 6.12 show markedly different effects for age and race at the two stages. Whites were substantially less likely than blacks to advance from grade school to high school but only slightly less likely to advance from some high school to graduation. The opposite pattern is found for age with no effect at the earlier stage, but older males are about 50% more likely than younger ones to advance to high school graduation. The father's education has strong positive effects at both stages, but the ordinal pattern is not as clear cut at the second stage.

Output 6.12 *Separate Logit Models for Two Levels of Advancement*

```
        Advancement from Grammar School to High School
   Parameter        DF    Estimate    Std Err   ChiSquare  Pr>Chi

   INTERCEPT         1      0.6424     0.1129     32.3764   0.0001
   WHITE             1     -0.9388     0.0897    109.5317   0.0001
   OLD               1     -0.1092     0.1110      0.9681   0.3252
   FAED     1        1      0.1781     0.0952      3.4960   0.0615
   FAED     2        1      0.9198     0.1895     23.5635   0.0001
   FAED     3        1      1.3376     0.1910     49.0237   0.0001
   FAED     4        0      0.0000     0.0000        .         .


        Advancement to High School Graduation
   Parameter        DF    Estimate    Std Err   ChiSquare  Pr>Chi

   INTERCEPT         1     -1.3217     0.1570     70.8575   0.0001
   WHITE             1     -0.1811     0.1245      2.1166   0.1457
   OLD               1      0.4427     0.1508      8.6214   0.0033
   FAED     1        1      0.4721     0.1348     12.2748   0.0005
   FAED     2        1      0.4425     0.2079      4.5303   0.0333
   FAED     3        1      1.0273     0.1949     27.7924   0.0001
   FAED     4        0      0.0000     0.0000        .         .
```

For this data, then, the constrained continuation ratio model is a failure, its attractive parsimony apparently spurious. Nevertheless, even when a single equation model is inappropriate, there can be conceptual advantages in viewing the process in terms of stages. Output 6.12 is probably more meaningfully interpreted than a multinomial logit model with an equal number of coefficients. Another potential advantage of the continuation ratio approach—one not applicable to the data in Table 6.2—is the possibility of stage-dependent explanatory variables. Variables like parental income, number of persons in the household, and presence of the father are likely to vary over time, and this information can be easily incorporated into the modeling process. In constructing the working data set, you simply redefine the variables to have different values at each of the stages.

There are several other points worth noting about the continuation ratio method. First, you may have observed that in the combined data set, the same people may appear more than once. For the education example, everyone who had some high school contributed two observations to the combined data set. Usually this raises red flags because of possible dependence among the multiple observations. While there isn't space here to go into the details, there is absolutely no problem of dependence. For each individual, the probability of a particular outcome is factored into a set of conditional probabilities that have the same structure as independent observations.

Second, the continuation ratio approach is closely related to discrete-time methods for event history analysis (a.k.a. survival analysis). In that setting, the aim is to model the length of time until some event occurs, and time is measured in discrete units like years. Each year is treated as a stage and "advancement" means getting to the next year without experiencing the event. For further details, see Chapter 7 of my book, *Survival Analysis Using the SAS System: A Practical Guide* (1995).

Third, just as there are cumulative probit and cumulative complementary log-log models, one can easily estimate continuation ratio models using the probit or complementary log-log functions. The complementary log-log model is particularly attractive for event history applications because it is the discrete-time equivalent of the proportional hazards model used in Cox regression. I'll close this chapter with a statistical curiosity: the complementary log-log continuation ratio model is mathematically equivalent to the cumulative complementary log-log model (McCullagh 1980).

Chapter 7

Discrete Choice Analysis

7.1   Introduction

In economics and marketing research, discrete choice analysis has become a popular approach to the study of consumer choice. Although the method is not well known in sociology or political science, it ought to be. There are many potential applications of this methodology that have been overlooked because of ignorance of the available tools.

In discrete choice problems, people choose from among a set of options that are available to them—political candidates for example—and the aim is to discover what variables affect their choices. While this may sound like a job for the multinomial logit model of Chapter 5, it differs in two respects:

- The explanatory variables can include characteristics of the choice options as well as variables describing the relationship between the chooser and the option.
- The set of available options can vary across individuals in the analysis.

Discrete choice analysis is usually based on the *conditional logit model*, a name that—unfortunately—has also been used for quite different models. The conditional logit models discussed in this chapter use the PHREG procedure for estimation. PHREG was designed to do Cox regression analysis of continuous-time survival data, using the method of partial likelihood to estimate a proportional hazards model. So what does that have to do with logit analysis? Well, it turns out that the stratified partial likelihood function is identical to the likelihood for conditional logit analysis. Furthermore, because PHREG has unique options for handling tied data, the range of conditional logit models that it will estimate is much broader than most Cox regression programs, or even programs specifically designed for discrete choice. The upshot is that PHREG is one of the best procedures in any statistical package for handling discrete choice problems.

7.2 Chocolate Example

The discrete choice model has often been used in studies of consumer preference. Consider the following experiment (SAS Institute 1995). Ten people were each given eight chocolate bars with varying characteristics. After eating the bars, they were asked to choose the one they liked best. The bars were distinguished by the following variables:

DARK 0=milk chocolate, 1=dark chocolate

SOFT 0=hard center, 1=soft center

NUTS 0=no nuts, 1=nuts

Each subject tasted eight chocolate bars with all possible combinations of these characteristics. The aim was to determine which characteristics of the bars affected people's choices. Here are the data:

```
DATA my.chocs;
   INPUT id choose dark soft nuts @@;
   DATALINES;
1 0 0 0 0    1 0 0 0 1    1 0 0 1 0    1 0 0 1 1
1 1 1 0 0    1 0 1 0 1    1 0 1 1 0    1 0 1 1 1
2 0 0 0 0    2 0 0 0 1    2 0 0 1 0    2 0 0 1 1
2 0 1 0 0    2 1 1 0 1    2 0 1 1 0    2 0 1 1 1
3 0 0 0 0    3 0 0 0 1    3 0 0 1 0    3 0 0 1 1
3 0 1 0 0    3 0 1 0 1    3 1 1 1 0    3 0 1 1 1
4 0 0 0 0    4 0 0 0 1    4 0 0 1 0    4 0 0 1 1
4 1 1 0 0    4 0 1 0 1    4 0 1 1 0    4 0 1 1 1
5 0 0 0 0    5 1 0 0 1    5 0 0 1 0    5 0 0 1 1
5 0 1 0 0    5 0 1 0 1    5 0 1 1 0    5 0 1 1 1
6 0 0 0 0    6 0 0 0 1    6 0 0 1 0    6 0 0 1 1
6 0 1 0 0    6 1 1 0 1    6 0 1 1 0    6 0 1 1 1
7 0 0 0 0    7 1 0 0 1    7 0 0 1 0    7 0 0 1 1
7 0 1 0 0    7 0 1 0 1    7 0 1 1 0    7 0 1 1 1
8 0 0 0 0    8 0 0 0 1    8 0 0 1 0    8 0 0 1 1
8 0 1 0 0    8 1 1 0 1    8 0 1 1 0    8 0 1 1 1
```

```
 9 0 0 0 0     9 0 0 0 1     9 0 0 1 0      9 0 0 1 1
 9 0 1 0 0     9 1 1 0 1     9 0 1 1 0      9 0 1 1 1
10 0 0 0 0    10 0 0 0 1    10 0 0 1 0     10 0 0 1 1
10 0 1 0 0    10 1 1 0 1    10 0 1 1 0     10 0 1 1 1
;
```

There are eight observations for each person. (To save space, each line contains four observations.) The first variable, ID, is a unique identifier for each person so we can keep track of who is making the choices. The second variable, CHOOSE, has a value of 1 if the person chose that particular chocolate bar, otherwise 0. So for every set of eight observations, only one of them has CHOOSE=1 while the other seven have CHOOSE=0.

To analyze the data with PHREG, we first recode CHOOSE so that all the 0's become 2's. That's because PHREG expects the chosen option to have a smaller number than the unselected options. If you forget to do this, the only consequence is to reverse the signs of the coefficients. The full program is

```
DATA chocs;
   SET my.chocs;
   choose=2-choose;
RUN;
PROC PHREG DATA=chocs NOSUMMARY;
   MODEL choose=dark soft nuts / TIES=DISCRETE;
   STRATA id;
RUN;
```

The NOSUMMARY option in the PROC statement merely suppresses output that's not informative for this kind of application. The TIES=DISCRETE option is essential to force PHREG to estimate a logit model rather than some inappropriate survival model. The STRATA statement tells PHREG how to group the observations together for each person. The results are shown in Output 7.1.

Output 7.1   *PHREG Output for Discrete Choice Model, Chocolate Data*

```
              Testing Global Null Hypothesis: BETA=0

                  Without        With
Criterion        Covariates    Covariates     Model Chi-Square

-2 LOG L           41.589        28.727       12.862 with 3 DF (p=0.0049)
Score                 .             .         11.600 with 3 DF (p=0.0089)
Wald                  .             .          8.928 with 3 DF (p=0.0303)

              Analysis of Maximum Likelihood Estimates

                  Parameter    Standard     Wald       Pr >       Risk
Variable   DF     Estimate      Error    Chi-Square  Chi-Square   Ratio

DARK        1     1.386294     0.79057    3.07490      0.0795     4.000
SOFT        1    -2.197225     1.05409    4.34502      0.0371     0.111
NUTS        1     0.847298     0.69007    1.50762      0.2195     2.333
```

PHREG output is very similar in format to LOGISTIC output. We first get global tests of the null hypothesis that all the coefficients are 0. In addition to the likelihood ratio and score tests, PHREG also gives a Wald test. In this case, all three are statistically significant, although the *p*-value for the Wald test is quite a bit higher than the other two. As in other models, the likelihood-ratio test is generally preferred.

In the lower panel, we find coefficients and associated statistics. Only the SOFT coefficient has a *p*-value below .05. However, because the global likelihood ratio chi-square is rather different from the Wald chi-square, the same divergence could occur for the individual chi-squares. To check that out, I computed likelihood ratio chi-squares for the three explanatory variables by re-estimating the model three times, deleting one of the explanatory variables each time. Then I took the differences between –2 LOG L for the model in Output 7.1 and for each of the reduced models. Results were

	Chi-Square	*p*-value
DARK	3.85	.05
SOFT	7.36	.007
NUTS	1.64	.20

With these preferred statistics, the results look a bit stronger.

As we'll see in the next section, the coefficients can be interpreted as effects on the log odds of choosing a bar of that particular kind. The "Risk Ratio" column contains the exponentiated values of the original coefficients, so these can be interpreted as adjusted odds ratios. We see, for example, that the odds of choosing a dark chocolate bar are four times the odds of a milk chocolate bar. The odds of choosing a soft bar are only about one-ninth the odds of choosing a hard bar. People were twice as likely to choose bars with nuts, but that coefficient was far from significant.

Notice that there's no intercept in the model. That's always true for PHREG output, and for conditional logit analysis in general. I'll explain why in the next section. Notice also that this data does not contain any variables describing the persons in the study. Even if variables like gender, education, or race were available in the data, they could not be included as variables in the model. Because a person's gender is the same for all eight chocolate bars, gender cannot help predict why a person chooses one bar rather than another. On the other hand, it would be possible to have interactions between gender and the other variables in the model by creating product terms in the DATA step and then including them in the model. For example, that could tell us if hardness were more important for men than for women. We'll see an example of interaction terms in Section 7.4.

7.3   Model and Estimation

Now that we've seen how to do a discrete choice analysis, let's look more closely at the model being estimated. Suppose we have $i=1, \dots , n$ individuals and each individual is presented with $j=1, \dots , J_i$ options. We write the number of possible choices as J_i to indicate that different individuals may have different sets of options. That wasn't true for the chocolate example, but it's an important feature of the model that distinguishes it from the multinomial logit model of Chapter 5. Let $y_{ij} =1$ if individual i chooses option j, otherwise 0, and let $\mathbf{x}_{ij}$ be a vector of explanatory variables describing option j for person i. This set of explanatory variables may include dummy variables for the various options and interactions between option characteristics and individual characteristics. However, it does *not* include an intercept term.

The *conditional logit model* introduced by McFadden (1973) is

$$\Pr(y_{ij} = 1) = \frac{e^{\beta \mathbf{x}_{ij}}}{e^{\beta \mathbf{x}_{i1}} + e^{\beta \mathbf{x}_{i2}} + \ldots + e^{\beta \mathbf{x}_{iJ_i}}}. \tag{7.1}$$

This equation is quite similar to equation (5.2) for the multinomial logit model. In that model, however, there was one $\mathbf{x}$ vector for each individual and separate coefficient vectors β_j for each of the possible outcomes. For the conditional logit model, there is only one coefficient vector but different $\mathbf{x}$ vectors for each outcome. Despite these apparent differences, the standard multinomial logit model can be shown to be a special case of the conditional logit model by appropriate coding of the explanatory variables, as illustrated below in Output 7.6 and 7.7.

From equation (7.1) we can see why there is no intercept term in the conditional logit model. Suppose we insisted on including an intercept by writing each of the terms in the numerator and denominator as $e^{\beta_0 + \beta \mathbf{x}_{ij}}$. This, of course, is equal to $e^{\beta_0} e^{\beta \mathbf{x}_{ij}}$. But because e^{β_0} appears in every term, this quantity cancels out of the fraction.

Equation (7.1) implies that the logit for comparing any two options j and k is given by

$$\log\left(\frac{\Pr(y_{ij} = 1)}{\Pr(y_{ik} = 1)}\right) = \beta(\mathbf{x}_{ij} - \mathbf{x}_{ik}).$$

Equivalently, the odds that person i will choose j over k is given by

$$\exp\{\beta(\mathbf{x}_{ij} - \mathbf{x}_{ik})\}$$

We estimate the model by maximum likelihood. The likelihood function is the product of n factors, each having the form of equation (7.1) for the particular option that is chosen. That's exactly the likelihood function that is calculated when PHREG is invoked in the manner described in the previous section.

Is this a reasonable model for individual choice? One justification is that the model can be derived from a latent variable model called the random utility model. Suppose that each individual i has a stable preference for each option j, denoted by μ_{ij}. But suppose the actual *utility* U_{ij} for a particular option varies randomly around μ_{ij} so that

$$U_{ij} = \mu_{ij} + \varepsilon_{ij}$$

where ε_{ij} is a random variable having a standard extreme value distribution. Assume further that the ε_{ij}'s are independent across the different options. If people choose the option with the highest utility U_{ij}, and if the logarithm of μ_{ij} is a linear function of the explanatory variables, it follows that the probability that person i chooses option j is given by equation (7.1).

If these assumptions are credible, then the conditional logit model is reasonable. There has been some concern, however, about the assumption of independence of the random variables ε_j. This assumption (together with the extreme-value assumption) implies a condition that is known as *independence of irrelevant alternatives*, frequently denoted IIA (read i-i-a, not 2a). This condition means that the odds of choosing option j rather than option k are not affected by what other options are available.

It's not hard to come up with counterexamples to the IIA condition. A classic example is the blue bus-red bus dilemma. Suppose I have two ways of getting to work, by car or by blue bus. My probability of taking the car is .8, which gives a car/blue bus odds of .8/.2=4. Now suppose another bus is introduced, identical in every way to the blue bus except that it's red, so I now have three options. Because I'm indifferent to bus color, it's reasonable to suppose that my probability of taking the car will still be .8 and that the remaining .2 will be equally divided between the two colors of buses. But then the car/blue bus odds are .8/.1=8, which violates the IIA condition.

Efforts to relax this assumption have centered on introducing correlations among the ε_j's in the random utility model, usually within the context of a multivariate normal distribution. However, such models tend to be much more computationally demanding than the conditional logit model and are not available in SAS. Also absent from SAS is the *nested logit model* (Maddala 1983), which treats the choice process as a sequence of nested choices. Consider the decision to buy a personal computer. A buyer might first choose whether to buy a desktop or a laptop machine. Having chosen a desktop, he might then choose whether to buy Macintosh or a Windows machine. After that choice, he must choose a manufacturer. The nested logit model assumes that the IIA assumption is satisfied for choices at the same level, but not necessarily for choices at different levels.

The IIA assumption can only be empirically tested when some sample members have different choice sets. That suggests that when everyone in the sample is presented with the same choice set, the IIA assumption may not be a serious problem. Here's a simple model that illustrates that claim. Suppose that the potential choice set contains only three alternatives, labeled 1, 2, and 3. When people are presented with alternatives 1 and 2 only, their relative odds are given by $\log(p_1 / p_2) = \alpha + \beta\mathbf{x}$, where $\mathbf{x}$ is a vector of explanatory variables. When people are presented with alternatives 1, 2, *and* 3, the relative odds of 1 versus 2 are given by $\log(p_1 / p_2) = \alpha + \mu + \beta\mathbf{x}$. Clearly, this violates the IIA condition because of the additional μ term. But as long as everyone in the sample is presented with the same set of alternatives, conventional logit analysis will produce consistent and efficient estimates of β.

7.4 Travel Example

Now let's look at a more complicated application of the conditional logit model. In a survey of transportation usage between three Australian cities, 210 people were asked which of four options they used on their most recent trip: air, train, bus, or car (Hensher and Bradley 1993). They were also asked about certain characteristics of all four travel options, regardless of whether they used them. As in the previous example, a separate observation is constructed for each option for each person, giving a total of 840 observations. The variables are:

ID	A unique identifier for each person
MODE	1=air, 2=train, 3=bus, 4=car
CHOICE	1=chose that mode, 0=didn't choose
TTME	Terminal waiting time
COST	Total cost for all stages
TIME	Total time in vehicle for all stages
HINC	Household income in thousands
PSIZE	Traveling party size

Output 7.2 displays the data for the first 20 observations (five persons). For each person, the last two variables are the same across all four options. The preceding three variables—TTME, COST, and TIME—describe relationships between the person and the option. For each person, they vary over options; and for each option, they vary over persons.

Output 7.2 *First 20 Observations in Travel Data Set*

OBS	ID	MODE	CHOICE	TTME	COST	TIME	HINC	PSIZE
1	1	1	0	69	59	100	35	1
2	1	2	0	34	31	372	35	1
3	1	3	0	35	25	417	35	1
4	1	4	1	0	10	180	35	1
5	2	1	0	64	58	68	30	2
6	2	2	0	44	31	354	30	2
7	2	3	0	53	25	399	30	2
8	2	4	1	0	11	255	30	2
9	3	1	0	69	115	125	40	1
10	3	2	0	34	98	892	40	1
11	3	3	0	35	53	882	40	1
12	3	4	1	0	23	720	40	1
13	4	1	0	64	49	68	70	3
14	4	2	0	44	26	354	70	3
15	4	3	0	53	21	399	70	3
16	4	4	1	0	5	180	70	3
17	5	1	0	64	60	144	45	2
18	5	2	0	44	32	404	45	2
19	5	3	0	53	26	449	45	2
20	5	4	1	0	8	600	45	2

Before invoking PHREG, I'm going to do some recoding of the data. Like PROC LOGISTIC, PHREG won't handle CLASS variables or interactions in the MODEL statement, so it's necessary to create appropriately coded variables in a DATA step:

```
DATA travel;
  SET my.travel;
  choice = 2-choice;
  air = mode EQ 1;
  train = mode EQ 2;
  bus = mode EQ 3;
  airhinc = air*hinc;
  airpsize = air*psize;
  trahinc = train*hinc;
  trapsize = train*psize;
  bushinc = bus*hinc;
  buspsize = bus*psize;
RUN;
```

As in the chocolate example, CHOICE is recoded so that 0 becomes 2. Dummy variables are created for three of the four modes (by using logical expressions with the EQ operator), and then interactions are created between the dummy variables and the person-specific characteristics.

Let's begin with a simple model that includes only those variables that vary over options:

```
PROC PHREG DATA=travel NOSUMMARY;
  MODEL choice = ttme time cost / TIES=DISCRETE;
  STRATA id;
RUN;
```

Results in Output 7.3 show highly significant negative effects of terminal time and travel time. Each additional minute of terminal waiting time reduces the odds of choosing that alternative by 2.3% (100×(1−.967)). Each additional minute of travel time reduces the odds by about 0.2%. The COST coefficient doesn't quite reach statistical significance, and it has the "wrong" sign—greater cost appears to increase the odds that an alternative is chosen.

Output 7.3   *PHREG Model for the Determinants of Travel Mode*

Variable	DF	Parameter Estimate	Standard Error	Wald Chi-Square	Pr > Chi-Square	Risk Ratio
TTME	1	-0.033977	0.00464	53.56004	0.0001	0.967
TIME	1	-0.002193	0.0004581	22.91506	0.0001	0.998
COST	1	0.008891	0.00488	3.32394	0.0683	1.009

Output 7.4 shows results for a model that has only the three dummy variables for travel mode. The coefficients represent the relative preferences for each mode compared with a car, the omitted mode. We see that bus travel is significantly less attractive than car travel—the odds of going by bus are only about half the odds of going by car. But there are no appreciable differences in the preferences for air, train, or car.

Output 7.4   *Travel Model with Mode Dummies Only*

Variable	DF	Parameter Estimate	Standard Error	Wald Chi-Square	Pr > Chi-Square	Risk Ratio
AIR	1	-0.017094	0.18491	0.00855	0.9263	0.983
TRAIN	1	0.065597	0.18117	0.13110	0.7173	1.068
BUS	1	-0.676340	0.22424	9.09732	0.0026	0.508

In Output 7.5, we see the results of combining these two models. The COST coefficient is now in the expected direction with a *p*-value below .05. The terminal time coefficient has increased markedly so that now each additional minute results in a 9% reduction in the odds of choice. The coefficients for the mode dummies are all much larger and highly significant. People overwhelmingly prefer *not* to go by car.

What's going on here? The coefficients for the mode dummies in Output 7.5 represent relative preferences for these modes *after* differences in the other variables are taken into account. Because terminal time is 0 for car travel, there's a strong correlation between terminal time and the mode dummies. It appears that the main reason people like to travel by car is the absence of terminal waiting. After that's taken into account, car travel seems to be unappealing. The coefficients for the time and cost variables can be interpreted as the within-mode effects of these variables (assuming that these effects are the same in all four modes).

Output 7.5   *Model Combining Mode Dummies and Mode Characteristics*

Variable	DF	Parameter Estimate	Standard Error	Wald Chi-Square	Pr > Chi-Square	Risk Ratio
AIR	1	4.739865	0.86753	29.85116	0.0001	114.419
BUS	1	3.306226	0.45833	52.03654	0.0001	27.282
TRAIN	1	3.953196	0.46856	71.18281	0.0001	52.102
TTME	1	-0.096887	0.01034	87.76460	0.0001	0.908
TIME	1	-0.003995	0.0008491	22.13082	0.0001	0.996
COST	1	-0.013912	0.00665	4.37460	0.0365	0.986

The next model removes the three time and cost variables and puts in the interactions between the mode dummies and the two variables that are constant over the four options—income and party size:

```
MODEL choice = air bus train airhinc bushinc trahinc airpsize
    buspsize trapsize/ TIES=DISCRETE;
```

This model illustrates the fact that the standard multinomial logit model discussed in Chapter 5 is a special case of the conditional logit model. Results in Output 7.6 are *identical* to what you get with the following CATMOD program, which deletes all records for nonchoices (leaving 210 records) and uses MODE as the dependent variable:

```
PROC CATMOD DATA=travel;
   WHERE choice=1;
   DIRECT hinc psize;
   MODEL mode=hinc psize / NOITER NOPROFILE;
RUN;
```

The comparable results are in Output 7.7. The intercepts in the CATMOD output correspond to the coefficients of the three mode dummies in the PHREG output. The main effects of HINC and PSIZE in the CATMOD output correspond to interactions of these variables with the mode dummies in the PHREG output.

Output 7.6   *Multinomial Logit Model with PHREG*

Variable	DF	Parameter Estimate	Standard Error	Wald Chi-Square	Pr > Chi-Square	Risk Ratio
AIR	1	0.943492	0.54985	2.94437	0.0862	2.569
TRAIN	1	2.493848	0.53572	21.67018	0.0001	12.108
BUS	1	1.977971	0.67172	8.67101	0.0032	7.228
AIRHINC	1	0.003544	0.01030	0.11827	0.7309	1.004
TRAHINC	1	-0.057308	0.01184	23.42113	0.0001	0.944
BUSHINC	1	-0.030325	0.01322	5.25970	0.0218	0.970
AIRPSIZE	1	-0.600554	0.19920	9.08916	0.0026	0.549
TRAPSIZE	1	-0.309813	0.19556	2.50980	0.1131	0.734
BUSPSIZE	1	-0.940414	0.32445	8.40106	0.0038	0.390

What does Output 7.6 tell us? The coefficients for the mode dummies are not particularly informative because they represent the relative log-odds of the four modes when both income and party size are 0, a clearly impossible condition. We see a highly significant negative effect of the train × income interaction, indicating that with increasing income there is a decreased preference for trains over cars. Specifically, each thousand-dollar increase in income reduces the odds of choosing a train over a car by 5.6%. A similar effect is found for income on bus preference, though not as large. Increasing party size also reduces the preferences for the public modes over the automobile, although the effect is not quite as significant for trains. For buses, each one-person increase in party size reduces the odds of choosing a bus over a car by over 60%. A plausible explanation is that costs increase directly with party size for the public modes but not for the automobile.

Output 7.7   *Multinomial Logit Model with CATMOD*

Effect	Parameter	Estimate	Standard Error	Chi-Square	Prob
INTERCEPT	1	0.9435	0.5498	2.94	0.0862
	2	2.4938	0.5357	21.67	0.0000
	3	1.9780	0.6717	8.67	0.0032
HINC	4	0.00354	0.0103	0.12	0.7309
	5	-0.0573	0.0118	23.42	0.0000
	6	-0.0303	0.0132	5.26	0.0218
PSIZE	7	-0.6006	0.1992	9.09	0.0026
	8	-0.3098	0.1956	2.51	0.1131
	9	-0.9404	0.3245	8.40	0.0037

Our last model in Output 7.8 tests this explanation by including the cost and time measures. Greene (1992) refers to this sort of model as a *mixed* model because it contains variables that are constant over outcomes and variables that vary over outcomes. This model could *not* be estimated with CATMOD. The coefficients for the time and cost measures are not much different from those in Output 7.5. On the other hand, the effects of income and party size on the odds of choosing a bus over a car have declined dramatically, to the point where they are no longer statistically significant.

Output 7.8   *A Mixed Model for Travel Choice*

Variable	DF	Parameter Estimate	Standard Error	Wald Chi-Square	Pr > Chi-Square	Risk Ratio
AIR	1	6.035160	1.13819	28.11581	0.0001	417.866
TRAIN	1	5.573527	0.71129	61.39953	0.0001	263.361
BUS	1	4.504675	0.79579	32.04261	0.0001	90.439
AIRHINC	1	0.007481	0.01320	0.32106	0.5710	1.008
TRAHINC	1	-0.059227	0.01489	15.81678	0.0001	0.942
BUSHINC	1	-0.020898	0.01635	1.63366	0.2012	0.979
AIRPSIZE	1	-0.922420	0.25851	12.73254	0.0004	0.398
TRAPSIZE	1	0.216273	0.23364	0.85687	0.3546	1.241
BUSPSIZE	1	-0.147925	0.34277	0.18624	0.6661	0.862
TTME	1	-0.101180	0.01114	82.45882	0.0001	0.904
TIME	1	-0.004131	0.0008928	21.40536	0.0001	0.996
COST	1	-0.008670	0.00788	1.21169	0.2710	0.991

7.5   Other Applications

The two discrete choice examples that we examined in the previous sections had two features in common:

- Each person had the same set of options.
- Each person chose one and only one option.

Neither of these features is essential to the discrete choice methodology. In the chocolate bar example, instead of receiving all eight chocolate bars, each person could have been given two chocolate bars and asked to decide which was better. Or some people could get two while others get three or four. In studies of travel mode choice, some cities might not have train service, which removes that option from the choice set of persons traveling to those cities. This creates no special difficulty for data processing and analysis. Each person has a distinct record for every available option—some people may have more records, others may have fewer. The only limitation is that, if you want to include dummy variables for each option, there has to be a substantial amount of overlap in people's option sets.

If the principal aim is to estimate the effects of the characteristics of the options on each person's choice, there's no need for the option sets to have any items in common. For example, one well-known study examined the factors affecting students' choices of where to attend graduate school (Punj and Staelin 1978). Each person's option set consisted of the schools to which he or she had been accepted. Obviously, this set varied enormously in size and composition. Explanatory variables included such things as student body size, tuition, financial aid, academic reputation, and distance from the applicant. While there was undoubtedly some overlap in students' option sets, the analysis could have proceeded even if every student had been accepted by a completely distinct set of colleges.

The methodology can also be extended to studies in which people choose two or more options from among their option sets. Imagine a multi-city study of people's preference for radio stations. Each person's option set consists of the stations broadcasting in his or her city, and the question asked is "Which radio stations do you listen to regularly?" Obviously, the number of choices will vary greatly from one person to another. Most discrete-choice software can't handle multiple choices. But PROC PHREG does it easily with the syntax we've already been using. The only difference is that the choice variable will have a value of 1 for more than one item in the choice set.

This is as good a point as any to note that there is a modification to the PHREG syntax that can reduce computation time. With large data sets, this can make a substantial difference. However, the modified syntax only works when the respondent makes a single choice per option set. For the travel data, the alternative syntax is:

```
PROC PHREG DATA=travel NOSUMMARY;
   MODEL choice*choice(2) = ttme time cost;
   STRATA id;
RUN;
```

which produces exactly the same results we saw in Output 7.3. In this program, I have removed the TIES=DISCRETE option and changed the specification of the dependent variable. The number in parenthesis should be the value of the variable that denotes a *non*choice. Why does this syntax work? Don't ask. The answer is both complicated and unenlightening.

7.6   Ranked Data

The discrete-choice approach can be extended even further. Instead of asking people to *choose* one or more items within an option set, we can ask them to *rank* the items on any criterion we specify. Here's an example. In Chapter 2, we studied 147 murder cases that went to a penalty jury to decide on a life-or-death sentence. In an effort to get an unbiased measure of the seriousness of the crimes, an auxiliary study was conducted in which 50 trial judges evaluated the murder cases. Each judge was asked to read documents describing 14 or 15 cases in some detail. Then they ranked the cases from 1 to 14 (or 15) in order of assessed culpability with 1 indicating the most serious. Each case was evaluated by four to six judges. There were 10 distinct groups of cases such that (a) every case in a group was evaluated by the same judges and (b) judges evaluating cases in a group saw none of the cases in the other groups. This group structure had no impact on the analysis, however.

Our goal is to estimate a model in which characteristics of the murder cases predict the judges' rankings. The model we'll use—sometimes called the *exploded logit model* (Punj and Staelin 1978, Allison and Christakis 1994)—can be motivated by supposing that judges construct their rankings by making a sequence of choices. They first choose the most serious offense from among the 15 in front of them and assign it a value of 1. They make this choice based on the conditional logit model:

$$\Pr(y_{ij} = 1) = \frac{e^{\beta \mathbf{x}_{ij}}}{e^{\beta \mathbf{x}_{i1}} + e^{\beta \mathbf{x}_{i2}} + \ldots + e^{\beta \mathbf{x}_{i,15}}} \; . \tag{7.2}$$

After removing the chosen case from the option set, each judge then chooses the most serious case from among the remaining 14. Again, the choice is governed by the conditional logit model, except that now there are only 14 terms in the denominator. This process continues until the last choice is made from among the two that are left. The likelihood for each judge's set of rankings is formed as the product of all the terms that are like the one in equation (7.2). And the overall likelihood is just the product of all the judges' likelihoods. Although the model can be derived in other ways that do not assume sequential choices, this is certainly the most intuitive way to think about it.

How can we estimate this model? It turns out that the likelihood function I just described is identical to the likelihood function for stratified Cox regression analysis. So we can use PHREG as in the earlier examples, except that now the dependent variable consists of ranks rather than a simple dichotomy. For the penalty trial data, I constructed a data set in which each of 736 records corresponded to a ranking of one murder case by one judge. The data included characteristics of the case and an ID number for the judge. To do the analysis I used the program:

```
PROC PHREG DATA=my.judgernk NOSUMMARY;
   MODEL rank=blackd whitvic death / TIES=DISCRETE;
   STRATA judgid;
RUN;
```

If every judge had given unique ranks to all cases, the TIES=DISCRETE option would be unnecessary. But in quite a few cases, the judge assigned tied ranks to several of the cases being ranked. Fortunately, PHREG is one of the few Cox regression programs that can handle tied ranks in an appropriate manner. Results are shown in Output 7.9.

Output 7.9 *PHREG Model for Rankings of Murder Cases*

Variable	DF	Parameter Estimate	Standard Error	Wald Chi-Square	Pr > Chi-Square	Risk Ratio
BLACKD	1	0.030821	0.09481	0.10569	0.7451	1.031
WHITVIC	1	0.234042	0.10246	5.21804	0.0224	1.264
DEATH	1	0.426861	0.09199	21.53048	0.0001	1.532

Recall that BLACKD is a dummy variable indicating whether the defendant was black, WHITVIC is a dummy variable indicating whether the victim was white, and DEATH is a dummy variable indicating whether the defendant received a death sentence. The case descriptions presented to the judges contained no direct information on any of these three variables. Still, it's not surprising that those cases that got a death sentence were ranked as more serious by the judges. Both juries and judges were responding to the same characteristics of the cases. The risk ratio for DEATH has the following interpretation. At any point in the choice sequence, cases with death sentences had odds of being chosen (as most serious) that were 53% higher than the odds for cases with life sentences.

It *is* a bit surprising that WHITVIC has a statistically significant coefficient. Cases with white victims had 26% greater odds of being chosen as more serious than cases with a nonwhite victim. This could be explained by either (a) judges somehow guessing the race of the victim from other case characteristics or (b) victim race being associated with other case characteristics that affected judges' rankings.

I also estimated the model with an additional variable CULP. This variable measured severity based on predicted values from a logit regression of the death penalty cases with DEATH as the dependent variable and numerous case characteristics as independent variables. As shown in Output 7.10, this is a better predictor of the judges' rankings than a death sentence itself. Each increase in the 5-point CULP scale increases the odds of being chosen as more serious by about 30%. Controlling for CULP, cases that received a death sentence are actually *less* likely to be chosen as more serious, although the coefficient is not statistically significant. The WHITVIC effect is virtually unchanged.

Output 7.10   *PHREG Ranking Model with Additional Variable*

Variable	DF	Parameter Estimate	Standard Error	Wald Chi-Square	Pr > Chi-Square	Risk Ratio
BLACKD	1	0.119404	0.09713	1.51133	0.2189	1.127
WHITVIC	1	0.236879	0.10458	5.13030	0.0235	1.267
DEATH	1	-0.181679	0.13766	1.74184	0.1869	0.834
CULP	1	0.258479	0.04233	37.29360	0.0001	1.295

This approach to the analysis of ranked data can also be used with partial rankings. For example, a ranker may be asked to choose the three best items out of a list of 10 and give them ranks of 1, 2, and 3. If all the rest are coded as 4, the problem is equivalent to tied ranks, which we already discussed. The PHREG syntax needs no modification.

Chapter 8

Logit Analysis of Longitudinal and Other Clustered Data

8.1   Introduction

In previous chapters, we assumed that all observations are independent—that is, the outcome for each observation is completely unrelated to the outcome for every other observation. While that assumption is quite appropriate for most data sets, there are many applications where the data can be grouped into natural or imposed clusters with observations in the same cluster tending to be more alike than observations in different clusters. Longitudinal data is, perhaps, the most common example of clustering. If we record an individual's responses at multiple points in time, we ordinarily expect those observations to be positively correlated. But there are many other applications in which the data has a cluster structure. For example, husbands and wives are clustered in families, and students are clustered in classrooms. In studies involving matching, each match group is a cluster. And, of course, cluster sampling naturally produces clustered observations.

There are several reasons why logit analysis should take clustering into account:

- Ignoring the clustering and treating the observations as though they are independent usually produces standard errors that are underestimated and test statistics that are overestimated. All methods for dealing with clustered data are designed to correct this problem.

- Conventional logit analysis applied to clustered data produces coefficient estimates that are inefficient. That means that there are, in principle, other methods whose coefficients have smaller true standard errors.

- In addition to these problems, clustered data also presents opportunities to correct for biases that may occur with any application of binary regression. One method for clustered data can correct for heterogeneity shrinkage. Another method can correct for bias due to omitted explanatory variables.

In this chapter, I'll discuss five different methods for clustered data that can be implemented in SAS:

- Robust standard errors with PROC GENMOD.
- Generalized estimating equations (GEE) with PROC GENMOD.
- Conditional logit (fixed-effects) models with PROC PHREG.
- Mixed models with the GLIMMIX macro.
- A hybrid method that combines fixed-effects with mixed models or GEE.

The emphasis in this chapter is on GEE and conditional logit models. Both methods produce standard errors and test statistics that are adjusted for dependence. Beyond that, they have very divergent characteristics that often produce strikingly different results. In brief, the conditional logit method is quite good at adjusting for bias induced by omitted explanatory variables but could make inefficient use of the data. GEE does nothing to adjust for bias but makes full use of the data. I'll elaborate on these and other distinctions as we work through the examples.

8.2 Longitudinal Example

Let's begin with an example of longitudinal (panel) data. The sample consisted of 316 people who survived residential fires in the Philadelphia area (Keane et al. 1996). They were interviewed at 3 months, 6 months, and 12 months after the fire. The outcome variable PTSD is coded 1 if the person had symptoms of post-traumatic stress disorder and 0 otherwise. The explanatory variables measured at each interview are

CONTROL   A scale of a person's perceived control over several areas of life.

PROBLEMS   The total number of problems reported in several areas of life.

SEVENT   The number of stressful events reported since the last interview.

In addition, there is one variable that was measured only at the initial interview:

COHES   A scale of family cohesion.

These are only a small fraction of the variables in the original study, and they were chosen solely for the sake of example. We shall ignore difficult questions of causal ordering here and simply assume that the dependent variable PTSD does not have any effect on the other four variables. For the moment, we'll also assume that any effects are contemporaneous so we don't have to worry about lags and leads.

Let's formulate a simple model. Let p_{it} be the probability that person i had PTSD symptoms at time t. Let $\mathbf{x}_{it}$ be a vector of explanatory variables for person i at time t. This vector can contain variables that differ at each interview and variables that are constant over interviews. It may also contain dummy variables to differentiate the three different interview times. Our initial model is just an ordinary logit model with subscripts added for time.

$$\log\left(\frac{p_{it}}{1-p_{it}}\right) = \boldsymbol{\beta}\mathbf{x}_{it} \; . \tag{8.1}$$

We'll first estimate this model *without* any special treatment for dependence among the observations. To accomplish this, the data is structured with a separate record for each person at each of the three time points, for a total of 948 records. Each record contains the variables described above, with COHES duplicated across the three records for each person. There is also a variable TIME equal to 1, 2, or 3 depending on whether the interview occurred at 3, 6, or 12 months after the fire. Finally, there is a variable called SUBJID, which contains a unique identification number for each *person*. We won't use that variable now, but it will be essential for the methods introduced later. The first 15 cases from the data set are shown in Output 8.1.

Output 8.1   *First 15 Cases in PTSD Data Set*

OBS	SUBJID	TIME	PTSD	CONTROL	PROBLEMS	SEVENT	COHES
1	18	1	1	2.55556	9.250	0.00	8.00
2	18	2	0	3.44444	4.375	0.00	8.00
3	18	3	0	3.33333	2.375	0.00	8.00
4	19	1	1	2.72222	7.750	1.00	7.00
5	19	2	1	2.77778	7.750	1.00	7.00
6	19	3	0	2.77778	7.500	1.00	7.00
7	23	1	0	3.38889	7.750	0.00	8.00
8	23	2	1	3.27778	7.250	1.00	8.00
9	23	3	0	3.33333	6.250	0.00	8.00
10	24	1	0	3.16667	6.875	0.00	9.00
11	24	2	0	3.88889	6.875	0.00	9.00
12	24	3	0	3.94444	4.375	0.00	9.00
13	31	1	0	2.88889	6.000	1.00	8.00
14	31	2	1	3.11111	7.125	2.00	8.00
15	31	3	0	3.22222	5.875	1.00	8.00

A GENMOD program for estimating the model is:

```
PROC GENMOD DATA=my.ptsd;
   CLASS time;
   MODEL ptsd = control problems sevent cohes time / D=B;
RUN;
```

Results in Output 8.2 show highly significant effects of four explanatory variables. The coefficients labeled TIME 1 and TIME 2 suggest that the odds of PTSD decline with time, but the differences are not statistically significant.

Output 8.2   *GENMOD Output for PTSD Data*

```
            Criteria For Assessing Goodness Of Fit

        Criterion            DF      Value      Value/DF

        Deviance             941    966.8455     1.0275
        Scaled Deviance      941    966.8455     1.0275
        Pearson Chi-Square   941    913.0034     0.9702
        Scaled Pearson X2    941    913.0034     0.9702
        Log Likelihood        .    -483.4227       .
```

Output 8.2   *Continued*

```
              Analysis Of Parameter Estimates

Parameter        DF    Estimate   Std Err   ChiSquare  Pr>Chi

INTERCEPT         1      1.4246    0.8287      2.9554   0.0856
CONTROL           1     -0.9594    0.2047     21.9760   0.0001
PROBLEMS          1      0.2956    0.0505     34.3080   0.0001
SEVENT            1      0.3557    0.0804     19.5912   0.0001
COHES             1     -0.1782    0.0373     22.8583   0.0001
TIME      1       1      0.3566    0.2055      3.0116   0.0827
TIME      2       1      0.2499    0.2041      1.4993   0.2208
TIME      3       0      0.0000    0.0000          .        .
```

The problem with this analysis is that it assumes that the three observations for each person are independent. That's unlikely at face value and contradicted by the data. As Table 8.1 shows, the association between PTSD at time 1 and time 2 is quite strong, and even stronger between time 2 and time 3.

Table 8.1   *Association between Symptoms of PTSD at Adjacent Time Points*

PTSD at Time 1	%With PTSD at Time 2	PTSD at Time 2	%With PTSD at Time 3
Yes	47%	Yes	51%
No	18%	No	10%

Of course, the real question is whether this association persists after controlling for the explanatory variables in the model. To answer that question, I included PTSD at time 1 in a logit model predicting PTSD at time 2, along with the other explanatory variables in Output 8.2. The coefficient for PTSD at time 1 was highly significant, indicating dependence over time (output not shown).

What are the consequences? Even with dependence among the observations, the coefficients in Output 8.2 should be consistent estimates of the true coefficients, and, therefore, approximately unbiased. They are not efficient, however. That means that there are other ways of estimating the coefficients that make better use of the data, thereby producing estimates with less sampling variability. A more serious problem is that the standard errors are likely to be underestimates of the true standard errors. And because the formula for the Wald chi-squares has the standard error in the denominator, they're likely to be overestimates. So, maybe the *p*-values aren't as small as they appear.

8.3   GEE Estimation

Beginning with Release 6.12 SAS/STAT, PROC GENMOD makes it easy to get efficient estimates of the coefficients and improved standard error estimates with clustered data by using the method of generalized estimating equations (Diggle et al. 1994). Here's a brief, nontechnical explanation of this method. In ordinary logit analysis, the maximum likelihood estimates can be obtained by an algorithm known as iteratively reweighted least squares. What that means is that each step in the algorithm is accomplished by weighted least squares, with both the weights and the constructed dependent variable changing at each iteration as functions of the results at the last iteration. In the matrix formulation of weighted least squares, there is a weight matrix **W,** which has off-diagonal elements equal to 0 and diagonal elements equal to $p_i(1-p_i)$, where p_i is the predicted probability from the previous iteration. The GEE algorithm extends this approach to do iterative *generalized* least squares. In this method, the matrix **W** has nonzero off-diagonal elements that are functions of the correlations among the observations. These correlations are re-estimated at each iteration, based on correlations among the Pearson residuals.

In GENMOD, GEE estimation is invoked with the REPEATED statement. Here is the program for our PTSD example:

```
PROC GENMOD DATA=my.ptsd;
  CLASS subjid time;
  MODEL ptsd = control problems sevent cohes time / D=B;
  REPEATED SUBJECT=subjid / WITHIN=time TYPE=UN CORRW;
RUN;
```

In the REPEATED statement, the SUBJECT option names a variable that contains a unique identification code for each cluster. This variable must first be named in the CLASS statement. It is assumed that observations are independent between clusters and correlated within clusters. The WITHIN option names a variable that distinguishes different items within a cluster. In this application, the items are distinguished by different times. This variable must also be named in the CLASS statement. The WITHIN option can be omitted if either (a) the data is appropriately sorted within each cluster (as it is in this example) or (b) the items in each cluster are all treated as equivalent (as with students in a classroom).

The TYPE option is used to specify the structure of the correlation matrix among the observations within each cluster. In this case, I've chosen UN for *unstructured*, which is appropriate if the number of time points is small. With three time points, there are three correlations to be estimated: 1-2, 2-3, and 1-3. When there are many time points, you would probably want to impose some structure by choosing either TYPE=EXCH for *exchangeable* (correlations between all time points assumed equal) or TYPE=AR for a lag–1 autoregressive structure. The CORRW option simply asks PROC GENMOD to print out the estimate of the "working" correlation matrix.

When a GENMOD program includes a REPEATED statement, GENMOD first reports the results from ordinary logit analysis as in Output 8.2. Then it displays the GEE results, shown in Output 8.3. In the middle panel, we see the estimates of the cross-time correlations used in the analysis. Somewhat surprisingly, the time 1 response is more highly correlated with time 3 than with time 2.

Output 8.3   *GEE Results for PTSD Data*

```
                    GEE Model Information

        Description                      Value

        Correlation Structure            Unstructured
        Subject Effect                   SUBJID (316 levels)
        Number of Clusters               316
        Clusters With Missing Values     0
        Correlation Matrix Dimension     3
        Maximum Cluster Size             3
        Minimum Cluster Size             3


                Working Correlation Matrix

                        COL1      COL2      COL3

        ROW1          1.0000    0.1861    0.2500
        ROW2          0.1861    1.0000    0.3819
        ROW3          0.2500    0.3819    1.0000
```

Output 8.3   Continued

```
              Analysis Of GEE Parameter Estimates
              Empirical Standard Error Estimates

                        Empirical  95% Confidence Limits
Parameter      Estimate  Std Err    Lower    Upper       Z   Pr>|Z|

INTERCEPT        1.6071   0.8682   -0.0945   3.3087   1.8511  0.0642
CONTROL         -0.9086   0.2157   -1.3314  -0.4858  -4.212   0.0000
PROBLEMS         0.2565   0.0500    0.1585   0.3545   5.1284  0.0000
SEVENT           0.2751   0.0866    0.1054   0.4449   3.1761  0.0015
COHES           -0.1908   0.0455   -0.2800  -0.1015  -4.190   0.0000
TIME      1      0.4153   0.1782    0.0661   0.7645   2.3312  0.0197
TIME      2      0.2714   0.1664   -0.0548   0.5977   1.6307  0.1029
TIME      3      0.0000   0.0000    0.0000   0.0000   0.0000  0.0000
Scale            0.9691      .        .        .        .       .
```

In the lower panel, we see that the coefficients are different from those in Output 8.2 but not markedly different. The associated statistics are displayed somewhat differently than standard GENMOD output. By default, we get upper and lower confidence limits (using the Wald method), and instead of chi-square statistics we get z-statistics. You can convert the z's to chi-squares just by squaring them, as I did in the second column of numbers in Table 8.2. Comparing them with the first column, taken from Output 8.2, we see that many of the chi-squares are substantially lower with GEE estimation, which is just what we would expect. The only statistic that changes enough to make a possible difference in conclusions is the chi-square for the time 1 comparison with time 3, which is actually larger with the GEE method.

Table 8.2   *Comparison of Chi-Square Values for Different Estimation Methods*

	Standard Logit	Generalized Estimating Equations			
		UN Robust SE's	UN Model SE's	EXCH Robust SE's	IND Robust SE's
CONTROL	21.98	17.74	20.24	20.00	17.85
PROBLEMS	34.31	26.30	25.89	25.24	33.00
SEVENT	19.59	10.09	13.30	10.57	15.62
COHES	22.86	17.56	18.88	17.21	14.60
TIME1	3.01	5.43	5.55	5.29	3.76
TIME2	1.50	2.66	3.05	2.70	2.11

You'll notice that the standard errors in Output 8.3 are labeled "Empirical Standard Errors." That means that they are robust estimates produced by the method of White (1980), which do not depend on the correctness of the structure imposed on the working correlation matrix. It's also possible to get *model-based* estimates of standard errors by putting the MODELSE option in the REPEATED statement. These standard errors, which are based directly on the assumed correlation structure, are then used in constructing confidence intervals and the *z*-statistics. The model-based standard errors ought to be better estimates if the assumed model for the correlation structure is correct, but worse if the assumed model is incorrect. It's certainly safer to stick with the robust estimates. In the third column of numbers in Table 8.2, I report the chi-squares calculated from the model-based standard errors. While there are some noticeable differences with the chi-squares calculated from the robust standard errors, none are so large as to alter any conclusions.

I also tried a model with TYPE=EXCH specified in the REPEATED statement, which produced the results shown in Output 8.4. As you can see from the working correlation matrix, this option specifies that the correlations are equal across time points, a fairly strong assumption for longitudinal data. Both the coefficients and the standard errors change slightly under this specification. Chi-squares calculated from the empirical standard errors are shown in the fourth column of Table 8.2.

Output 8.4 *GEE Results for an Exchangeable Correlation Structure*

```
                    Working Correlation Matrix

                         COL1      COL2      COL3

          ROW1         1.0000    0.2727    0.2727
          ROW2         0.2727    1.0000    0.2727
          ROW3         0.2727    0.2727    1.0000
```

Output 8.4 *Continued*

```
              Analysis Of GEE Parameter Estimates
              Empirical Standard Error Estimates
                          Empirical  95% Confidence Limits
   Parameter      Estimate  Std Err    Lower     Upper        Z  Pr>|Z|

   INTERCEPT        1.7927   0.8619    0.1033    3.4820   2.0798  0.0375
   CONTROL         -0.9601   0.2147   -1.3809   -0.5393   -4.472  0.0000
   PROBLEMS         0.2497   0.0497    0.1523    0.3471   5.0244  0.0000
   SEVENT           0.2810   0.0864    0.1116    0.4503   3.2519  0.0011
   COHES           -0.1871   0.0451   -0.2755   -0.0987   -4.148  0.0000
   TIME      1      0.4100   0.1782    0.0607    0.7593   2.3008  0.0214
   TIME      2      0.2699   0.1662   -0.0558    0.5955   1.6243  0.1043
   TIME      3      0.0000   0.0000    0.0000    0.0000   0.0000  0.0000
```

Lastly, I fitted a model with TYPE=IND (for independence), which forces the cross-time correlations to be 0. Under this constraint, GEE estimation reduces to ordinary ML logit estimation, so the coefficients and model-based standard errors are the same as those in Output 8.2. Nevertheless, the robust standard error estimates still take account of the correlations among the observations. Chi-squares based on these standard errors are shown in the last column of Table 8.2. (I have also written a macro named ROBUST that will produce robust standard errors for PROC LOGISTIC. See the Appendix for details.)

8.4   Fixed-Effects with Conditional Logit Analysis

Although GEE estimation is a wonderful addition to the GENMOD procedure, it doesn't correct for bias resulting from omitted explanatory variables at the cluster level. To be more specific, when you have multiple observations per person—as in the PTSD example—it is possible to statistically control for *all* stable characteristics of persons, regardless of whether those characteristics can be measured. Needless to say, this is an extremely attractive possibility, and one that is easily implemented with the PHREG procedure. Unfortunately, as we shall see, there are significant limitations that keep this approach from being the universally preferred method.

I begin with a slight elaboration of the model of equation (8.1):

$$\log\left(\frac{p_{it}}{1 - p_{it}}\right) = \alpha_i + \beta \mathbf{x}_{it} . \tag{8.2}$$

What's new here is the α_i term that represents all differences among individuals that are stable over time. Because α_i is the same for a given person at all three time points, a positive correlation is induced among the observed outcomes.

At this point, there are two ways to go. We could treat α_i as a random variable with a specified probability distribution (say, normal with mean 0 and variance σ^2), which leads to a random-effects or mixed model, much like the linear models estimated by the MIXED procedure. In fact, there is a macro named GLIMMIX that makes it possible to use the MIXED procedure with dichotomous outcomes. I'll discuss it briefly in Section 8.7.

That's not the approach taken in this section, however. Instead, we treat α_i as a set of fixed constants, one for each individual in the sample, an approach that is sometimes referred to as a fixed-effects model. But how can we estimate it? If the left-hand side of equation (8.2) were a continuous variable, we could use ordinary least squares, with a dummy variable for each individual i (less one). For example, if the dependent variable were CONTROL instead of PTSD, we could fit a model to the 948 observations with 316 dummy variables. That may seem like an outrageous number of variables in the model, but it's perfectly legitimate. An equivalent method that is more computationally tractable is to transform all variables so that they are expressed as deviations from each individual's means. Then, the model is run on the transformed variables. PROC GLM can accomplish this automatically by using the ABSORB statement.

Unfortunately, the dummy variable or mean deviation method isn't satisfactory for logit analysis, unless the number of clusters (dummy variables) is small and the number of observations per cluster is relatively large. It certainly wouldn't be appropriate for the PTSD example. The difficulty is caused by the "incidental parameters problem" (Kalbfleisch and Sprott 1970). In the asymptotic theory of maximum likelihood estimation, it is usually assumed that the number of observations gets large while the number of parameters to be estimated remains constant. However, when equation (8.2) is applied to panel data, each additional individual adds an additional parameter to the model. This can lead to very substantial biases in the parameter estimates.

One solution to the incidental parameters problem is called conditional likelihood estimation (Chamberlain 1980). In constructing the likelihood function, we condition on the number of 1's and 0's that are observed for each individual. For example, if a person had PTSD symptoms at time 1 but not at time 2 and time 3, we ask "Given that this person had only one occasion with PTSD symptoms, what's the probability that it occurred at time 1 and not at times 2 and 3?" We write an expression for this probability as a function of the explanatory variables and the β parameters, and we multiply these probabilities together for all individuals to get the overall likelihood. When this is done, the α_i parameters cancel from the likelihood function. We say that they have been *conditioned out* of the likelihood. Presto, no more incidental parameters problem.

How can we implement this method? Luckily, the conditional likelihood function has a form that's identical to the conditional logit model that we examined for discrete choice models in Chapter 7. And as we saw there, the conditional logit model has a likelihood that's identical to certain discrete-time survival models that can be estimated with the PHREG procedure. So, once again we turn to PROC PHREG. Here's the code for estimating the fixed-effects version of our model for the PTSD data:

```
DATA ptsd;
  SET my.ptsd;
  ptsd=2-ptsd;
  t1 = time EQ 1;
  t2 = time EQ 2;
RUN;
PROC PHREG DATA=ptsd NOSUMMARY;
  MODEL ptsd = control problems sevent cohes t1 t2 /
    TIES=DISCRETE;
  STRATA subjid;
RUN;
```

The DATA step is necessary to change the coding of PTSD so that the 0's become 2's, and to create two dummy variables for time (because PHREG doesn't have a CLASS statement). As with the conditional logit model, we specify TIES=DISCRETE and use the STRATA statement to name the variable containing the unique identifier for each person. Results are shown in Output 8.5.

Output 8.5 *PHREG Output for Fixed-Effects Logit Model*

		Analysis of Maximum Likelihood Estimates				
Variable	DF	Parameter Estimate	Standard Error	Wald Chi-Square	Pr > Chi-Square	Risk Ratio
CONTROL	1	-1.098258	0.42210	6.76998	0.0093	0.333
PROBLEMS	1	0.213900	0.10267	4.34008	0.0372	1.238
SEVENT	1	0.202666	0.13427	2.27829	0.1312	1.225
COHES	0	0	.	.	.	.
T1	1	0.794082	0.29717	7.14016	0.0075	2.212
T2	1	0.436466	0.25967	2.82521	0.0928	1.547

Two things are immediately evident in the PHREG output: there's no coefficient for COHES and the chi-squares are a lot lower than those we saw in Table 8.2. The reason we don't get a COHES coefficient is that COHES is constant over time. This is a quite general and often maddening characteristic of fixed-effects models: they can't produce coefficients for variables that don't vary within clusters. The explanation is both simple and intuitive. In forming the conditional likelihood, we pose the question "Given that k events happened to this individual, what factors explain why they happened at these particular times and not at other times?" Clearly, variables that are constant over time cannot explain why events happened at some times and not others. That doesn't mean that the time-constant variables aren't controlled. As I noted earlier, the method actually controls for *all* time constant variables, not just those we happen to have measured. Or as it's sometimes stated, each individual serves as his or her own control.

The main reason the chi-squares are small is that the standard errors are substantially larger than they were for GEE estimation. If you compare the coefficients, they're not all that different from those in Output 8.4. So why are the standard errors larger? Because fixed-effects estimation discards a lot of data that's used by GEE. For one thing, any person whose PTSD values didn't change over the three periods is automatically excluded from the likelihood function. Why? Again, the conditional likelihood is trying to explain why a person with a certain number of occasions with PTSD symptoms had them at some times and not at other times. But if we know that a person had symptoms at all three interviews or at none of the interviews, there's no variation in timing to explain. In fact, there were 37 persons with PTSD symptoms at all three interviews and 144 persons without symptoms at all three interviews. That's 57% of the sample who contribute nothing to the estimation. Even those who had PTSD symptoms at some times and not at other times don't contribute as much information as they did in the GEE analysis. Only within-person variation is used, not between-person variation. The result is standard errors that are about twice as large as in the GEE analysis.

The contrast between fixed-effects and GEE estimation is a classic trade-off between bias and inefficiency. Fixed-effects estimates are much less prone to bias because the conditional likelihood discards information that is potentially contaminated by confounding variables. On the other hand, if confounding variables are not a problem, then the fixed-effects approach can ignore much potentially useful information. That seems to be the case in the PTSD example where the fixed-effects coefficients differ only slightly from the GEE coefficients. For this example, then, GEE seems to be the superior method.

8.5 Postdoctoral Training Example

The techniques that work for panel data also work for other kinds of clustered data. In this section, we'll apply the GEE method and the fixed-effects method to data in which newly minted Ph.D.s are clustered within universities. The sample consisted of 557 male biochemists who got their doctorates from 106 American universities in the late 1950s and early 1960s (McGinnis, Allison and Long 1982). The outcome variable PDOC is coded 1 if they got postdoctoral training and 0 otherwise. The sample is about evenly split, with 49% getting some form of postdoctoral training immediately after receiving their degrees. Other variables examined here are

AGE Age in years at completion of the Ph.D.
MAR 1 if married, 0 otherwise
DOC Measure of the prestige of the doctoral institution in bioscience fields
UND Measure of selectivity of the person's undergraduate institution
AG 1 if degree is from an agricultural department, 0 otherwise
ARTS Number of articles published while a graduate student
CITS Number of citations to published articles
DOCID ID number of the doctoral institution

The first 20 observations in the data set are shown in Output 8.6.

Output 8.6   *First 20 Observations in Postdoctoral Data Set*

OBS	PDOC	AGE	MAR	DOC	UND	AG	ARTS	CITS	DOCID
1	0	29	1	362	7	0	1	2	1402
2	1	32	1	210	6	0	1	4	1250
3	1	26	1	359	6	0	0	1	1399
4	0	25	1	181	3	0	0	1	1221
5	1	30	1	429	7	0	0	1	1469
6	1	28	1	359	6	0	1	0	1399
7	1	30	1	210	4	0	0	0	1250
8	1	40	1	347	4	0	0	0	1387
9	0	30	1	210	5	0	1	2	1250
10	1	28	1	359	7	0	5	32	1399
11	0	29	1	447	4	0	0	0	1487
12	1	28	1	276	5	0	1	0	1316
13	0	41	1	261	3	0	0	0	1301
14	1	27	1	226	7	0	0	1	1266
15	1	35	1	359	6	0	0	1	1399
16	1	30	0	341	5	0	7	16	1381
17	0	28	0	226	1	0	1	1	1266
18	1	28	1	429	4	0	3	3	1469
19	0	27	0	359	3	0	0	0	1399
20	1	27	0	205	4	0	0	0	1245

Using PROC GENMOD, I first estimated a conventional logit model. The results are shown in Output 8.7. Except for article and citation counts, all variables are statistically significant at the .05 level. Older, married Ph.D.s with degrees from agricultural departments were less likely to receive postdoctoral training. Those from high prestige institutions or who were undergraduates at selective institutions were more likely to receive postdoctoral training.

Output 8.7   *GENMOD Estimates for Conventional Logit Model*

Analysis Of Parameter Estimates

Parameter	DF	Estimate	Std Err	ChiSquare	Pr>Chi
INTERCEPT	1	2.3974	0.9092	6.9529	0.0084
AGE	1	-0.0991	0.0254	15.1943	0.0001
MAR	1	-0.5645	0.2684	4.4242	0.0354
DOC	1	0.0027	0.0009	8.3989	0.0038
AG	1	-1.1070	0.2030	29.7214	0.0001
UND	1	0.1215	0.0600	4.1000	0.0429
ARTS	1	-0.0739	0.0809	0.8345	0.3610
CITS	1	-0.0030	0.0170	0.0314	0.8593

Because many of the members in the sample got their degrees from the same institutions, it's reasonable to suspect some dependence among the observations. There are many characteristics of universities besides prestige that are likely to have some impact on the probability of postdoctoral training. The omission of these variables from the model would produce a correlation in postdoctoral training among those men from the same institution. To adjust for this possible correlation, I estimated the model by GEE:

```
PROC GENMOD DATA=my.postdoc;
   CLASS docid;
   MODEL pdoc = age mar doc ag und arts cits / D=B;
   REPEATED SUBJECT=docid / TYPE=EXCH;
RUN;
```

As we saw in the last example, the TYPE=EXCH option specifies a single correlation that applies to any pair of persons within each cluster. In applications like this one, where there is no natural ordering of persons within clusters, the EXCH option is the only sensible specification.

Output 8.8   *GEE Estimates for Postdoctoral Example*

```
                    GEE Model Information

        Description                   Value

        Correlation Structure         Exchangeable
        Subject Effect                DOC (106 levels)
        Number of Clusters            106
        Correlation Matrix Dimension  53
        Maximum Cluster Size          53
        Minimum Cluster Size          1
```

Output 8.8 *Continued*

```
              Analysis Of GEE Parameter Estimates
              Empirical Standard Error Estimates


                        Empirical  95% Confidence Limits
Parameter    Estimate    Std Err     Lower     Upper      Z   Pr>|Z|

INTERCEPT     2.5332     0.9414     0.6881    4.3784   2.6909  0.0071
AGE          -0.1020     0.0247    -0.1504   -0.0536  -4.130   0.0000
MAR          -0.5561     0.2727    -1.0906   -0.0216  -2.039   0.0414
DOC           0.0026     0.0012     0.0002    0.0050   2.1383  0.0325
AG           -0.9208     0.2624    -1.4351   -0.4065  -3.509   0.0004
UND           0.1176     0.0489     0.0218    0.2134   2.4067  0.0161
ARTS         -0.0733     0.0796    -0.2292    0.0826   -.9213  0.3569
CITS         -0.0038     0.0164    -0.0360    0.0284   -.2305  0.8177
Scale         1.0143        .          .         .        .       .
```

From the top panel of Output 8.8, we see that of the 106 universities represented in the sample, the largest had 53 doctorates. As we found in the PTSD example, the coefficients don't change much with GEE, but the estimated standard errors get larger for all but one of the coefficients. Table 8.3 converts the z-statistics to chi-squares so that the two methods can be more easily compared. Some of the chi-squares are dramatically lower for GEE while others change very little. Those that changed the most—like AG and DOC—are still highly significant.

Table 8.3 *Chi-Squares for Different Methods, Postdoctoral Example*

	Standard Logit	GEE Robust SE's	Fixed Effects	Mixed Model
AGE	15.19	17.06	12.00	16.63
MAR	4.42	4.16	2.87	4.35
DOC	8.40	4.57	---	4.99
AG	29.72	12.31	5.98	14.94
UND	4.10	5.79	3.48	4.05
ARTS	.83	.85	.79	.82
CITS	.03	.05	.21	.06

Next, we apply the fixed-effects method using PROC PHREG. The attraction of the fixed-effects approach is that we control for *all* characteristics of universities, not just prestige. Failure to control for these characteristics could bias some or all of the coefficients in the model.

We implement the method with the program

```
DATA postdoc;
   SET my.postdoc;
   pdoc=2-pdoc;
RUN;
PROC PHREG DATA=postdoc NOSUMMARY;
   MODEL pdoc = age mar ag und arts cits / TIES=DISCRETE;
   STRATA docid;
RUN;
```

As in the previous example, the DATA step converts 0 to 2 on the dependent variable so that the signs of the coefficients are correct. To implement the method, we specify the DISCRETE option for ties and stratify on the DOCID variable for doctoral institution. I excluded the DOC variable from the model because it's constant over cases within each university. If I had put it in, PHREG wouldn't have reported any numbers for it.

The results in Output 8.9 show little difference in the coefficients as compared with the GEE results. Apparently, other characteristics of universities either have little effect on postdoctoral training or are uncorrelated with the measured variables in the model. Nevertheless, the standard errors are higher and the chi-squares lower than those we got with GEE, as shown in the third column of Table 8.3. That's due in part to the fact that 108 biochemists were excluded from the analysis because either everyone or no one at their universities got postdoctoral training. Of these, 20 were necessarily excluded because they were the only representatives from their universities. In any case, the decline in chi-squares is enough to move the *p*-values above the .05 level for two of the variables, MAR and UND. Again, it seems that fixed-effects is not the best method for this data because it produces little reduction in bias but a big increase in standard errors.

Output 8.9 *Fixed-Effects Results for Postdoctoral Data*

```
            Analysis of Maximum Likelihood Estimates

           Parameter   Standard     Wald      Pr >       Risk
Variable DF  Estimate      Error  Chi-Square Chi-Square  Ratio

AGE      1  -0.107564    0.03105   11.99722    0.0005    0.898
MAR      1  -0.531398    0.31378    2.86814    0.0903    0.588
AG       1  -0.935536    0.38271    5.97570    0.0145    0.392
UND      1   0.135225    0.07246    3.48247    0.0620    1.145
ARTS     1  -0.086798    0.09759    0.79102    0.3738    0.917
CITS     1  -0.010681    0.02279    0.21969    0.6393    0.989
```

8.6   Matching

In the postdoctoral example, the data was clustered into naturally occurring groups. *Matching* is another form of clustering in which individuals are grouped together by design. Matching was once commonly used in the social sciences to control for potentially confounding variables. Now, most researchers use some kind of regression procedure, primarily because of the difficulty of matching on several variables. However, with the recent development of the *propensity score* method, that objection to matching is largely obsolete (Rosenbaum and Rubin 1983, Smith 1997).

Here's a typical application of the propensity score method. Imagine that your goal is to compare academic achievement of students in public and private schools, controlling for several measures of family background. You have measures on all the relevant variables for a large sample of eighth grade students, 10% of whom are in private schools. The first step in a propensity score analysis is to do a logit regression in which the dependent variable is the type of school and the independent variables are the family background characteristics. Based on that regression, the propensity score is the predicted probability of being in a private school. Each private school student is then matched to one or more public school students according to their closeness on the propensity score. In most cases, this method produces two groups that have nearly equal means on all the variables in the propensity score regression. One can then do a simple bivariate analysis of achievement versus school type. Alternatively, other variables not in the propensity score regression could be included in some kind of regression analysis. In many situations, this method could have important advantages over conventional regression analysis in reducing both bias and sampling variability (Smith 1997).

The propensity score method is an example of *treatment-control* matching. In this kind of matching, the individuals within each match group necessarily differ on the explanatory variable of central interest. Another sort of matching is *case-control* matching in which individuals within each match group necessarily differ on the *dependent* variable. Case-control studies have long been popular in the biomedical sciences for reasons I explained in Section 3.12. In a case-control study, the aim is to model the determinants of some dichotomous outcome, for instance, a disease condition. People who have the condition are called cases; people who do not are called controls. In Section 3.12, we saw that it's legitimate to take all the available cases and a random subsample of the controls, pool the two groups into a single sample, and do a conventional logit analysis for the dichotomous outcome. Although not an essential feature of the method, each case is often matched to one or more controls on variables—such as age—that are known to affect the outcome but are not of direct interest.

Although it's usually desirable to adjust for matching in the analysis, the appropriate adjustment methods are quite different for treatment-control and case-control matching. In brief, there are several ways to do it for treatment-control matching but only one way for case-control matching. Let's begin with a treatment-control example. Metraux and Culhane (1997) constructed a data set of 8,402 women who stayed in family shelters in New York City for at least one 7-day period during 1992. The data contained information on several pre-stay characteristics, events that occurred during the stay, and housing type subsequent to the stay. As our dependent variable, we'll focus on whether or not the woman exited to public housing (PUBHOUSE), which was the destination for 48% of the sample. Our principal independent variable is STAYBABY, equal to 1 if a woman gave birth during her stay at the shelter and 0 otherwise. Nine percent of the sample had a birth during the stay. Other independent variables are:

BLACK	1=black race, 0=nonblack
KIDS	Number of children in the household
DOUBLEUP	1=living with another family prior to shelter stay, 0 otherwise
AGE	Age of woman at beginning of shelter stay
DAYS	Number of days in shelter stay

The conventional approach to analysis would be to estimate a logit regression model for the entire sample of 8,402 women. Results for doing that with PROC GENMOD are shown in Output 8.10. We see that although the odds of exiting to public housing increase with the number of children in the household, a birth during the stay reduces the odds by about 100(exp(−.40)−1)=−33%. Both of these effects are overshadowed by the enormous impact of the length of stay. Each additional day increases the odds of exiting to public housing by about 1%. (Not surprisingly, DAYS also has a correlation of .25 with STAYBABY—the longer a woman's stay, the more likely it is that she gave birth during the stay.)

Output 8.10 *Logistic Regression of Exit to Public Housing with GENMOD*

```
                  Analysis Of Parameter Estimates

Parameter    DF    Estimate    Std Err    ChiSquare    Pr>Chi

INTERCEPT    1     -1.7441     0.1543      127.7919    0.0001
STAYBABY     1     -0.4030     0.0990       16.5794    0.0001
BLACK        1     -0.1606     0.0586        7.5141    0.0061
KIDS         1      0.1835     0.0219       70.0112    0.0001
DOUBLEUP     1     -0.1904     0.0601       10.0156    0.0016
AGE          1     -0.0227     0.0052       18.8247    0.0001
DAYS         1      0.0114     0.0003     1973.0827    0.0001
```

Now let's estimate the effect of STAYBABY in a matched sample. I compared all 791 women who had a baby during the stay with an equal number of women who did not. To control for the effect of DAYS, I matched each woman who had a baby with a random draw from among those women whose length of stay was identical (or as close as possible). In this subsample, then, the correlation between STAYBABY and DAYS is necessarily .00. Rosenbaum and Rubin (1983) argue that adjustment by matching is "usually more robust to departures from the assumed form of the underlying model than model-based adjustment on random samples . . . primarily because of reduced reliance on the model's extrapolations." Despite the fact that 6,820 cases are discarded in the matched analysis, we'll see that very little precision is lost in the estimation of the STAYBABY coefficient. I could have used the propensity score method to control for *all* the variables in Output 8.10, but I wanted to keep things simple, and the adjustment for DAYS would have dominated anyway.

Next, I estimated a logit model for this matched-pair subsample without adjusting for the matching (Output 8.11). Although the level of significance declines greatly for most of the variables, the loss of precision is quite small for the STAYBABY coefficient; its standard error only increases by about 18% relative to that in Output 8.10. The coefficient declines somewhat in magnitude, but the matched subsample may be less prone to bias in this estimate than that in the full sample. Note that if we deleted DAYS from this model, the results for STAYBABY would hardly change at all because the two variables are uncorrelated, by design.

Output 8.11 *Regression of PUBHOUSE with Matched-Pair Data without Adjustment for Matching*

Analysis Of Parameter Estimates					
Parameter	DF	Estimate	Std Err	ChiSquare	Pr>Chi
INTERCEPT	1	-0.0317	0.3357	0.0089	0.9248
STAYBABY	1	-0.3107	0.1167	7.0914	0.0077
BLACK	1	-0.1322	0.1253	1.1139	0.2912
KIDS	1	0.1789	0.0465	14.8089	0.0001
DOUBLEUP	1	-0.1046	0.1216	0.7397	0.3898
AGE	1	-0.0188	0.0110	2.9045	0.0883
DAYS	1	0.0043	0.0004	95.4934	0.0001

The problem with the analysis in Output 8.11 is that the matched pairs are not independent, which could lead to bias in the standard error estimates. One way to adjust for the matching is to use the GEE method discussed in Section 8.5. Here's how:

```
PROC GENMOD DATA=my.casecont;
  CLASS casenum;
  MODEL pubhouse=staybaby black kids doubleup age days / D=B;
  REPEATED SUBJECT=casenum / TYPE=UN CORRW;
RUN;
```

CASENUM is the unique identifier for each matched pair. Although I specified an unstructured correlation matrix (TYPE=UN), all types of correlation structure are equivalent when there are only two observations per cluster.

Output 8.12 *Regression of PUBHOUSE with Matched-Pair Data with GEE Adjustment for Matching*

```
                        GEE Model Information

         Description                    Value

         Correlation Structure          Unstructured
         Subject Effect                 CASENUM (791 levels)
         Number of Clusters             791
         Correlation Matrix Dimension   2
         Maximum Cluster Size           2
         Minimum Cluster Size           2


                      Working Correlation Matrix

                               COL1      COL2

                   ROW1      1.0000    0.0705
                   ROW2      0.0705    1.0000


                 Analysis Of GEE Parameter Estimates
                 Empirical Standard Error Estimates

                        Empirical  95% Confidence Limits
     Parameter   Estimate  Std Err     Lower      Upper        Z   Pr>|Z|

     INTERCEPT   -0.0125   0.3487    -0.6959     0.6709   -.0359   0.9714
     STAYBABY    -0.3100   0.1074    -0.5206    -0.0995   -2.886   0.0039
     BLACK       -0.1462   0.1197    -0.3808     0.0884   -1.221   0.2220
     KIDS         0.1790   0.0469     0.0871     0.2709   3.8186   0.0001
     DOUBLEUP    -0.1138   0.1168    -0.3427     0.1151   -.9742   0.3300
     AGE         -0.0188   0.0108    -0.0400     0.0024   -1.740   0.0819
     DAYS         0.0043   0.0007     0.0030     0.0056   6.5214   0.0000
     Scale        1.2250        .          .          .        .        .
```

Results in Output 8.12 differ only slightly from those in Output 8.11, which were not adjusted for matching. In particular, the coefficient for STAYBABY is about the same, while its estimated standard error is slightly reduced, from .1167 to .1074. Consistent with the small change is the estimated "residual" correlation between within-pair observations of only .07. One reason why the results don't differ more is that the inclusion of DAYS in Output 8.11 is itself a partial adjustment for matching. When DAYS is omitted from the model, the residual correlation is .20.

In my opinion, GEE is usually the best method for adjusting for treatment-control matching. Although the example consisted of matched pairs, the method is identical for one-to-many matching or many-to-many matching. One alternative to GEE is the mixed model discussed in Section 8.7, but this is likely to give very similar results in most applications. Another widely recommended alternative is the conditional logit (fixed effects) model of Section 8.4. Unfortunately, this method often involves a substantial loss of data with concomitant increases in standard errors. The shelter stay data provides a good example of this loss. The PHREG program for the fixed-effects model with matched-pair data is:

```
DATA b;
  SET my.casecont;
  pubhouse=1-pubhouse;
RUN;
PROC PHREG DATA=b NOSUMMARY;
 MODEL pubhouse= staybaby black kids doubleup age /
        TIES=DISCRETE;
 STRATA casenum;
RUN;
```

Because PHREG predicts the probability of the *smaller* value, the DATA step is necessary to make the coefficients have the correct sign. There is no need to include DAYS in the model because it is the same (or almost the same) for both members of every matched pair.

Output 8.13 *PHREG Output for Treatment-Control Matched Pairs*

			Analysis of Maximum Likelihood Estimates			
Variable	DF	Parameter Estimate	Standard Error	Wald Chi-Square	Pr > Chi-Square	Risk Ratio
STAYBABY	1	-0.384991	0.13665	7.93701	0.0048	0.680
BLACK	1	-0.327532	0.19385	2.85470	0.0911	0.721
KIDS	1	0.201547	0.07141	7.96579	0.0048	1.223
DOUBLEUP	1	-0.328253	0.20425	2.58269	0.1080	0.720
AGE	1	-0.028323	0.01806	2.45837	0.1169	0.972

The results in Output 8.13 are quite similar to those in Output 8.12, but the standard error of STAYBABY is about 27% higher than it was before. The increase is attributable to the fact that the conditional logit method essentially discards all matched pairs in which both members have the same value of the dependent variable PUBHOUSE. In Section 8.4, I argued that this loss of information must be balanced by the potential decrease in bias that comes from controlling all stable characteristics of the cluster that might be correlated with the treatment variable, in this case, STAYBABY. Because the matching is balanced in this application (with one treatment and one control per cluster), it's impossible for STAYBABY to be correlated with cluster characteristics. So, there's no potential benefit from the conditional logit method.

The situation is quite different for case-control designs. In that setting, every matched pair has both of the two values of the *dependent* variable. If you try to apply GEE to such data, the estimated working residual correlation is –1 and the method breaks down. On the other hand, the conditional logit method suffers no loss of data because there are no clusters in which both members have the same value on the dependent variable. So conditional logit is the only way to go for case-control matching.

As an example of the case-control design, we again use the data on shelter stays, but with STAYBABY as the dependent variable rather than an independent variable. Output 8.14 shows the results from estimating a logit model with LOGISTIC for the full data set of 8,402 women. We see evidence that the probability of having a baby during the shelter stay is higher for blacks, women with more children in the household, younger women, and those with longer shelter stays.

Output 8.14 *Logit Regression of STAYBABY for Full Sample*

```
                         Response Profile

                   Ordered
                   Value   STAYBABY      Count

                     1        1           791
                     2        0          7611


       Model Fitting Information and Testing Global Null Hypothesis BETA=0

                              Intercept
                  Intercept      and
     Criterion      Only      Covariates    Chi-Square for Covariates

     AIC          5245.229     4728.880              .
     SC           5252.265     4771.097              .
     -2 LOG L     5243.229     4716.880      526.349 with 5 DF (p=0.0001)
     Score           .            .         592.384 with 5 DF (p=0.0001)
```

Output 8.14 *Continued*

```
               Analysis of Maximum Likelihood Estimates

            Parameter Standard     Wald      Pr >     Standardized    Odds
Variable DF Estimate   Error  Chi-Square Chi-Square    Estimate      Ratio

INTERCPT 1   -2.6802   0.2204   147.8532   0.0001          .            .
BLACK    1    0.2857   0.0860    11.0466   0.0009       0.074728     1.331
KIDS     1    0.1558   0.0287    29.5257   0.0001       0.115842     1.169
DOUBLEUP 1    0.1497   0.0832     3.2351   0.0721       0.040090     1.161
AGE      1   -0.0467   0.00772   36.6776   0.0001      -0.146754     0.954
DAYS     1    0.00447  0.000224 399.7093   0.0001       0.404779     1.004
```

Now let's re-estimate the model for the 791 pairs of women who are matched by number of days of shelter stay. The LOGISTIC output without adjustment for matching is shown in Output 8.15.

Output 8.15 *Logit Regression of STAYBABY for Matched Pairs, No Adjustment*

```
                         Response Profile

                  Ordered
                  Value   STAYBABY      Count

                    1        1           791
                    2        0           791


    Model Fitting Information and Testing Global Null Hypothesis BETA=0

                               Intercept
                   Intercept      and
    Criterion        Only      Covariates    Chi-Square for Covariates

    AIC            2195.118     2154.347            .
    SC             2200.484     2186.546            .
    -2 LOG L       2193.118     2142.347      50.771 with 5 DF (p=0.0001)
    Score             .            .         49.882 with 5 DF (p=0.0001)
```

Output 8.15 Continued

```
                    Analysis of Maximum Likelihood Estimates

              Parameter Standard     Wald       Pr >     Standardized    Odds
  Variable DF  Estimate   Error   Chi-Square Chi-Square    Estimate     Ratio

  INTERCPT 1     0.6315  0.2870     4.8418     0.0278          .           .
  BLACK    1     0.3436  0.1101     9.7329     0.0018      -0.088556    1.410
  KIDS     1     0.1717  0.0386    19.8173     0.0001      -0.135385    1.188
  DOUBLEUP 1     0.1638  0.1094     2.2430     0.1342      -0.043971    1.178
  AGE      1    -0.0464  0.00977   22.5180     0.0001       0.143084    0.955
  DAYS     1  -0.000044  0.0003     0.0212     0.8842       0.004313    1.000
```

I included DAYS in the model just to demonstrate that matching on this variable eliminates its effect on the dependent variable. The other variables have coefficient estimates that are quite similar to those for the full sample. The standard errors are about 30% larger than in the full sample, but that's not bad considering that we have discarded 81% of the cases.

We still haven't adjusted for matching, however. To do that, we use PROC PHREG to estimate a conditional logit model:

```
DATA c;
  SET my.casecont;
  staybaby=1-staybaby;
RUN;
PROC PHREG DATA=c NOSUMMARY;
  MODEL staybaby=black kids doubleup age;
  STRATA casenum;
RUN;
```

The DATA step reverses the coding of the dependent variable so that the signs of the coefficients are correct. Notice that the MODEL statement does not contain the TIES=DISCRETE option that was used in earlier examples of conditional logit analysis. That option is unnecessary when the data consists of matched *pairs* with each pair containing a 1 and a 0 on the dependent variable. Under any other matching design (for example, one-to-many or many-to-many matching), the DISCRETE option is essential. The results in Output 8.16 are very close to those in Output 8.15, which did not adjust for matching.

Output 8.16 *Logit Regression of STAYBABY for Matched Pairs, Adjusted for Matching*

```
                  Testing Global Null Hypothesis: BETA=0

              Without      With
 Criterion   Covariates  Covariates   Model Chi-Square

 -2 LOG L     1096.559    1043.201      53.358 with 4 DF (p=0.0001)
 Score            .           .         51.408 with 4 DF (p=0.0001)
 Wald             .           .         47.919 with 4 DF (p=0.0001)


                  Analysis of Maximum Likelihood Estimates

               Parameter   Standard     Wald       Pr >       Risk
 Variable  DF   Estimate     Error   Chi-Square  Chi-Square   Ratio

 BLACK      1   0.353492    0.10921   10.47629    0.0012      1.424
 KIDS       1   0.186585    0.03994   21.82912    0.0001      1.205
 DOUBLEUP   1   0.186489    0.11141    2.80200    0.0941      1.205
 AGE        1  -0.049648    0.01019   23.72808    0.0001      0.952
```

8.7   Mixed Logit Models

There is another approach to dichotomous clustered data that is likely to become increasingly attractive in the next few years. In my judgment, however, it's not quite ready for prime time. In this approach, clustering is treated as a random effect in a mixed model—so named because it includes both fixed and random effects. Mixed models are quite similar to the GEE method discussed earlier but have two potential advantages. First, much more complex models are possible, with multiple levels of clustering, overlapping clusters, and random coefficients. Second, estimation of mixed models can correct for heterogeneity shrinkage discussed in Section 3.11. In other words, mixed models are subject specific rather than population averaged like the models estimated by GEE.

The problem with mixed logit models is that they are not easy to estimate. While the MIXED procedure in SAS does an excellent job of estimating mixed models when the dependent variable is continuous and normally distributed, it does not handle dichotomous data. There are several commercial *multi-level modeling* packages that will estimate mixed logit models, but all involve approximations that may produce substantial biases with certain data configurations (McCulloch 1997, Rodriguez and Goldman 1995).

There is also a SAS macro called GLIMMIX (which can be downloaded at www.sas.com) that serves as a front-end to the MIXED procedure, enabling it to estimate models for dependent variables with binomial, Poisson, and other distributions. Like other mixed logit programs, GLIMMIX has been criticized for the accuracy of its approximations. It's also quite slow and much worse than built-in procedures at handling errors in data, syntax, or model specification—characteristics it shares with many other macro-based procedures. Nevertheless, because of the potential of this methodology, I'll present two examples here. (Incidentally, earlier versions of the GLIMMIX macro do not work with Release 6.12 of SAS. You should download the version specifically labeled for the release of SAS that you are using.)

In its simplest form, the mixed logit model looks just like the fixed-effects model of equation (8.2):

$$\log\left(\frac{p_{it}}{1-p_{it}}\right) = \alpha_i + \beta \mathbf{x}_{it} \, .$$

The difference is that now, instead of treating α_i as representing a set of fixed constants, we assume that each α_i is a random variable with a specified probability distribution. For the models estimated with GLIMMIX, the α_i's are assumed to be independent of the $\mathbf{x}_{it}$ and to have a normal distribution with a mean of 0. In the simpler models, they are also assumed to be independent of each other and have a constant variance of σ^2.

Let's estimate this model for the PTSD data in Section 8.2. After reading in the GLIMMIX macro, the SAS code for specifying the model is:

```
DATA ptsd;
  SET my.ptsd;
  n=1;
RUN;

%GLIMMIX(DATA=ptsd, STMTS=%STR(

  CLASS subjid time;
  MODEL ptsd/n = control problems sevent cohes time /
     SOLUTION;
  RANDOM subjid;

))
```

The DATA step defines a new variable N that is always equal to 1. This is necessary because GLIMMIX—like older SAS releases with PROC GENMOD—presumes that the logit model is estimated from grouped data. The MODEL statement that follows uses the grouped-data syntax PTSD/N, where N is the number of observations in each group—in this case, 1.

GLIMMIX works by repeated calls to the MIXED procedure, and the statements specifying the model are identical to those used in the MIXED procedure for an analogous linear model. These statements are listed as arguments to the %STR function. The SOLUTION option in the MODEL statement is necessary to get coefficient estimates— otherwise only *F*-statistics are reported. The RANDOM statement specifies the random effects, in this case, one random variable for each person in the data set. Because the default in GLIMMIX is a logit model with a binomial error distribution, no further options are necessary. The results are shown in Output 8.17.

The first thing we find in the output is an estimate of the common variance of the random effects, 2.613. If this were 0, we'd be back to an ordinary logit model, which is displayed in Output 8.2. To test the null hypothesis that the variance is 0, we can compare deviances for the models with and without this parameter. In Output 8.17, the deviance is 550.01 as compared with 966.85 in Output 8.2. The difference between the two deviances is 416.84. This can be regarded as a chi-square of 416.84 (with 1 d.f. for the single parameter), which is significant by anyone's standards.

Output 8.17 *GLIMMIX Output for PTSD Data*

```
                    Covariance Parameter Estimates

                        Cov
                        Parm            Estimate

                        SUBJID          2.61300590

                     GLIMMIX Model Statistics

            Description                        Value

            Deviance                         550.0122
            Scaled Deviance                  996.5090
            Pearson Chi-Square               417.7434
            Scaled Pearson Chi-Square        756.8652
            Extra-Dispersion Scale             0.5519
```

Output 8.17 *Continued*

```
                        Parameter Estimates

Effect        TIME    Estimate    Std Error    DF         t     Pr > |t|

INTERCEPT               2.4074      0.9676     315      2.49     0.0134
CONTROL                -1.2604      0.2362     626     -5.34     0.0001
PROBLEMS                0.3088      0.0570     626      5.42     0.0001
SEVENT                  0.3339      0.0862     626      3.87     0.0001
COHES                  -0.2353      0.0566     626     -4.15     0.0001
TIME          1         0.6188      0.1915     626      3.23     0.0013
TIME          2         0.3756      0.1797     626      2.09     0.0369
TIME          3         0.0000         .        .        .         .

                      Tests of Fixed Effects

              Source       NDF    DDF    Type III F    Pr > F

              CONTROL       1      626       28.48      0.0001
              PROBLEMS      1      626       29.35      0.0001
              SEVENT        1      626       15.00      0.0001
              COHES         1      626       17.26      0.0001
              TIME          2      626        5.26      0.0054
```

The coefficients in Output 8.17 are all somewhat larger than those produced by GEE estimation in Output 8.3, exemplifying the fact that the mixed model approach corrects for heterogeneity shrinkage. The *F*-statistics in the lower part of the table can be directly compared with the chi-squares in Table 8.2 because the denominator degrees of freedom is so large. (The *F*-distribution with 1 numerator d.f. converges to a chi-square distribution as the denominator d.f. gets large.) All the mixed model chi-squares are larger than the GEE chi-squares for the EXCH option, which is the most comparable model.

Now let's try GLIMMIX on the postdoctoral data. The SAS code looks pretty much the same:

```
DATA postdoc;
  SET my.postdoc;
  n=1;
RUN;
```

```
%GLIMMIX(DATA=postdoc,STMTS=%STR(

    CLASS docid;
    MODEL pdoc/n=age mar doc ag und arts cits / SOLUTION;
    RANDOM docid;

))
```

The results in Output 8.18 are quite similar to the GEE estimates in Output 8.7. Although all the coefficients in 8.18 are larger than those in 8.7, the differences are trivial. The estimated variance of the random term (.455) is much lower than the 2.61 we got for the PTSD data. Again, we can test whether the variance is significantly different from 0 by taking the difference between the deviance for this model (618.2) and the deviance for the conventional logit model (688.6). The resulting chi-square of 70.39 (1 d.f.) is highly significant but not nearly as large as for the PTSD data. This reflects the fact that the within-cluster correlation is not nearly as strong here. The *F*-statistics are compared with the chi-square statistics for other methods in the last column of Table 8.3. They tend to be a bit higher than the chi-squares for the other corrected methods but still lower than those from conventional logit estimation.

Output 8.18 *GLIMMIX Results for Postdoctoral Data*

```
                            Cov
                            Parm          Estimate

                            DOCID        0.45524856

                      GLIMMIX Model Statistics

            Description                      Value

            Deviance                        618.2550
            Scaled Deviance                 664.8388
            Pearson Chi-Square              480.9393
            Scaled Pearson Chi-Square       517.1767
            Extra-Dispersion Scale            0.9299
```

Output 8.18 *Continued*

```
                        Parameter Estimates

Effect          Estimate      Std Error      DF          t      Pr > |t|

INTERCEPT         2.5706         0.9504      104       2.70       0.0080
AGE              -0.1055         0.0259      442      -4.08       0.0001
MAR              -0.5640         0.2704      442      -2.09       0.0375
DOC               0.0028         0.0012      442       2.23       0.0261
AG               -0.9687         0.2506      442      -3.86       0.0001
UND               0.1225         0.0609      442       2.01       0.0448
ARTS             -0.0746         0.0826      442      -0.90       0.3668
CITS             -0.0043         0.0178      442      -0.24       0.8071


                       Tests of Fixed Effects

        Source      NDF      DDF      Type III F      Pr > F

        AGE           1      442          16.63       0.0001
        MAR           1      442           4.35       0.0375
        DOC           1      442           4.99       0.0261
        AG            1      442          14.94       0.0001
        UND           1      442           4.05       0.0448
        ARTS          1      442           0.82       0.3668
        CITS          1      442           0.06       0.8071
```

Now let's try a random coefficients model—something that can't be done with any of the other methods we've looked at. More specifically, let's suppose that the effect of getting a degree from an agricultural school varies randomly across different universities. If β is the coefficient for AG, our new model says that $\beta_j = \tau_0 + \tau_j$ where j refers to 108 different universities and each τ_j is a normally distributed random variable with a mean of 0 and a variance of ω^2. This is in addition to the random "main effect" of university that was in the previous model. In SAS code, the model is

```
%GLIMMIX(DATA=postdoc,STMTS=%STR(

    CLASS docid;
    MODEL pdoc/n=age mar doc ag und arts cits/SOLUTION;
    RANDOM docid docid*ag;

))
```

The results in Output 8.19 suggest that there may indeed be differences across universities in the effect of agricultural school on postdoctoral training. The AG*DOCID interaction is almost as large as the main effect of DOCID. To test its significance, we can compare the deviance for this model with that of the previous one. The resulting chi-square is about 7.0 with 1 d.f., which is significant at beyond the .01 level. I didn't bother reporting the coefficients and *F*-statistics because they're not much different from those in Output 8.18.

Output 8.19 *Results for a Random Coefficients Model*

```
              Covariance Parameter Estimates

              Cov Parm          Estimate

              DOCID            0.45938901
              AG*DOCID         0.20137669
              GLIMMIX Model Statistics

       Description                         Value

       Deviance                         612.4306
       Scaled Deviance                  664.3210
       Pearson Chi-Square               474.4997
       Scaled Pearson Chi-Square        514.7034
       Extra-Dispersion Scale             0.9219
```

8.8   Comparison of Methods

Table 8.4 summarizes differences among the four methods for handling clustered data. All four methods produce consistent estimates of the standard errors of the coefficients in the presence of clustering. But GEE goes further than robust variance estimation because it also produces coefficient estimates that have less sampling variability. On the other hand, GEE produces estimates of population-averaged coefficients rather than subject-specific coefficients. Population-averaged coefficients are subject to heterogeneity shrinkage—attenuation toward 0 in the presence of heterogeneity in the population. Heterogeneity shrinkage can be corrected by either conditional logit analysis or mixed models. Conditional logit analysis goes further by reducing bias that arises from correlations between individual and cluster-level variables (spuriousness). But conditional logit analysis can also discard a considerable portion of the data, thereby increasing the standard errors.

Table 8.4   *Effectiveness of Different Methods for Logit Analysis of Clustered Data*

| | Coefficient Bias | | | |
	Corrects Spuriousness	Corrects Shrinkage	Corrects S.E. Bias	Efficiency
Conditional Logit	✔	✔	✔	
Mixed Models		✔	✔	✔
GEE			✔	✔
Robust S.E.'s			✔	

The best method to use depends greatly on the design, the data, and the goals of the analysis. While the mixed-models approach seems to solve many problems, such models are usually difficult to specify and estimate, especially because they are only available in macro form in SAS. In randomized experiments, there is little danger of spuriousness, so conditional logit analysis is relatively unattractive. With observational (nonexperimental) data, on the other hand, spuriousness is nearly always a serious concern, making conditional logit analysis especially attractive. I typically use both GEE and conditional logit analysis to get greater insight into the data. But as we saw in the matching section, some designs make GEE impossible while others make conditional logit analysis unappealing.

8.9   A Hybrid Method

The four methods just considered are now fairly well known and understood. Recently, a fifth approach has been proposed, one that appears to combine the virtues of the conditional logit method with those of GEE or the mixed model. Neuhaus and Kalbfleisch (1998) have the most explicit discussion of the method for binary data, but the general strategy was previously considered by Bryk and Raudenbusch (1992) and applied to a study of criminal recidivism by Horney et al. (1995). The method can be summarized in four steps:

1. Calculate the means of the time-varying explanatory variables for each individual.

2. Calculate the deviations of the time-varying explanatory variables from the individual-specific means.

3. Estimate the model with variables created in steps 1 and 2, along with any additional time-constant explanatory variables.

4. Use GEE or a mixed model to adjust for residual dependence.

The coefficients and standard errors for the deviation variables are typically very similar to those obtained with conditional logit analysis. But unlike conditional logit analysis, this method also allows for the inclusion of time-constant explanatory variables. In addition, the hybrid method is usually much less computationally intensive than conditional logit analysis.

Before estimating the model, one must calculate the individual-specific means and the deviations from those means. Here's how to do it for the PTSD data:

```
PROC MEANS DATA=my.ptsd NWAY NOPRINT;
   CLASS subjid;
   VAR control problems sevent;
   OUTPUT OUT=means MEAN=mcontrol mproblem msevent;
PROC SORT DATA=my.ptsd;
   BY subjid;
PROC SORT DATA=a;
   BY subjid;
DATA combine;
   MERGE my.ptsd means;
   BY subjid;
   dcontrol=control-mcontrol;
   dproblem=problems-mproblem;
   dsevent=sevent-msevent;
RUN;
```

The PROC MEANS step produces a data set called MEANS, which contains 316 observations. Each of these observations has four variables: the individual's ID number and the individual's means for the three time-varying explanatory variables (CONTROL, PROBLEMS, and SEVENT). After sorting the data sets by ID number, a DATA step merges the MEANS data set with the original data set and computes the deviation variables. The new data set (COMBINE) has 948 observations, with the means replicated across the three observations for each individual.

We can now estimate a logit model that includes both the mean and the deviations from the means. Because there may still be residual dependence in the dependent variable, this should be accommodated with either GEE or a mixed model. The SAS code for a mixed model using the GLIMMIX macro is:

```
%GLIMMIX(DATA=combine, STMTS=%STR(

    CLASS subjid;
    MODEL ptsd/n = dcontrol dproblem dsevent mcontrol mproblem
        msevent cohes t2 t3 / SOLUTION;
    RANDOM subjid;

))
```

The results are shown in Output 8.20. The coefficients for the three deviation variables are quite close to those in Output 8.5 for the conditional logit model. However, the standard errors are somewhat lower for the hybrid model, leading to lower *p*-values. (The *F*-statistics in the lower part of the output should be directly comparable to one degree of freedom chi-square statistics). In this example, coefficients for the three mean variables are also somewhat similar to those for the deviation variables, but this will not always be the case. In fact, I've seen examples in which the deviation variables and the mean variables have highly significant coefficients that are opposite in sign.

Output 8.20 *GLIMMIX Estimates for Hybrid PTSD Model*

Effect	Estimate	Std Error	DF	t	Pr > |t|
INTERCEPT	1.4313	1.6568	311	0.86	0.3883
DCONTROL	-1.1672	0.2984	627	-3.91	0.0001
DPROBLEM	0.2058	0.0729	627	2.82	0.0049
DSEVENT	0.1996	0.0980	627	2.04	0.0422
MCONTROL	-1.1105	0.4076	627	-2.72	0.0066
MPROBLEM	0.4533	0.0917	627	4.95	0.0001
MSEVENT	0.7570	0.1771	627	4.27	0.0001
COHES	-0.2239	0.0585	627	-3.83	0.0001
T2	-0.4025	0.1808	627	-2.23	0.0263
T3	-0.8438	0.2135	627	-3.95	0.0001

Output 8.20 Continued

```
                       Tests of Fixed Effects

          Source      NDF    DDF    Type III F    Pr > F

          DCONTROL     1     627       15.30      0.0001
          DPROBLEM     1     627        7.97      0.0049
          DSEVENT      1     627        4.14      0.0422
          MCONTROL     1     627        7.42      0.0066
          MPROBLEM     1     627       24.47      0.0001
          MSEVENT      1     627       18.27      0.0001
          COHES        1     627       14.65      0.0001
          T2           1     627        4.96      0.0263
          T3           1     627       15.62      0.0001
```

While the deviation coefficients can be interpreted in the same way as the conditional logit coefficients, the coefficients for the mean variables are usually difficult to interpret causally. Under the assumptions of the conventional mixed model of Section 8.7, the coefficients for the mean variables and the corresponding deviation variables should be identical. Hence, the degree to which they differ can be the basis of a specification test for the conventional model. We can test the null hypothesis that they are the same by including a CONTRAST statement in the hybrid model program:

```
CONTRAST 'spec test' dcontrol 1 mcontrol -1,
    dproblem 1 mproblem -1, dsevent 1 msevent -1;
```

This produced an *F*-statistic of 4.68 with 3 and 627 degrees of freedom, yielding a *p*-value of .0031. Apparently, at least one pair of coefficients is different, suggesting that the conventional mixed model could lead to biased estimates of the coefficients.

Although the hybrid method seems to produce useful results that are quite similar to those of the conditional logit model, its statistical properties have not yet been thoroughly investigated. In particular, I have not seen any proof of its statistical consistency or efficiency.

Chapter 9

Poisson Regression

9.1   Introduction

In this relatively short chapter we examine Poisson regression, a method appropriate for dependent variables that have only non-negative integer values: 0, 1, 2, ... Usually these numbers represent counts of something, like number of people in an organization, number of visits to a physician, or number of arrests in the past year. While such data are fairly common in the social sciences, there is another reason why the Poisson regression is important: it is a fundamental building block for loglinear analysis of contingency tables, a topic we will examine in some detail in the next chapter.

For years, people analyzed count data by ordinary linear regression and, in most cases, that method was adequate for the task. But Poisson regression has the advantage of being precisely tailored to the discrete, often highly-skewed distribution of the dependent variable. On the other hand, Poisson regression has the disadvantage of being susceptible to problems of overdispersion that do not affect ordinary regression. Overdispersion, discussed in detail later, can produce severe underestimates of standard errors and overestimates of test statistics. While there are simple (as well as complex) corrections for overdispersion, it's a problem that must always be checked when you do Poisson regression.

9.2   The Poisson Regression Model

The Poisson regression model gets its name from the assumption that the dependent variable has a Poisson distribution, defined as follows. Let y be a variable that can have only non-negative integer values. We assume that the probability that y is equal to some number r is given by

$$\Pr(y = r) = \frac{\lambda^r e^{-\lambda}}{r!}, \qquad r = 0, 1, 2, \ldots \tag{9.1}$$

where λ is the expected value (mean) of y and $r! = r(r-1)(r-2)\ldots(1)$. Although y can only take on integer values, λ can be any positive number. For $\lambda = 1.5$, the probabilities for the Poisson distribution are graphed in Figure 9.1.

Figure 9.1   *Poisson Distribution for $\lambda = 1.5$*

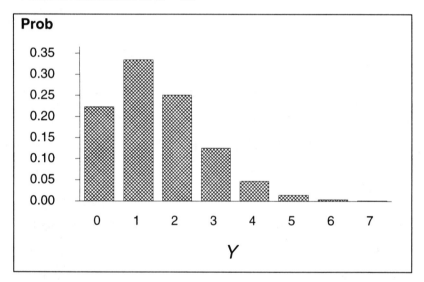

As λ gets larger, the mode moves away from 0 and the distribution looks more and more like a normal distribution. An unusual property of the Poisson distribution is that the mean and variance are equal:

$$E(y) \;=\; \mathrm{var}(y) \;=\; \lambda \tag{9.2}$$

Next we need to specify how the parameter λ depends on the explanatory variables. First, we write λ_i with a subscript i to allow the parameter to vary across individuals ($i = 1$, $\ldots$, n). Then, because λ can't be less than 0, it is standard to let λ be a loglinear function of the x variables:

$$\log \lambda_i = \beta_0 + \beta_1 x_{i1} + \beta_2 x_{i2} + \ldots + \beta_k x_{ik}. \tag{9.3}$$

This ensures that λ will be greater than 0 for any values of the x's or the β's.

That's all there is to the model. Note that the model does not say that the marginal distribution of y will necessarily be Poisson. (The marginal distribution is what you get when you ignore any explanatory variables. Output 9.1 and 9.2 are realizations of marginal distributions.) Instead, y has a Poisson distribution *conditional* on the values of the explanatory variables. If the x variables have large coefficients and large variances, the marginal distribution of y may look very different from a Poisson distribution.

As usual, we'll estimate the model by maximum likelihood. This is easily accomplished with PROC GENMOD.

9.3   Scientific Productivity Example

In Chapter 8, we studied a sample of 557 biochemists who got their doctorates in the late 1950s and early 1960s. Two of the variables in the data set are good candidates for Poisson regression: ARTS—the number of articles published by the biochemists before they received their degrees (counted in *Chemical Abstracts*) and CITS—the number of citations to those articles (counted in *Science Citation Index*). Output 9.1 and 9.2 show the marginal frequency distributions for these two variables.

Output 9.1   *Frequency Distribution of Article Counts*

ARTS	Frequency	Percent	Cumulative Frequency	Cumulative Percent
0	332	59.6	332	59.6
1	111	19.9	443	79.5
2	57	10.2	500	89.8
3	33	5.9	533	95.7
4	9	1.6	542	97.3
5	5	0.9	547	98.2
6	3	0.5	550	98.7
7	3	0.5	553	99.3
10	2	0.4	555	99.6
11	1	0.2	556	99.8
15	1	0.2	557	100.0

Both distributions are highly skewed, especially citation counts. Neither distribution would pass a statistical test for the Poisson distribution, but as I noted earlier, that's not essential for the model to be correct.

Output 9.2 *Frequency Distribution of Citation Counts*

CITS	Frequency	Percent	Cumulative Frequency	Cumulative Percent
0	187	33.6	187	33.6
1	188	33.8	375	67.3
2	36	6.5	411	73.8
3	26	4.7	437	78.5
4	13	2.3	450	80.8
5	23	4.1	473	84.9
6	5	0.9	478	85.8
7	19	3.4	497	89.2
8	4	0.7	501	89.9
9	4	0.7	505	90.7
10	8	1.4	513	92.1
11	5	0.9	518	93.0
12	3	0.5	521	93.5
13	1	0.2	522	93.7
14	1	0.2	523	93.9
15	5	0.9	528	94.8
16	4	0.7	532	95.5
17	1	0.2	533	95.7
20	5	0.9	538	96.6
22	2	0.4	540	96.9
23	3	0.5	543	97.5
25	1	0.2	544	97.7
27	2	0.4	546	98.0
30	1	0.2	547	98.2
32	3	0.5	550	98.7
33	1	0.2	551	98.9
37	3	0.5	554	99.5
40	1	0.2	555	99.6
57	1	0.2	556	99.8
74	1	0.2	557	100.0

The next step is to do Poisson regressions for articles and citations as predicted by the other independent variables described in Section 8.5. Here's the GENMOD code for the two regressions:

```
PROC GENMOD DATA=my.postdoc;
```

```
    MODEL arts = age mar doc ag und / DIST=POISSON;
PROC GENMOD DATA=my.postdoc;
    MODEL cits = age mar doc ag und / D=P;
RUN;
```

To fit a Poisson regression, we use the DIST=POISSON option, which can be abbreviated D=P. When a Poisson regression is requested, the loglinear model in equation (9.3) is the default. Results appear in Output 9.3 and 9.4.

Output 9.3   *Poisson Regression for Article Counts*

```
                  Criteria For Assessing Goodness Of Fit

           Criterion              DF         Value        Value/DF

           Deviance               548     1072.2986         1.9567
           Scaled Deviance        548     1072.2986         1.9567
           Pearson Chi-Square     548     1474.6055         2.6909
           Scaled Pearson X2      548     1474.6055         2.6909
           Log Likelihood           .     -541.0603            .


                    Analysis Of Parameter Estimates

     Parameter    DF    Estimate    Std Err    ChiSquare   Pr>Chi

     INTERCEPT     1      0.4241     0.4645      0.8337     0.3612
     AGE           1     -0.0312     0.0131      5.6970     0.0170
     MAR           1      0.0087     0.1306      0.0044     0.9470
     DOC           1     -0.0001     0.0005      0.0737     0.7861
     AG            1      0.0319     0.1001      0.1019     0.7495
     UND           1      0.0698     0.0303      5.2948     0.0214
     SCALE         0      1.0000     0.0000         .          .
```

In Output 9.3, we see that only one variable is a significant predictor of publication counts, the selectivity of the undergraduate institution. Because the dependent variable is logged, we can interpret the coefficients much like logistic regression coefficients. If we calculate $100(e^{\beta}-1)$, we get the percent change in the expected number of publications with each 1-unit increase in the independent variable. For the 7-point UND scale, the increase in number of publications for each 1-point increase is about 7.2%.

Note that the deviance is almost twice as large as the degrees of freedom in Output 9.3. It's probably not appropriate to calculate a *p*-value for this statistic because the predicted number of articles is quite small for many of the biochemists. As we saw in fitting logistic regression models with individual level data, when predicted values are small, the deviance is not well approximated by a chi-square distribution. Nevertheless, the large ratio of deviance to degrees of freedom does suggest a problem with the model, one that we'll pursue in the next section. The problem is even more severe in Output 9.4 for citation counts, where the deviance is more than seven times the degrees of freedom. In this regression, all the variables are highly significant. Older students at agricultural schools have lower average citation counts, while married students at prestigious institutions and from selective undergraduate institutions have higher average citation counts. More precisely, the expected citation count for those in agricultural schools is $100(\exp(-.4469)-1)=36\%$ lower than for those in medical schools. On the other hand, married students have citation counts that are $100(\exp(.29)-1)=34\%$ higher, on average, than those for unmarried students. Before we take these results too seriously, however, we need to consider the problem of overdispersion, exemplified by the large deviance relative to the degrees of freedom.

Output 9.4   *Poisson Regression for Citation Counts*

```
                Criteria For Assessing Goodness Of Fit

        Criterion              DF        Value       Value/DF

        Deviance               548     4053.1740       7.3963
        Scaled Deviance        548     4053.1740       7.3963
        Pearson Chi-Square     548     7174.8868      13.0929
        Scaled Pearson X2      548     7174.8868      13.0929
        Log Likelihood          .       448.8995          .


                    Analysis Of Parameter Estimates

    Parameter    DF    Estimate    Std Err    ChiSquare   Pr>Chi

    INTERCEPT     1      1.3407     0.2427      30.5250    0.0001
    AGE           1     -0.0417     0.0069      36.7273    0.0001
    MAR           1      0.2899     0.0699      17.1957    0.0001
    DOC           1      0.0009     0.0002      15.5009    0.0001
    AG            1     -0.4469     0.0558      64.0349    0.0001
    UND           1      0.1269     0.0156      66.0324    0.0001
    SCALE         0      1.0000     0.0000          .          .
```

9.4 Overdispersion

I now claim that the standard errors, chi-squares, and *p*-values in the previous section are essentially worthless because of overdispersion. We encountered overdispersion with grouped-data logit models in Chapter 4 where I argued that the problem was primarily restricted to clustered data. For Poisson regression, it's *always* a potential problem, and often a quite serious one.

Basically the problem arises because equation (9.2) says that, for a given set of values on the explanatory variables, the variance of the dependent variable is equal to its mean. In fact, the variance is often much higher than that. Equivalently, we can say that overdispersion occurs because there's no random disturbance term in equation (9.3) that would allow for omitted explanatory variables. (A disturbance term would produce a larger variance in *y*.) While overdispersion doesn't bias the coefficients, it does lead to underestimates of the standard errors and overestimates of chi-square statistics. Overdispersion also implies that conventional maximum likelihood estimates are not efficient, meaning that other methods can produce coefficients with less sampling variability.

What can be done about overdispersion? If you're willing to ignore the lack of efficiency of conventional estimates, it's a simple matter to correct the standard errors and chi-squares (Agresti 1996, p. 92). The correction is the same as for the grouped binomial case: Take the ratio of the goodness-of-fit chi-square to its degrees of freedom, and call the result *C*. Divide the chi-square statistic for each coefficient by *C*. Multiply the standard error of each coefficient by the square root of *C*. The only ambiguity is that we have two goodness-of-fit chi-squares, the deviance and the Pearson chi-square. Which one should we use? Most of the time they'll be fairly close, but the theory of quasi-likelihood estimation suggests the use of the Pearson chi-square (McCullagh and Nelder 1989).

In GENMOD, the corrections just described can be automatically invoked by putting either PSCALE (for Pearson) or DSCALE (for deviance) as options in the MODEL statement. For our biochemist example, the full code using the PSCALE option is:

```
PROC GENMOD DATA=my.postdoc;
  MODEL arts = age mar doc ag und / D=P PSCALE;
PROC GENMOD DATA=my.postdoc;
  MODEL cits = age mar doc ag und / D=P PSCALE;
RUN;
```

Results are shown in Outputs 9.5 and 9.6. Each output now includes a scale parameter which, as noted, is just the square root of the Pearson chi-square divided by the degrees of freedom. For articles, the chi-squares for the coefficients are all reduced by about 40%, with the result that none of the coefficients is statistically significant. For citations, the chi-square adjustments are much more severe, with reductions of over 70%. The only significant coefficients are for agricultural school and for undergraduate selectivity. Clearly, reliance on the unadjusted test statistics would have been disastrous.

Output 9.5   *Poisson Regression for Articles with Overdispersion Correction*

```
                   Analysis Of Parameter Estimates

     Parameter    DF    Estimate    Std Err    ChiSquare  Pr>Chi

     INTERCEPT     1      0.4241     0.7619      0.3098    0.5778
     AGE           1     -0.0312     0.0215      2.1172    0.1457
     MAR           1      0.0087     0.2143      0.0016    0.9677
     DOC           1     -0.0001     0.0007      0.0274    0.8686
     AG            1      0.0319     0.1641      0.0379    0.8457
     UND           1      0.0698     0.0497      1.9677    0.1607
     SCALE         0      1.6404     0.0000        .         .

     NOTE: The scale parameter was estimated by the square root of Pearson's
     Chi-Squared/DOF.
```

Output 9.6   *Poisson Regression for Citations with Overdispersion Correction*

```
                   Analysis Of Parameter Estimates

     Parameter    DF    Estimate    Std Err    ChiSquare  Pr>Chi

     INTERCEPT     1      1.3407     0.8781      2.3314    0.1268
     AGE           1     -0.0417     0.0249      2.8051    0.0940
     MAR           1      0.2899     0.2530      1.3134    0.2518
     DOC           1      0.0009     0.0009      1.1839    0.2766
     AG            1     -0.4469     0.2021      4.8908    0.0270
     UND           1      0.1269     0.0565      5.0434    0.0247
     SCALE         0      3.6184     0.0000        .         .

     NOTE: The scale parameter was estimated by the square root of Pearson's
     Chi-Squared/DOF.
```

Somewhat surprisingly, ordinary linear regression is not susceptible to the problem of overdispersion because it automatically estimates a scale parameter that is used in calculating standard errors and test statistics. The scale parameter is just the estimated standard deviation of the disturbance term, sometimes called the root mean squared error. To illustrate this point, I used OLS to regress the logarithm of citation counts on the same explanatory variables. Because the logarithm of 0 is undefined, I first added .5 to everyone's citation count:

```
DATA postdoc;
  SET my.postdoc;
  lcits=log(cits+.5);
RUN;
PROC GENMOD DATA=postdoc;
  MODEL lcits = age mar doc ag und;
RUN;
```

When no DIST option is specified in the MODEL statement, GENMOD uses OLS to estimate a normal linear model. The results shown in Output 9.7, while not identical to those in 9.6, are at least in the same ballpark. In general, Poisson regression with a correction for overdispersion is preferable to ordinary least squares. But OLS may be better than Poisson regression without the overdispersion correction.

Output 9.7   *OLS Results for Log-Linear Citation Model*

```
              Analysis Of Parameter Estimates

 Parameter    DF     Estimate    Std Err   ChiSquare   Pr>Chi

 INTERCEPT    1       0.6403     0.4647     1.8984    0.1683
 AGE          1      -0.0193     0.0127     2.3186    0.1278
 MAR          1       0.0873     0.1382     0.3987    0.5277
 DOC          1       0.0005     0.0005     1.3294    0.2489
 AG           1      -0.2765     0.1034     7.1546    0.0075
 UND          1       0.0597     0.0311     3.6899    0.0547
 SCALE        1       1.1279     0.0339        .         .
```

9.5 Negative Binomial Regression

The adjustment for overdispersion discussed in the last section is a huge improvement over conventional Poisson regression but it's not ideal. The coefficients are still inefficient, meaning that they have more sampling variability than necessary. Efficient estimates are produced by a method known as negative binomial regression that is becoming increasingly popular for count data.

The negative binomial model is a generalization of the Poisson model. We modify equation (9.3) to include a disturbance term, which accounts for the overdispersion:

$$\log \lambda_i = \beta_0 + \beta_1 x_{i1} + \beta_2 x_{i2} + \ldots + \beta_k x_{ik} + \sigma \varepsilon_i.$$

We assume that the dependent variable y_i has a Poisson distribution with expected value λ_i, *conditional on* ε_i. Finally, we assume that $\exp(\varepsilon_i)$ has a standard gamma distribution (Agresti 1990, p. 74). It follows that the unconditional distribution of y_i is a negative binomial distribution.

The negative binomial regression model may be efficiently estimated by maximum likelihood. In Version 7 of SAS/STAT software, GENMOD is expected to have this capability, invoked with the DIST=NEGBIN option. In the meantime, there is a user-contributed macro (Hilbe 1994) that accomplishes the task by repeated calls to GENMOD. (As of this writing, the macro can be downloaded at www.sas.com/techsup/download/stat/negbinom.sas). The syntax is very simple. For the article and citation data, we use:

```
%HILBENB(DSIN=my.postdoc,YVAR=arts,XVARS=age mar doc ag und)
%HILBENB(DSIN=my.postdoc,YVAR=cits,XVARS=age mar doc ag und)
```

Results are shown in Outputs 9.8 and 9.9. For articles, the results are quite close to those we got with the simple adjustment in Ouput 9.5. For citations, the differences with the simple adjustment in Output 9.6 are more substantial but still not dramatic.

Output 9.8   *Negative Binomial Regression for Article Counts*

```
Number of iterations:          11
Alpha:                     1.9739
Deviance:                451.9967    Deviance/DF:              0.8248
Pearson Chi2:            548.2168    Pearson Chi2/DF:          1.0004
LogLikelihood:          -695.3805


PARM         DF     ESTIMATE     STDERR       CHISQ        PVAL


INTERCEPT     1       0.2589     0.6811      0.1445      0.7039
AGE           1      -0.0277     0.0191      2.1156      0.1458
MAR           1       0.0167     0.2184      0.0059      0.9390
DOC           1       0.0000     0.0007      0.0045      0.9468
AG            1       0.0376     0.1643      0.0524      0.8190
UND           1       0.0694     0.0483      2.0630      0.1509
```

Output 9.9   *Negative Binomial Regression for Citation Counts*

```
Number of iterations:           8
Alpha:                     3.6741
Deviance:                395.6792    Deviance/DF:              0.7220
Pearson Chi2:            548.0080    Pearson Chi2/DF:          1.0000
LogLikelihood:         -1216.8250




PARM         DF     ESTIMATE     STDERR       CHISQ        PVAL


INTERCEPT     1       1.5665     0.8127      3.7156      0.0539
AGE           1      -0.0445     0.0219      4.1264      0.0422
MAR           1       0.2277     0.2445      0.8672      0.3517
DOC           1       0.0010     0.0008      1.5600      0.2117
AG            1      -0.4602     0.1897      5.8822      0.0153
UND           1       0.1080     0.0567      3.6334      0.0566
```

9.6   Adjustment for Varying Time Spans

The Poisson distribution (or its generalization to the negative binomial) is well suited for describing counts of events that occur in some interval of time. In the preceding example, articles and citations were counted over a certain period of time. Other examples include the number of arrests in a five-year period, the number of colds that occur in one year, or the number of arguments between spouses in one month. If the length of the time interval is the same for every individual in the sample, the methods already described work just fine. But if events are counted over different lengths of time for different individuals, there is clearly a need for some kind of standardization. For ordinary regression analysis, we could simply divide each individual's event count by the length of the interval and regress the resulting ratio on the independent variables. However, that won't work for Poisson regression because the division by time implies that the resulting variable no longer has a Poisson distribution.

Instead, we incorporate time into the model. If t_i is the length of the observation interval for individual i, the number of events (y_i) that occur during that interval is assumed to have the Poisson distribution

$$\Pr(y_i = r) = \frac{(\lambda_i t_i)^r e^{-\lambda_i t_i}}{r!}, \qquad r = 0, 1, 2, \ldots \tag{9.4}$$

which implies that the expected value of y_i is $\lambda_i t_i$. We continue to assume equation (9.3), which says that the logarithm of λ is a linear function of the x's. That implies that

$$\begin{aligned} \log E(y_i) &= \log(\lambda_i t_i) = \log(t_i) + \log(\lambda_i) \\ &= \log(t_i) + \beta_0 + \beta_1 x_{i1} + \beta_2 x_{i2} + \ldots + \beta_k x_{ik}. \end{aligned} \tag{9.5}$$

This equation says that the logarithm of the observation time should be on the right-hand side of the equation, with a coefficient of 1.0. Notice that if t_i is the same for everyone, this term can be absorbed into the intercept β_0.

Now it's easy enough to include log t as an independent variable in the regression model, but how do you force its coefficient to be 1.0? In GENMOD, you simply declare log t to be an OFFSET variable by using an option in the MODEL statement. Here's an example. Levinson et al. (1997) collected data on patient visits to 125 physicians. We'll take as our dependent variable the "number of utterances devoted by doctor or patient to prognostic material," which was obtained by investigator coding of 121 audio tapes (Christakis and Levinson 1998). The frequency distribution of this variable, called LENGTHPX, is shown in Output 9.10.

Output 9.10 *Distribution of Number of Utterances About Prognosis*

LENGTHPX	Frequency	Percent	Cumulative Frequency	Cumulative Percent
0	52	41.6	52	41.6
1	11	8.8	63	50.4
2	16	12.8	79	63.2
3	5	4.0	84	67.2
4	8	6.4	92	73.6
5	3	2.4	95	76.0
6	6	4.8	101	80.8
7	4	3.2	105	84.0
8	3	2.4	108	86.4
9	5	4.0	113	90.4
10	1	0.8	114	91.2
11	1	0.8	115	92.0
12	2	1.6	117	93.6
14	1	0.8	118	94.4
15	1	0.8	119	95.2
17	1	0.8	120	96.0
20	2	1.6	122	97.6
21	1	0.8	123	98.4
24	2	1.6	125	100.0

We'll consider the following independent variables:

PTAGE — Patient's age

PTSEX — Patient's sex (1=male, 0=female)

EZCOMPT — Doctor's rating of how easy it was to communicate with the patient (1-5)

MDLIKEPT — Doctor's rating of how much he or she liked the patient (1-5)

SURGEON — 1 if doctor was a surgeon, otherwise 0

CLAIMS — Number of malpractice claims filed against the doctor

MINUTES — Length of the visit in minutes

To standardize for length of the session, we must define a new variable LMIN equal to the natural logarithm of MINUTES:

```
DATA prog2;
  SET my.prognosi;
  lmin=LOG(minutes);
RUN;
```

We then use LMIN as an OFFSET variable in the call to GENMOD:

```
PROC GENMOD DATA=prog2;
   MODEL lengthpx=ptage ptsex ezcompt mdlikept surgeon claims /
      OFFSET=lmin D=P;
RUN;
```

Results in Output 9.11 indicate that there are more utterances about prognosis when the patient is male, when the physician rates the patient easy to communicate with, when the physician is a surgeon, and when many malpractice claims have been filed against the physician. More specifically, surgeons have nearly four times as many prognosis utterances as non-surgeons (exp(1.34)=3.83) and there are about 75% more utterances for male patients than for females (exp(.55)=1.73). Notice that no coefficient is reported for LMIN because it is constrained to be 1.0.

Output 9.11 *Poisson Regression with Offset Variable*

```
                      The GENMOD Procedure

                      Model Information


         Description                    Value

         Data Set                       WORK.PROG2
         Distribution                   POISSON
         Link Function                  LOG
         Dependent Variable             LENGTHPX
         Offset Variable                LMIN
         Observations Used              121
         Missing Values                 4



            Criteria For Assessing Goodness Of Fit

      Criterion              DF        Value       Value/DF

      Deviance               114     682.0299       5.9827
      Scaled Deviance        114     682.0299       5.9827
      Pearson Chi-Square     114     899.6258       7.8915
      Scaled Pearson X2      114     899.6258       7.8915
      Log Likelihood          .      115.9561          .
```

Output 9.11 *Continued*

```
            Analysis Of Parameter Estimates

Parameter    DF    Estimate    Std Err    ChiSquare    Pr>Chi

INTERCEPT     1     -3.7237     0.3378     121.5305     0.0001
PTAGE         1     -0.0014     0.0031       0.2222     0.6373
PTSEX         1      0.5482     0.1048      27.3515     0.0001
EZCOMPT       1      0.1981     0.0760       6.7853     0.0092
MDLIKEPT      1     -0.0864     0.0744       1.3505     0.2452
SURGEON       1      1.3431     0.1304     106.1394     0.0001
CLAIMS        1      0.0519     0.0232       5.0106     0.0252
```

However, these results are called into question by the fact that the deviance is nearly six times the degrees of freedom, suggesting substantial overdispersion and consequent underestimation of the standard errors. To correct this problem, I reran the model with the PSCALE option in the MODEL statement, producing the results in Output 9.12.

Output 9.12 *Poisson Regression with Correction for Overdispersion*

```
            Analysis Of Parameter Estimates

Parameter    DF    Estimate    Std Err    ChiSquare    Pr>Chi

INTERCEPT     1     -3.7237     0.9489     15.4003     0.0001
PTAGE         1     -0.0014     0.0086      0.0282     0.8667
PTSEX         1      0.5482     0.2945      3.4660     0.0626
EZCOMPT       1      0.1981     0.2136      0.8598     0.3538
MDLIKEPT      1     -0.0864     0.2090      0.1711     0.6791
SURGEON       1      1.3431     0.3662     13.4499     0.0002
CLAIMS        1      0.0519     0.0651      0.6349     0.4256
SCALE         0      2.8092     0.0000         .          .
```

With this correction, only SURGEON is statistically significant at the .05 level, although PTSEX comes close. As an alternative to the PSCALE option for correcting for overdispersion, I could have used the negative binomial macro, which also allows for the inclusion of an OFFSET variable. When I did that, results were very similar to those in Output 9.12.

Chapter 10

Loglinear Analysis of Contingency Tables

10.1 Introduction

In Chapter 4, we saw how to analyze contingency tables that included a dichotomous variable treated as dependent on the other variables. The strategy was to directly estimate a logit model in PROC LOGISTIC or PROC GENMOD. We extended that approach in Chapter 5 to handle dependent variables with more than two categories by estimating a multinomial logit model with PROC CATMOD. In this chapter, we see how to estimate *loglinear* models for contingency tables. What distinguishes loglinear models from logit models is that loglinear models do not have an explicit dependent variable, at least not one that corresponds to any conceptual variable. As I've mentioned previously, every logit model for a contingency table has a loglinear model that is exactly equivalent. But the class of loglinear models also includes models that don't correspond to any logit models, so we are dealing with a much wider class of models.

Why do we need loglinear models? When loglinear analysis was first developed in the late 1960s and early 1970s, there wasn't much software available for logit analysis. And what *was* available wasn't very suitable for analyzing contingency tables. By contrast, loglinear models were easily estimated with widely available software. Now, however, you're usually better off estimating a logit model directly. Logit models are simpler and correspond more directly to substantive theory. However, there are some situations, when a logit model just doesn't do the job. For example, you might want to explore the relationships among several attitude measures that have no obvious causal ordering. But a logit model requires that you choose one variable as the dependent variable and the others as independent variables.

Even if you do have a clear-cut dependent variable, the particular logit model you want to estimate may be awkward for conventional software. For example, the adjacent-categories model described in Chapter 6 is a special case of the multinomial logit model. But the maximum likelihood algorithm in CATMOD will not impose the necessary constraints to get this model. As we shall see, the adjacent-categories model is easily estimated as a loglinear model when the data comes in the form of a contingency table. Loglinear models are particularly well suited to the analysis of two-way tables in which the row variable has the same categories as the column variables (a square table). For example, there is a large literature on loglinear models for mobility tables in which the row variable represents parent's occupation and the column variable represents child's occupation (for example, Hout 1983).

The treatment of loglinear analysis in this book is far from comprehensive. The topic is so vast that I can do no more than scratch the surface here. My goals are, first, to give you some idea of what loglinear models are like and how they are related to logit models. Second, I will show you how to estimate fairly conventional loglinear models by using the GENMOD procedure. Third, I will present some examples in which a loglinear model has significant advantages over a logit model.

10.2   A Loglinear Model for a 2 × 2 Table

Let's start with the 2 × 2 table we analyzed in Chapter 4 (reproduced here as Table 10.1), which shows sentence by race for 147 death penalty cases. How can we represent this by a loglinear model?

Table 10.1   *Death Sentence by Race of Defendant*

	Blacks	Nonblacks	Total
Death	28	22	50
Life	45	52	97
Total	73	74	147

Let's consider the table in more general form as

m_{11}	m_{12}
m_{21}	m_{22}

where m_{ij} is the *expected* number of cases falling into row i and column j. What I mean by this is that if n is the sample size and p_{ij} is the probability of falling into cell (i, j), then $m_{ij}=np_{ij}$.

There are a couple of different but equivalent ways of writing a loglinear model for these four frequency counts. The way I'm going to do it is consistent with how PROC GENMOD estimates the model. Let R_i be a dummy variable for the rows, having a value of 1 if $i=1$ and 0 if $i=2$. Similarly, let C_j be a dummy variable for the columns with a value of 1 if $j=1$ and 0 if $j=2$. We can then write the "saturated" loglinear model for this 2×2 table of frequency counts as:

$$\log m_{ij} = \beta_0 + \beta_1 R_i + \beta_2 C_j + \beta_3 R_i C_j \qquad i, j = 1, 2. \qquad (10.1)$$

Note that $R_i C_j$ is the product (interaction) of R_i and C_j. Equation (10.1) actually represents four different equations:

$$\begin{aligned}
\log m_{11} &= \beta_0 + \beta_1 + \beta_2 + \beta_3 \\
\log m_{12} &= \beta_0 + \beta_1 \\
\log m_{21} &= \beta_0 \quad + \beta_2 \\
\log m_{22} &= \beta_0.
\end{aligned} \qquad (10.2)$$

In a moment, we'll see how to estimate the four β parameters by using PROC GENMOD. But before doing that, let's talk about why we might be interested in these parameters at all. All we've done in equation (10.2) is transform the four expected frequencies into four different quantities. The reason for doing this is that the β's show us things about the table that aren't so easily seen by looking at the frequency counts.

We are particularly interested in β_3, the coefficient for the interaction term. If we solve equation (10.2) for β_3, we get:

$$\beta_3 = \log\left(\frac{m_{11}m_{22}}{m_{12}m_{21}}\right) \qquad (10.3)$$

The quantity in parenthesis is the cross-product ratio. In Chapter 2, we saw that the cross-product ratio is equal to the odds ratio. In this case, it's the ratio of the odds of a death sentence for blacks to the odds of a death sentence for nonblacks. Recall that an odds ratio of 1.0 corresponds to independence between the two variables. Because the logarithm of 1 is 0, independence of the row and column variables is equivalent to $\beta_3=0$. So, we can test whether the two variables are independent by testing whether $\beta_3=0$.

All this has been expressed in terms of *expected* frequency counts, the m_{ij}. What about the observed frequency counts, which I'll denote by n_{ij}? For the model we've just been considering, the maximum likelihood estimator of β_3 has the same form as equation (10.3) except that expected frequencies are replaced by observed frequencies:

$$\hat{\beta}_3 = \log\left(\frac{n_{11}n_{22}}{n_{12}n_{21}}\right) \tag{10.4}$$

For the data in Table 10.1, $\hat{\beta}_3 = \log[(28\times52)/(45\times22)] = .3857$. Similar expressions can readily be obtained for the other β parameters in the model, but we're not usually very interested in them.

Although it's simple enough in this case to get all the maximum likelihood estimates by hand calculations, we can also do it with PROC GENMOD. Here is the SAS code:

```
DATA penalty;
   INPUT n death black;
   DATALINES;
28 1 1
22 1 0
45 0 1
52 0 0
;
PROC GENMOD DATA=penalty;
   MODEL n = death black death*black / DIST=POISSON;
RUN;
```

Each cell in the table is a separate record in the data set. DEATH is a dummy variable for a death sentence, and BLACK is a dummy variable for race. The MODEL statement includes the main effects of row and column, as well as their interaction. The DIST option in the MODEL statement says that each frequency count has a Poisson distribution whose expected value m_{ij} is given by equation (10.2). For frequency counts in contingency tables, the Poisson distribution is appropriate for a variety of different sampling designs. As we saw in Chapter 9, the default in GENMOD for a Poisson distribution is LINK=LOG. That means that the logarithm of the expected value of the dependent variable is assumed to be a linear function of the explanatory variables, which is exactly what equation (10.1) says.

Output 10.1 *GENMOD Output for Loglinear Model for a 2 × 2 Table*

```
        Data Set                        WORK.PENALTY
        Distribution                    POISSON
        Link Function                   LOG
        Dependent Variable              N
        Observations Used               4


           Criteria For Assessing Goodness Of Fit


     Criterion            DF         Value      Value/DF


     Deviance              0        0.0000           .
     Scaled Deviance       0        0.0000           .
     Pearson Chi-Square    0        0.0000           .
     Scaled Pearson X2     0        0.0000           .
     Log Likelihood        .      391.0691           .



              Analysis Of Parameter Estimates


  Parameter    DF    Estimate    Std Err   ChiSquare  Pr>Chi


  INTERCEPT    1       3.9512      0.1387   811.8410   0.0001
  DEATH        1      -0.8602      0.2543    11.4392   0.0007
  BLACK        1      -0.1446      0.2036     0.5043   0.4776
  DEATH*BLACK  1       0.3857      0.3502     1.2135   0.2706
  SCALE        0       1.0000      0.0000        .        .


  NOTE:   The scale parameter was held fixed.
```

Examining Output 10.1, we see that the deviance for this model is 0. That's because it's a *saturated* model; there are four estimated parameters for the four cells in the table, so the model perfectly reproduces the frequency counts. The estimate for the interaction is .3857, the same value obtained from hand calculation of equation (10.4). This estimate has an associated Wald chi-square of 1.214, which is nearly identical to the traditional Pearson chi-square (1.218) for testing whether the two variables are independent (obtained with PROC FREQ). That's not surprising because both statistics are testing the same null hypothesis.

Instead of a loglinear model, we could estimate a logit model for this table, taking death sentence as the dependent variable:

```
PROC GENMOD DATA=penalty;
  WEIGHT n;
  MODEL death=black / D=BINOMIAL LINK=LOGIT;
RUN;
```

This produces Output 10.2.

Output 10.2 *GENMOD Output for Logit Model for 2 × 2 Table*

Analysis Of Parameter Estimates					
Parameter	DF	Estimate	Std Err	ChiSquare	Pr>Chi
INTERCEPT	1	-0.8602	0.2543	11.4392	0.0007
BLACK	1	0.3857	0.3502	1.2135	0.2706

Remarkably, the estimates in Output 10.2 are identical to some of the estimates in Output 10.1. The coefficient for BLACK in the logit model is the same as the BLACK*DEATH coefficient in the loglinear model, along with identical standard errors and chi-squares. Similarly, the intercept (and associated statistics) in the logit model is the same as the DEATH coefficient in the loglinear model. This is a general phenomenon. As I've said before, every logit model for a contingency table has a corresponding loglinear model. But the main effects in the logit model become 2-way interactions (with the dependent variable) in the loglinear model. The intercept in the logit model becomes a main effect of the dependent variable in the loglinear model.

Now let's do something peculiar just to emphasize the point. We'll estimate another logit model, but we'll switch the variables and make BLACK the dependent variable and DEATH the independent variable:

```
PROC GENMOD DATA=penalty;
  WEIGHT n;
  MODEL black=death / D=BINOMIAL LINK=LOGIT;
RUN;
```

Output 10.3 *GENMOD Output for Logit Model for 2 × 2 Table with Variables Reversed*

```
            Analysis Of Parameter Estimates

Parameter    DF    Estimate    Std Err   ChiSquare  Pr>Chi

INTERCEPT     1     -0.1446     0.2036     0.5043    0.4776
DEATH         1      0.3857     0.3502     1.2135    0.2706
```

In Output 10.3, we see again that the slope coefficient (along with its standard error and chi-square) is identical to the two-way interaction in the loglinear model. Unlike bivariate linear regression, where the regression line changes when you reverse the dependent and independent variables, the bivariate logit model is symmetrical with respect to the two variables. We also see that the intercept term corresponds to the main effect of BLACK in the loglinear model.

Why do the logit models share parameters with the loglinear model? The algebra that demonstrates this is really quite simple. The dependent variable in the logit model is the logarithm of the odds. For example, the log-odds of a death sentence for racial group j is $\log(m_{1j}/m_{2j})$. Substituting from the loglinear model in equation (10.1), we get:

$$\log\left(\frac{m_{1j}}{m_{2j}}\right) = \log(m_{1j}) - \log(m_{2j})$$

$$= \left(\beta_0 + \beta_1 R_1 + \beta_2 C_j + \beta_3 R_1 C_j\right) - \left(\beta_0 + \beta_1 R_2 + \beta_2 C_j + \beta_3 R_2 C_j\right).$$

But because $R_1=1$ and $R_2=0$, this reduces to:

$$\log\left(\frac{m_{1j}}{m_{2j}}\right) = \beta_1 + \beta_3 C_j.$$

Similarly, if we reverse the independent and dependent variables, we obtain:

$$\log\left(\frac{m_{i1}}{m_{i2}}\right) = \beta_2 + \beta_3 R_i.$$

These results show that the loglinear model for the 2 × 2 table implies two logit models, one for the row variable as dependent on the column variable and the other for the column variable as dependent on the row variable.

10.3 Loglinear Models for a Four-Way Table

Now let's look at a much more complicated table, the $2 \times 2 \times 4 \times 4$ table that we previously analyzed by way of a logit model in Section 4.5. Our main goal will be to duplicate the results of the logit model with a loglinear model. To refresh your memory, the sample consisted of 4,991 high school seniors in Wisconsin. The dependent variable was whether or not they planned to attend college in the following year. The three independent variables were coded as follows:

IQ   1=low, 2=lower middle, 3=upper middle, 4=high

SES   1=low, 2=lower middle, 3=upper middle, 4=high

PARENT   1=low parental encouragement, 2= high encouragement.

The data, shown in Section 4.5, was read in as 32 records, each record containing a unique combination of values of the independent variables, along with the number of seniors who had those values and the number of those seniors who planned to attend college. Unfortunately, that's not the format we need for a loglinear analysis. Instead, we need 64 records, one for each cell in the four-way table, with values for all the variables and the frequency count in that cell. Here's a DATA step that inputs the previous data set (WISC) and outputs the new data set in the appropriate format (WISCTAB).

```
DATA wisctab;
   SET wisc;
   college=1;
   freq=coll;
   OUTPUT;
   college=0;
   freq=total-coll;
   OUTPUT;
   DROP total coll;
PROC PRINT;
RUN;
```

Output 10.4 shows what this new data set looks like.

Output 10.4 *Data for a Four-Way Contingency Table*

OBS	IQ	PARENT	SES	COLLEGE	FREQ
1	1	1	1	1	4
2	1	1	1	0	349
3	1	1	2	1	2
4	1	1	2	0	232
5	1	1	3	1	8
6	1	1	3	0	166
7	1	1	4	1	4
8	1	1	4	0	48
9	1	2	1	1	13
10	1	2	1	0	64
11	1	2	2	1	27
12	1	2	2	0	84
13	1	2	3	1	47
14	1	2	3	0	91
15	1	2	4	1	39
16	1	2	4	0	57
17	2	1	1	1	9
18	2	1	1	0	207
19	2	1	2	1	7
20	2	1	2	0	201
21	2	1	3	1	6
22	2	1	3	0	120
23	2	1	4	1	5
24	2	1	4	0	47
25	2	2	1	1	33
26	2	2	1	0	72
27	2	2	2	1	64
28	2	2	2	0	95
29	2	2	3	1	74
30	2	2	3	0	110
31	2	2	4	1	123
32	2	2	4	0	90
33	3	1	1	1	12
34	3	1	1	0	126
35	3	1	2	1	12
36	3	1	2	0	115
37	3	1	3	1	17
38	3	1	3	0	92
39	3	1	4	1	9
40	3	1	4	0	41
41	3	2	1	1	38
42	3	2	1	0	54
43	3	2	2	1	93
44	3	2	2	0	92

Output 10.4 Continued

45	3	2	3	1	148
46	3	2	3	0	100
47	3	2	4	1	224
48	3	2	4	0	65
49	4	1	1	1	10
50	4	1	1	0	67
51	4	1	2	1	17
52	4	1	2	0	79
53	4	1	3	1	6
54	4	1	3	0	42
55	4	1	4	1	8
56	4	1	4	0	17
57	4	2	1	1	49
58	4	2	1	0	43
59	4	2	2	1	119
60	4	2	2	0	59
61	4	2	3	1	198
62	4	2	3	0	73
63	4	2	4	1	414
64	4	2	4	0	54

Here is the SAS code for estimating a loglinear model that is equivalent to the first logit model of Section 4.5:

```
PROC GENMOD DATA=wisctab;
   CLASS iq ses;
   MODEL freq=iq|ses|parent college iq*college ses*college
        parent*college / D=P TYPE3;
RUN;
```

As before, we are fitting a Poisson regression model for the frequency counts, with the default logarithmic link. The first term on the right-hand side of the MODEL equation—IQ|SES|PARENT—is shorthand for IQ*SES*PARENT IQ*SES IQ*PARENT SES*PARENT IQ SES PARENT. In other words, we fit the 3-way interaction, the three 2-way interactions, and the main effects of each of the independent variables. These parameters pertain only to the relationships among the independent variables in the logit model, not to the effects of the independent variables on the dependent variable (college choice). We include them in the model because to do otherwise would assert that they are 0. Because we cannot force these parameters to be 0 in a logit model, neither do we do it in the corresponding loglinear model. The general principle is this: *Whenever you want a loglinear model to be equivalent to some logit model, you must include all possible interactions among* *the independent variables in the logit model.* Even though we include these interactions, they rarely have any substantive interest because they describe relationships among the independent variables *conditional on the values of the dependent variable.* Ordinarily, this has no useful causal interpretation.

The parameters that do have a useful interpretation are specified in the MODEL statement as COLLEGE IQ*COLLEGE SES*COLLEGE PARENT*COLLEGE. These correspond to the intercept and the three main effects of the independent variables on the dependent variable in the logit model. So, all the parameters in the corresponding logit model involve the dependent variable when specified in the loglinear model. Notice that IQ and SES are listed as CLASS variables so that, for each variable, three dummy variables will be constructed to represent the four categories. This is unnecessary for COLLEGE and PARENT because they are dichotomous.

Results are shown in Output 10.5. Values that are the same as those in Output 4.10, obtained by direct fitting of the logit model, are shown in boldface. The numbers to the right of the parameter names correspond to the values of the CLASS variables. Apparently, the loglinear model contains many more parameters than the logit model, but the ones that count are identical in the two models. Notice also that the deviance and Pearson chi-squares are identical for the logit and loglinear models.

Output 10.5 *GENMOD Output for Loglinear Analysis of Four-Way Table*

```
                        The GENMOD Procedure

                         Model Information

          Description                      Value

          Data Set                         WORK.WISCTAB
          Distribution                     POISSON
          Link Function                    LOG
          Dependent Variable               FREQ
          Observations Used                64



                     Class Level Information

                  Class     Levels   Values

                   IQ          4     1 2 3 4
                   SES         4     1 2 3 4
```

Output 10.5 Continued

```
                  Criteria For Assessing Goodness Of Fit

            Criterion            DF        Value      Value/DF

            Deviance             24       25.2358      1.0515
            Scaled Deviance      24       25.2358      1.0515
            Pearson Chi-Square   24       24.4398      1.0183
            Scaled Pearson X2    24       24.4398      1.0183
            Log Likelihood        .      18912.8805       .


                     Analysis Of Parameter Estimates

   Parameter           DF    Estimate    Std Err   ChiSquare   Pr>Chi

   INTERCEPT            1      1.4076     0.4093    11.8287    0.0006
   IQ        1         1      2.4070     0.5036    22.8476    0.0001
   IQ        2         1      1.8198     0.4967    13.4206    0.0002
   IQ        3         1      1.7044     0.4969    11.7656    0.0006
   IQ        4         0      0.0000     0.0000       .          .
   SES       1         1      3.4289     0.4775    51.5546    0.0001
   SES       2         1      3.3431     0.4600    52.8290    0.0001
   SES       3         1      1.6470     0.5007    10.8213    0.0010
   SES       4         0      0.0000     0.0000       .          .
   IQ*SES    1  1      1      0.2993     0.5817     0.2647    0.6069
   IQ*SES    1  2      1     -0.7469     0.5692     1.7217    0.1895
   IQ*SES    1  3      1      0.2001     0.6061     0.1090    0.7413
   IQ*SES    1  4      0      0.0000     0.0000       .          .
   IQ*SES    2  1      1     -0.3036     0.5794     0.2745    0.6004
   IQ*SES    2  2      1     -0.6241     0.5633     1.2277    0.2679
   IQ*SES    2  3      1      0.0101     0.6070     0.0003    0.9867
   IQ*SES    2  4      0      0.0000     0.0000       .          .
   IQ*SES    3  1      1     -0.7575     0.5905     1.6454    0.1996
   IQ*SES    3  2      1     -1.4171     0.5746     6.0828    0.0137
   IQ*SES    3  3      1     -0.2082     0.6113     0.1160    0.7334
   IQ*SES    3  4      0      0.0000     0.0000       .          .
   IQ*SES    4  1      0      0.0000     0.0000       .          .
   IQ*SES    4  2      0      0.0000     0.0000       .          .
   IQ*SES    4  3      0      0.0000     0.0000       .          .
   IQ*SES    4  4      0      0.0000     0.0000       .          .
   PARENT              1      1.3895     0.2144    42.0060    0.0001
   PARENT*IQ  1        1     -1.3237     0.2746    23.2379    0.0001
   PARENT*IQ  2        1     -0.7906     0.2632     9.0218    0.0027
   PARENT*IQ  3        1     -0.8352     0.2616    10.1935    0.0014
   PARENT*IQ  4        0      0.0000     0.0000       .          .
   PARENT*SES 1        1     -2.0023     0.2641    57.4604    0.0001
   PARENT*SES 2        1     -1.7432     0.2474    49.6418    0.0001
```

Output 10.5 *Continued*

PARENT*SES	3		1	-0.7940	0.2636	9.0726	0.0026
PARENT*SES	4		0	0.0000	0.0000	.	.
PARENT*IQ*SES	1	1	1	0.2425	0.3363	0.5198	0.4709
PARENT*IQ*SES	1	2	1	0.6967	0.3196	4.7533	0.0292
PARENT*IQ*SES	1	3	1	0.1915	0.3316	0.3336	0.5636
PARENT*IQ*SES	1	4	0	0.0000	0.0000	.	.
PARENT*IQ*SES	2	1	1	0.3940	0.3240	1.4789	0.2239
PARENT*IQ*SES	2	2	1	0.4903	0.3061	2.5662	0.1092
PARENT*IQ*SES	2	3	1	0.0860	0.3228	0.0709	0.7900
PARENT*IQ*SES	2	4	0	0.0000	0.0000	.	.
PARENT*IQ*SES	3	1	1	0.5263	0.3284	2.5689	0.1090
PARENT*IQ*SES	3	2	1	0.9028	0.3082	8.5797	0.0034
PARENT*IQ*SES	3	3	1	0.2568	0.3215	0.6380	0.4244
PARENT*IQ*SES	3	4	0	0.0000	0.0000	.	.
PARENT*IQ*SES	4	1	0	0.0000	0.0000	.	.
PARENT*IQ*SES	4	2	0	0.0000	0.0000	.	.
PARENT*IQ*SES	4	3	0	0.0000	0.0000	.	.
PARENT*IQ*SES	4	4	0	0.0000	0.0000	.	.
COLLEGE			1	-3.1005	0.2123	213.3353	0.0001
COLLEGE*IQ	1		1	-1.9663	0.1210	264.2400	0.0001
COLLEGE*IQ	2		1	-1.3722	0.1024	179.7284	0.0001
COLLEGE*IQ	3		1	-0.6331	0.0976	42.0831	0.0001
COLLEGE*IQ	4		0	0.0000	0.0000	.	.
COLLEGE*SES	1		1	-1.4140	0.1210	136.6657	0.0001
COLLEGE*SES	2		1	-1.0580	0.1029	105.7894	0.0001
COLLEGE*SES	3		1	-0.7516	0.0976	59.3364	0.0001
COLLEGE*SES	4		0	0.0000	0.0000	.	.
PARENT*COLLEGE			1	2.4554	0.1014	586.3859	0.0001
SCALE			0	1.0000	0.0000	.	.

NOTE: The scale parameter was held fixed.

LR Statistics For Type 3 Analysis

Source	DF	ChiSquare	Pr>Chi
IQ	3	175.6015	0.0001
SES	3	379.7224	0.0001
IQ*SES	9	17.5638	0.0406
PARENT	1	34.1173	0.0001
PARENT*IQ	3	86.1646	0.0001
PARENT*SES	3	257.0933	0.0001
PARENT*IQ*SES	9	13.7343	0.1321
COLLEGE	1	1078.3695	0.0001
COLLEGE*IQ	3	361.5648	0.0001
COLLEGE*SES	3	179.8467	0.0001
PARENT*COLLEGE	1	795.6139	0.0001

Because the deviance is not 0, we know that this is not a saturated model, unlike the model we considered for the 2 × 2 table. To get a saturated model, we would have to include three 3-way interactions with COLLEGE and one 4-way interaction with COLLEGE. These would correspond to three 2-way interactions and one 3-way interaction in the logit model.

10.4   Fitting the Adjacent Categories Model as a Loglinear Model

We now know how to fit a logit model to a contingency table by fitting an equivalent loglinear model, but a natural question is "Why bother?" As we've just seen, the loglinear model is cluttered with "nuisance parameters" and is more cumbersome to specify in the MODEL statement. Even worse, the requirement of fitting the full multi-way interaction for the independent variables often leads to annoying convergence problems. Specifically, if there are any cell frequencies of 0 in the multi-way contingency table for the independent variables, the model will not converge. This problem does not arise when fitting the logit model directly.

Despite these difficulties, there are situations in which it is easy to fit the loglinear model but difficult to fit the corresponding logit model. One such model is the adjacent-categories model that we considered in Chapter 6. Recall that the adjacent-categories model is one of three alternative logit models for dependent variables with multiple, ordered categories. If the dependent variable has J ordered categories, the model says that for individual i:

$$\log\left(\frac{p_{ij}}{p_{i,j+1}}\right) = \alpha_j + \beta\mathbf{x}_i \qquad j = 1,...,J-1$$

In other words, if we contrast adjacent categories of the dependent variable, the effect of the independent variables on their relative odds is the same regardless of which pair we consider.

This model is a special case of the multinomial logit model that does not impose any ordering on the categories of the dependent variable. (We get the general model by putting a j subscript on the β coefficient). In Chapter 6, we saw how we could estimate the adjacent categories model in PROC CATMOD by the method of weighted least squares. But the maximum likelihood algorithm in CATMOD cannot impose the necessary constraints on the multinomial model.

Now, we'll see how to easily estimate the adjacent categories model as a loglinear model by maximum likelihood. In Chapter 6, we looked at the effect of calendar year (1974, 1984, 1994) and marital status (married, unmarried) on reported happiness (very happy=1, pretty happy=2, not too happy=3). The contingency table is found in Table 6.1. Here's how the data is read into a SAS data set:

```
DATA happy;
  INPUT year married happy count;
  happyq=happy;
  DATALINES;
1 1 1 473
1 1 2 493
1 1 3  93
1 0 1  84
1 0 2 231
1 0 3  99
2 1 1 332
2 1 2 387
2 1 3  62
2 0 1 150
2 0 2 347
2 0 3 117
3 1 1 571
3 1 2 793
3 1 3 112
3 0 1 257
3 0 2 889
3 0 3 234
;
```

Notice that I defined a new variable HAPPYQ to be identical to HAPPY, the three-category dependent variable. By defining two versions of the dependent variable, we can treat it as both quantitative and qualitative in the same model. The model is specified as follows:

```
PROC GENMOD DATA=happy;
  CLASS year happy;
  MODEL count=year|married happy year*happyq married*happyq /
    D=P TYPE3;
RUN;
```

HAPPY and YEAR are declared as CLASS variables, but HAPPYQ is treated as a quantitative variable. Because MARRIED has only two categories, it doesn't need to be a CLASS variable. The term YEAR|MARRIED ensures that the model is equivalent to a logit model by fitting all possible terms pertaining to the two independent variables. The effects of YEAR and MARRIED on happiness are specified by the terms YEAR*HAPPYQ and MARRIED*HAPPYQ. By also including HAPPY in the model as a CLASS variable, we allow for different intercepts for the two adjacent pairs of categories. Results are shown in Output 10.6. As in Output 10.5, those parameters that correspond to the equivalent logit model are shown in bold face.

Output 10.6 *GENMOD Output for Adjacent Categories Model*

```
                        The GENMOD Procedure

                        Model Information

          Description                     Value

          Data Set                        WORK.HAPPY
          Distribution                    POISSON
          Link Function                   LOG
          Dependent Variable              COUNT
          Observations Used               18




                     Class Level Information

            Class      Levels  Values

            YEAR          3     1 2 3
            HAPPY         3     1 2 3




            Criteria For Assessing Goodness Of Fit

    Criterion              DF       Value      Value/DF

    Deviance                7      35.7555       5.1079
    Scaled Deviance         7      35.7555       5.1079
    Pearson Chi-Square      7      35.9250       5.1321
    Scaled Pearson X2       7      35.9250       5.1321
    Log Likelihood          .   28747.4570          .
```

Output 10.6 *Continued*

```
                       Analysis Of Parameter Estimates

     Parameter            DF   Estimate   Std Err   ChiSquare   Pr>Chi

     INTERCEPT             1     5.6206    0.0492   13029.5637   0.0001
     YEAR            1     1    -1.1262    0.1182      90.7120   0.0001
     YEAR            2     1    -0.6319    0.1144      30.4822   0.0001
     YEAR            3     0     0.0000    0.0000        .         .
     MARRIED               1     1.5386    0.0918     281.0696   0.0001
     MARRIED*YEAR    1     1     0.8596    0.0710     146.7800   0.0001
     MARRIED*YEAR    2     1     0.1449    0.0677       4.5795   0.0324
     MARRIED*YEAR    3     0     0.0000    0.0000        .         .
     HAPPY           1     1     0.0247    0.0739       0.1117   0.7382
     HAPPY           2     1     1.0899    0.0475     526.0558   0.0001
     HAPPY           3     0     0.0000    0.0000        .         .
     HAPPYQ*YEAR     1     1    -0.0391    0.0525       0.5556   0.4560
     HAPPYQ*YEAR     2     1    -0.0900    0.0526       2.9284   0.0870
     HAPPYQ*YEAR     3     0     0.0000    0.0000        .         .
     MARRIED*HAPPYQ        1    -0.8020    0.0453     312.9691   0.0001
     SCALE                 0     1.0000    0.0000        .         .

 NOTE:  The scale parameter was held fixed.


                    LR Statistics For Type 3 Analysis

             Source            DF   ChiSquare   Pr>Chi

             YEAR               2     99.0743   0.0001
             MARRIED            1    493.8851   0.0001
             MARRIED*YEAR       2    157.8319   0.0001
             HAPPY              1   1423.9318   0.0001
             HAPPYQ*YEAR        2      2.9687   0.2266
             MARRIED*HAPPYQ     1    335.5684   0.0001
```

Looking first at the deviance (and Pearson chi-square), we see strong evidence that the fitted model is unsatisfactory: the deviance is more than five times the degrees of freedom and the *p*-value is less than .00001. (All *p*-values reported in this chapter were computed by using a SAS macro, not with PROC GENMOD). This is nearly identical to what we found in Output 6.7 when we estimated the equivalent logit model by weighted least squares. Although there is little evidence for an effect of YEAR, the chi-squares for MARRIED are quite large. The parameter estimate for the marital status effect (MARRIED*HAPPYQ) is –.8020. Again this is quite close to the WLS estimate of –.8035 in Output 6.7. Because higher values of HAPPYQ indicate lower happiness and MARRIED=1 for married, otherwise 0, the negative sign of the coefficient tells us that married people are happier. To be more specific, if we contrast the categories "very happy" and "pretty happy," the odds of a married person being in the latter category are exp(–.8020)=.45 times the odds of an unmarried person. To put it another way, married people are about twice as likely (on the odds scale) as unmarried people to be in the happier category. Because of the constraints on the model, the same statement can be made about the contrast between "pretty happy" and "not too happy"— married people are about twice as likely as unmarried people to be in the happier category.

Given the poor fit of the model, we must be wary of these interpretations. But how can the model be improved? There are two possibilities. We can allow an interaction between year and marital status in their effects on happiness, which corresponds to a three-way interaction in the loglinear model. Or, we can relax the adjacent-categories constraint and fit a regular multinomial logit model. To fit the interaction model, we use the statement:

```
MODEL count=year|married happy year*happyq married*happyq
       married*year*happyq / D=P TYPE3;
```

That model produces a deviance of 29.64 with 5 d.f. Not much of an improvement, and still an unacceptable fit. We can fit the unrestricted multinomial model without a three-way interaction by simply deleting the Q from the HAPPY variable, thereby treating it as a CLASS variable:

```
MODEL count=year|married happy year*happy married*happy /
       D=P TYPE3;
```

This produces a deviance of 4.16 with 4 d.f., for a *p*-value of .38. Furthermore, there is a highly significant reduction in deviance when we move from the adjacent-categories model to the multinomial model. This suggests that either YEAR or MARRIED does not have a uniform effect on both pairs of adjacent categories. To see where the problem lies, take a look at the parameter estimates of the multinomial model in Output 10.7.

Output 10.7 *Selected Parameter Estimates for Multinomial Model*

Parameter			DF	Estimate	Std Err	ChiSquare	Pr>Chi
HAPPY	1		1	0.0917	0.0781	1.3780	0.2404
HAPPY	2		1	1.3038	0.0662	387.7154	0.0001
HAPPY	3		0	0.0000	0.0000	.	.
YEAR*HAPPY	1	1	1	-0.1135	0.1098	1.0680	0.3014
YEAR*HAPPY	1	2	1	-0.4025	0.1028	15.3312	0.0001
YEAR*HAPPY	1	3	0	0.0000	0.0000	.	.
YEAR*HAPPY	2	1	1	0.0653	0.1114	0.3437	0.5577
YEAR*HAPPY	2	2	1	-0.1941	0.1028	3.5613	0.0591
YEAR*HAPPY	2	3	0	0.0000	0.0000	.	.
YEAR*HAPPY	3	1	0	0.0000	0.0000	.	.
YEAR*HAPPY	3	2	0	0.0000	0.0000	.	.
YEAR*HAPPY	3	3	0	0.0000	0.0000	.	.
MARRIED*HAPPY	1		1	1.5725	0.0950	274.0672	0.0001
MARRIED*HAPPY	2		1	0.7092	0.0867	66.8277	0.0001
MARRIED*HAPPY	3		0	0.0000	0.0000	.	.

To save space, Output 10.7 has been edited to display only those parameter estimates that correspond to the multinomial logit model. Of course, those include all model terms that contain HAPPY. In the first two coefficients for MARRIED, we see that the coefficient for category 1 (versus category 3) is 1.5725, about twice as large as the coefficient of .7092 for category 2. That's what we would expect from the adjacent-categories model, so apparently the problem is not with this variable. However, things aren't quite so simple with YEAR. In the previous model, we found no evidence for any effect of year on happiness, but now we see that the 1974 contrast between categories 2 and 3 of HAPPY is highly significant, and the 1984 contrast between categories 2 and 3 is marginally significant. But the contrasts between categories 1 and 3 of HAPPY are both far from significant. Clearly, there is some kind of effect of year on happiness, but it doesn't conform to the adjacent categories assumption. What appears to be happening is that each 10-year increment in time is associated with an increase in the odds of being in the middle category (pretty happy) and a corresponding reduction of the odds of being in either of the two extreme categories.

We can represent this interpretation by a more parsimonious model that (a) treats happiness as quantitative in its association with marital status and (b) linearizes the effect of year on a dichotomous version of happiness—pretty happy versus the other two responses:

```
DATA happy2;
  SET happy;
  yearq=year;
```

```
      pretty=happy eq 2;
   RUN;
   PROC GENMOD DATA=happy2;
      CLASS year happy;
      MODEL count=year|married happy yearq*pretty married*happyq
        / D=P TYPE3;
   RUN;
```

Output 10.8   *Selected Parameter Estimates for a Parsimonious Model*

Parameter		DF	Estimate	Std Err	ChiSquare	Pr>Chi
HAPPY	1	1	0.0852	0.0645	1.7452	0.1865
HAPPY	2	1	0.7303	0.0845	74.6359	0.0001
HAPPY	3	0	0.0000	0.0000	.	.
YEARQ*PRETTY		1	0.1722	0.0320	28.9847	0.0001
MARRIED*HAPPYQ		1	-0.7944	0.0448	314.9991	0.0001

This model has a deviance of 9.66 with 8 d.f. for a *p*-value of .29, certainly an acceptable fit. The relevant parameter estimates are shown in Output 10.8. The coefficient for MARRIED is about what it was in the original adjacent categories model and has the same interpretation: for any contrast of adjacent categories, married people have about twice the odds of being in the happier category as unmarried people. The YEARQ coefficient can be interpreted as follows: with each additional decade, the odds of being in the middle category (as compared to the two extremes) rises by about 18%=100[exp(.1722)–1].

We have achieved the parsimony of this final model by carefully adjusting it to fit observed patterns that might have arisen from random variation. So, we should not feel extremely confident that this is the correct model. Nevertheless, this exercise should give you some idea of the range of possibilities for models like this. While the loglinear approach can be rather cumbersome, it is also remarkably flexible.

10.5   Loglinear Models for Square, Ordered Tables

Loglinear models have been particularly popular for the analysis of mobility tables like the one shown in Table 10.2, which is based on data collected in Britain by Glass (1954) and his collaborators. The column variable is the respondent's occupational status, classified into five categories with 1 being the highest and 5 the lowest. The same classification was used for the father's occupation, the row variable in the table. For obvious reasons, we call this a square table. Our aim is to fit loglinear models that describe the relationship between father's status and son's status. In the process, we'll see how to estimate some models proposed by Goodman (1970).

Table 10.2   *Cross-Classification of Respondent's Occupational Status by Father's Occupational Status, 3,497 British Males.*

		Son's Status				
		1	2	3	4	5
Father's Status	1	50	45	8	18	8
	2	28	174	84	154	55
	3	11	78	110	223	96
	4	14	150	185	714	447
	5	0	42	72	320	411

One model that nearly every researcher knows how to fit (but may not realize it) is the *independence model*, which asserts that the two variables are independent. Here is SAS code to fit the independence model:

```
DATA mobility;
     INPUT n dad son;
     DATALINES;
50   1 1
45   1 2
8    1 3
18   1 4
8    1 5
28   2 1
174  2 2
84   2 3
154  2 4
55   2 5
11   3 1
78   3 2
110  3 3
223  3 4
96   3 5
14   4 1
150  4 2
185  4 3
714  4 4
447  4 5
0    5 1
42   5 2
```

```
72  5 3
320 5 4
411 5 5
;
PROC GENMOD DATA=mobility;
  CLASS dad son;
      MODEL n = dad son /D=P;
RUN;
```

As usual, each cell of the table is read in as a separate record, with the variable N containing the frequency counts and with values of 1 through 5 for the row and column variables, DAD and SON. In PROC GENMOD, these are declared as CLASS variables so that, at this point, no ordering of the categories is assumed. The MODEL statement includes the main effects of DAD and SON but no interaction. This allows for variation in the marginal frequencies but doesn't allow for any relationship between the two variables. Not surprisingly, the fit of this model is terrible. With 16 d.f., the deviance is 810.98 and the Pearson chi-square is 1199.36. (It's hardly worth the effort calculating *p*-values because they would obviously be smaller than any sensible criterion.) Note that the Pearson chi-square is the same value that would be obtained by traditional methods of computing chi-square in a two-way table and the same value that is reported by PROC FREQ under the CHISQ option.

In rejecting the independence model, we conclude that there is indeed a relationship between father's status and son's status. But how can we modify the model to represent this relationship? We could fit the *saturated* model by the statement:

```
MODEL n=dad son dad*son / D=P;
```

but that wouldn't accomplish much. The deviance and Pearson chi-square would both be 0, and we'd have estimates for 16 parameters describing the relationship between the two variables. We might as well just look at the original table. Can't we get something more parsimonious?

The first alternative model that Goodman considered is the *quasi-independence model*, also called the *quasi-perfect mobility model* when applied to a mobility table. This model takes note of the fact that the main diagonal cells in Table 10.2 tend to have relatively high frequency counts. We might explain this by postulating a process of occupational inheritance such that sons take up the same occupation as the father. The quasi-independence model allows for such inheritance but asserts that there is no additional relationship between father's status and son's status. That is, if the son doesn't have the same status as the father, then father's status doesn't tell us anything about son's status.

There are two ways to fit the quasi-independence model. One way is to include a separate parameter for each of the main diagonal cells. The other, equivalent way (which we will take) is to simply delete the main diagonal cells from the data being fitted. Here's how:

```
PROC GENMOD DATA=mobility;
   WHERE dad NE son;
   CLASS dad son;
      MODEL n = dad son /D=P;
RUN;
```

In the WHERE statement, NE means "not equal to."

Although the quasi-independence model fits much better than the independence model, the fit is still bad. With 11 d.f., the deviance is 249.4 and the Pearson chi-square is 328.7. We conclude: although 69% of the original deviance is attributable to the main diagonal cells, there is something else going on in the table besides status inheritance.

To represent that something else, Goodman proposed 21 other models as possible candidates. Let's consider two of them. The *QPN* model is based on the ordering of occupational status. In Table 10.2, the upper triangle represents downward mobility while the lower triangle represents upward mobility. The QPN model says that, besides ignoring the main diagonal cells, there is independence *within* each of these two triangles. To fit the model, we create a new variable distinguishing the two portions of the table:

```
DATA b;
   SET mobility;
   up=son GT dad;
PROC GENMOD DATA=b;
   WHERE dad NE son;
   CLASS dad son;
      MODEL n = dad son son*up dad*up/D=P;
RUN;
```

We get a considerable improvement in fit from this model (output not shown). With 6 d.f., the deviance is 14.0 ($p=.03$) and the Pearson chi-square is 9.9 ($p=.13$). While the p value for the deviance is below the .05 criterion, keep in mind that we are working with a rather large sample and even minor deviations from the model are likely to be statistically significant. What is the substantive interpretation of this model? In addition to allowing for status inheritance (by deleting the main diagonal), it seems to be saying that father's status could affect whether the son moves up or down but does not determine the exact destination.

Another of Goodman's models is the *diagonals parameter model*. This model is motivated by the observation that the cells in Table 10.2 that are farther away from the main diagonal tend to have smaller frequencies. To represent this, we include a distinct parameter corresponding to each absolute difference between father's status and son's status:

```
DATA c;
   SET mobility;
   band=ABS(dad-son);
PROC GENMOD DATA=c;
   WHERE dad NE son;
   CLASS dad son band;
        MODEL n = dad son band /D=P;
RUN;
```

The results are shown in Output 10.9. The fit is not terrible but it's not great either—the *p*-value for the likelihood ratio chi-square is .014. The only parameters of interest to us are those for BAND. We see that cells that are directly adjacent to the main diagonal (BAND=1) have frequencies that are estimated to be exp(2.4824)=12 times those in the off-diagonal corners. For BAND=2 and BAND=3, the frequency counts are estimated to be 7 times and 3 times those in the corners.

Output 10.9   *Results from Fitting the Diagonals Parameter Model*

```
                Criteria For Assessing Goodness Of Fit

        Criterion           DF        Value      Value/DF

        Deviance             8       19.0739       2.3842
        Scaled Deviance      8       19.0739       2.3842
        Pearson Chi-Square   8       15.9121       1.9890
        Scaled Pearson X2    8       15.9121       1.9890
        Log Likelihood       .     8473.7383          .
```

Output 10.9 *Continued*

```
                    Analysis Of Parameter Estimates

        Parameter        DF    Estimate    Std Err   ChiSquare   Pr>Chi

        INTERCEPT         1      3.0797     0.3680     70.0315    0.0001
        DAD       1       1     -1.3915     0.1293    115.7369    0.0001
        DAD       2       1     -0.2227     0.0802      7.7116    0.0055
        DAD       3       1     -0.4620     0.0743     38.6411    0.0001
        DAD       4       1      0.5450     0.0814     44.7860    0.0001
        DAD       5       0      0.0000     0.0000        .          .
        SON       1       1     -2.1280     0.1478    207.3948    0.0001
        SON       2       1     -0.5790     0.0756     58.6140    0.0001
        SON       3       1     -0.8890     0.0726    149.8054    0.0001
        SON       4       1      0.2367     0.0768      9.4917    0.0021
        SON       5       0      0.0000     0.0000        .          .
        BAND      1       1      2.4824     0.3707     44.8335    0.0001
        BAND      2       1      1.9539     0.3733     27.3900    0.0001
        BAND      3       1      1.1482     0.3740      9.4258    0.0021
        BAND      4       0      0.0000     0.0000        .          .
```

Before concluding our analysis, let's consider one additional model that was not discussed in Goodman's article, the *quasi-uniform association model*. This model incorporates the ordering of the occupational statuses in a very explicit manner. The conventional uniform association model says that if the cells in the table are properly ordered, then the odds ratio (cross-product ratio) in every 2×2 subtable of adjacent cells is exactly the same. Our modification of that model is to delete the main diagonals before we fit it. Here's the SAS code:

```
DATA d;
  SET mobility;
  sonq=son;
  dadq=dad;
PROC GENMOD DATA=d;
  WHERE dad NE son;
  CLASS dad son;
      MODEL n = dad son sonq*dadq /D=P OBSTATS;
RUN;
```

As in some earlier examples, we define new versions of the row and column variables so that we can treat those variables as both categorical and quantitative. The model includes the main effects of SON and DAD as categorical, thereby ensuring that the marginal frequencies are fitted exactly. The relationship between the two variables is specified by an interaction between the quantitative versions of the two variables. The OBSTATS option requests predicted values and residuals.

With 10 d.f., the quasi-uniform association model has a deviance of 19.3 (p=.04) and a Pearson chi-square of 16.2 (p=.094) (output not shown). While not quite as good a fit as the QPN model, it's still decent for a sample of this size, and it has the virtue of providing a single number to describe the association between father's status and son's status in the off-diagonal cells: .3374. Exponentiating, we find that the estimated odds ratio in any 2 × 2 subtable is 1.40. Thus for adjacent categories, being in the higher category for DAD increases the odds of being in the higher category for SON by 40%.

Comparing the observed and predicted frequencies in Output 10.10, we find that the numbers are close for most of the cells. (For the three lines shown in boldface, the observed frequency lies outside the 95% confidence interval based on the fitted model.)

Output 10.10 *Selected OBSTATS Output for Quasi-Uniform Association Model*

N	Pred	Lower	Upper
45	36.2948	28.0890	46.8979
8	**16.1264**	**12.6337**	**20.5846**
18	21.3776	16.3270	27.9904
8	**5.2014**	**3.6963**	**7.3195**
28	24.7939	18.3938	33.4210
84	84.8482	72.6289	99.1233
154	157.6170	138.6531	179.1746
55	53.7409	45.1977	63.8990
11	11.8078	8.8657	15.7262
78	90.9439	78.3197	105.6030
223	206.5569	184.0375	231.8317
96	98.6915	85.9194	113.3623
14	13.9113	10.1391	19.0870
150	150.1456	131.5876	171.3208
185	183.5770	162.5983	207.2623
447	448.3662	410.6894	489.4994
0	**2.4871**	**1.6884**	**3.6636**
42	37.6157	31.1354	45.4449
72	64.4486	55.1532	75.3105
320	329.4487	297.8315	364.4223

10.6 Marginal Tables

To understand the literature on loglinear models, it's helpful to have some appreciation of *marginal tables* and their relationship to the parameters in the loglinear model and to the maximum likelihood estimates. A marginal table is just a contingency table that is obtained by summing the frequencies in some larger contingency table over one or more of the variables. For example, if we have a three-way table for variables X, Y, and Z, there are several possible marginal tables:

- the $X \times Y$ table, obtained by summing over Z
- the $X \times Z$ table, obtained by summing over Y
- the $Y \times Z$ table, obtained by summing over X
- the X table, obtained by summing over both Y and Z
- the Y table, obtained by summing over both X and Z
- the Z table, obtained by summing over both Y and X

Why are these tables important? Because every term in a loglinear model has a corresponding marginal table. For example, to fit a saturated model for the $X \times Y \times Z$ table in GENMOD, we specify:

```
MODEL f = x y z x*y x*z y*z x*y*z / D=P;
```

Each term in this model corresponds to a specific table or subtable, with the three-way interaction corresponding to the full three-way table. Because this is a saturated model, the predicted cell frequencies are identical to the observed cell frequencies in the full table. In the notation of Section 10.2 (with i representing a value of variable X, j representing a value of Y, and k representing a value of Z), we have $\hat{m}_{ijk} = n_{ijk}$ for all i, j, and k. Clearly, this must also be true for any marginal table: the summed predicted frequencies will be equal to the summed observed frequencies.

Now consider an unsaturated model that deletes the three-way interaction:

```
MODEL f = x y z x*y x*z y*z / D=P;
```

For this model, the maximum likelihood estimates of the expected frequencies in the three-way table will not, in general, be equal to the observed frequencies: $\hat{m}_{ijk} \neq n_{ijk}$. However, for all the marginal tables corresponding to the terms in the model, the summed predicted frequencies will equal the summed observed frequencies (the + signs in the subscripts below indicate that the frequencies are summed over that variable):

$$\hat{m}_{ij+} = n_{ij+}$$
$$\hat{m}_{i+k} = n_{i+k}$$
$$\hat{m}_{+jk} = n_{+jk} \quad \text{for all } i, j, \text{ and } k$$
$$\hat{m}_{i++} = n_{i++}$$
$$\hat{m}_{+j+} = n_{+j+}$$
$$\hat{m}_{++k} = n_{++k}$$

You can readily see this with the independence model for a 2×2 table. Table 10.3 displays observed and predicted frequencies for the independence model applied to Table 10.1. Clearly, both the observed and predicted frequencies sum to the one-way marginal totals.

Table 10.3   *Observed (and Predicted) Frequencies for Independence Model*

	Blacks	Nonblacks	Total
Death	28 (24.8)	22 (25.2)	50
Life	45 (48.2)	52 (48.8)	97
Total	73	74	147

One final property of marginal tables is this: the marginal tables that correspond to the terms in the loglinear model are the *sufficient statistics* for that model. That means that the maximum likelihood estimates can be calculated using only the information in the appropriate marginal tables. For example, in Table 10.3 the maximum likelihood estimate of the expected frequency in each cell is obtained by multiplying the row total times the column total and dividing by the grand total (147). The parameter estimates can then be obtained from the estimated expected frequencies. So, we only need the marginal tables to fit the independence model. Of course, to calculate a chi-square, we need the full table so that we can compare the expected frequencies with the observed frequencies.

For all these reasons, the estimation of a loglinear model is often referred to as a process of *fitting marginal tables*. Many journal articles that report results of a loglinear analysis describe the fitted models by specifying the fitted marginal tables for each model, not by specifying the parameters included in the model.

10.7 The Problem of Zeros

Contingency tables sometimes have cells with frequency counts of 0. These may cause problems or require special treatment. There are two kinds of zeros:

- *Structural zeros*: These are cells for which a nonzero count is impossible because of the nature of the phenomenon or the design of the study. The classic example is a cross-tabulation of sex by type of surgery in which structural zeros occur for male hysterectomies and female vasectomies.

- *Random zeros*: In these cells, nonzero counts are possible (at least as far we know), but a zero occurs because of random variation. Random zeros are especially likely to arise when the sample is small and the contingency table has many cells.

Structural zeros are easily accommodated with PROC GENMOD. Simply delete the structural zeros from the data set before estimating the model. Random zeros can be a little trickier. Most of the time they don't cause any difficulty, except that the expected cell counts may be very small, thereby degrading the chi-square approximation to the deviance and Pearson's statistic. However, more serious problems arise when random zeros show up in fitted marginal tables. *When a fitted marginal table contains a frequency count of zero, at least one ML parameter estimate is infinite and the fitting algorithm will not converge.* We already encountered this problem in Section 3.4 for the binary logit model. There, we saw that if there is a 0 in the 2×2 table describing the relationship between the dependent variable and any dichotomous independent variable, the coefficient for that variable is infinite and the algorithm will not converge. The identical problem arises when fitting a logit model by means of its equivalent loglinear model, and the potential solutions are the same. However, problems arise more frequently when fitting loglinear models because it's necessary to fit the full marginal table describing the relationships among all the independent variables. As we've seen, loglinear models typically contain many nuisance parameters, any of which could have infinite estimates causing problems with convergence.

Here's a simple, hypothetical example. Consider the following three-way table for dichotomous variables *X*, *Y*, and *Z*:

		X			
		1		0	
		Z		Z	
Y		1	0	1	0
1		20	5	4	0
0		5	5	11	0
Total		25	10	15	0

Considering the two-way marginal tables, neither the *XY* table nor the *YZ* table has any zeros. But the *XZ* table clearly has one random zero, producing two random zeros in the three-way table.

Now suppose we want to estimate a logit model for *Y* dependent on *X* and *Z*. We can read the table into SAS as follows:

```
DATA zero;
   INPUT x y z f;
   DATALINES;
1   1   1   20
1   0   1   5
1   1   0   5
1   0   0   5
0   1   1   4
0   0   1   11
0   1   0   0
0   0   0   0
;
```

We can estimate the logit model directly with:

```
PROC GENMOD DATA=zero;
   FREQ f;
   MODEL y = x z / D=B;
RUN;
```

This produces the results in Output 10.11. There is no apparent problem here. The coefficient for *X* is large and statistically significant, while the coefficient for *Z* is smaller and not quite significant. Both goodness-of-fit statistics are 0 with 0 degrees of freedom. That's because the model has three parameters, but there are only three combinations of *X* and *Z* for which we observe the dependent variable *Y*.

Output 10.11 *Logit Output for Data with Marginal Zeros*

```
            Criteria For Assessing Goodness Of Fit

Criterion                DF        Value      Value/DF

Deviance                  0       0.0000          .
Pearson Chi-Square        0       0.0000          .
Log Likelihood            .     -28.1403          .


            Analysis Of Parameter Estimates

Parameter    DF    Estimate    Std Err    ChiSquare   Pr>Chi

INTERCEPT     1     -2.3979     0.9954      5.8027     0.0160
X             1      2.3979     0.7687      9.7306     0.0018
Z             1      1.3863     0.8062      2.9566     0.0855
```

Now let's estimate the equivalent loglinear model:

```
PROC GENMOD DATA=zero;
   MODEL f=x z y x*z y*z y*x / D=P OBSTATS;
RUN;
```

As Output 10.12 shows, all the parameters pertaining to *Y* (and associated statistics) are the same in both the loglinear and logit versions of the model. But, all the nuisance parameters are very large, with huge chi-squares. The goodness of fit chi-squares are again 0, but the reported degrees of freedom is 1 rather than 0.

Output 10.12 *Loglinear Output for Data with Marginal Zeros*

```
            Criteria For Assessing Goodness Of Fit

Criterion                DF        Value      Value/DF

Deviance                  1       0.0000       0.0000
Pearson Chi-Square        1       0.0000       0.0000
Log Likelihood            .      65.9782          .
```

Output 10.12 Continued

Analysis Of Parameter Estimates					
Parameter	DF	Estimate	Std Err	ChiSquare	Pr>Chi
INTERCEPT	1	-23.6020	0.7006	1134.7429	0.0001
X	1	25.2115	0.5394	2184.9366	0.0001
Z	1	25.9999	0.6325	1689.9898	0.0001
Y	1	-2.3979	0.9954	5.8027	0.0160
X*Z	0	-25.9999	0.0000	.	.
Z*Y	1	1.3863	0.8062	2.9566	0.0855
X*Y	1	2.3979	0.7687	9.7306	0.0018

The four parameter estimates greater than 20 all stem from the 0 in the marginal table for X and Z. While there's no guarantee, my experience with PROC GENMOD is that it invariably produces the right estimates and standard errors for the parameters that do *not* pertain to the marginal table with zeros. However, other software may not do the same. Even if the logit parameter estimates are correct, the incorrect degrees of freedom for the deviance and Pearson statistics may invalidate comparisons with other models.

The solution is to treat the random zeros that arise from marginal zeros as if they were structural zeros—that is, delete them from the data before fitting the model. How do we know which random zeros in the full table come from zeros in the fitted marginal tables? In this example, it's fairly evident, but more complicated tables may present some difficulties. One approach is to examine the table produced by the OBSTATS option and check for records in which the observed frequency is 0 and the estimated frequency is very small. Output 10.13 shows the OBSTATS table produced for the model in Output 10.12. We see that the last two lines do, in fact, have observed frequencies of 0 and predicted frequencies near 0.

Output 10.13 *OBSTATS Output for Model with Marginal Zeros*

F	Pred	Xbeta	Std	HessWgt	Lower	Upper
			Observation Statistics			
20	20.0000	2.9957	0.2236	20.0000	12.9031	31.0002
5	5.0000	1.6094	0.4472	5.0000	2.0811	12.0127
5	5.0000	1.6094	0.4472	5.0000	2.0811	12.0127
5	5.0000	1.6094	0.4472	5.0000	2.0811	12.0127
4	4.0000	1.3863	0.5000	4.0000	1.5013	10.6576
11	11.0000	2.3979	0.3015	11.0000	6.0918	19.8628
0	5.109E-12	-25.9999	0.7071	5.109E-12	1.278E-12	2.043E-11
0	5.62E-11	-23.6020	0.7006	5.62E-11	1.424E-11	2.219E-10

Now let's refit the model without these two zeros:

```
PROC GENMOD DATA=zero;
  WHERE f NE 0;
  MODEL f=x z y x*z y*z y*x / D=P;
RUN;
```

Results in Output 10.14 give the correct logit parameter estimates and the correct degrees of freedom, 0. None of the estimated parameters is unusually large. Note, however, that we do not get an estimate for the X*Z interaction, because we've eliminated one component of the *XZ* table. Deletion of cells with zero frequency should only be used when the parameters corresponding to the marginal tables with zeros are nuisance parameters. Otherwise, follow the strategies discussed in Section 3.4.

Output 10.14 *Loglinear Output for Model with Zeros Deleted*

Criteria For Assessing Goodness Of Fit			
Criterion	DF	Value	Value/DF
Deviance	0	0.0000	.
Pearson Chi-Square	0	0.0000	.
Log Likelihood	.	65.9782	.

Output 10.14 Continued

```
                 Analysis Of Parameter Estimates

Parameter    DF    Estimate    Std Err    ChiSquare    Pr>Chi

INTERCEPT     1      2.3979      0.7006     11.7128     0.0006
X             1     -0.7885      0.5394      2.1370     0.1438
Z             1     -0.0000      0.6325      0.0000     1.0000
Y             1     -2.3979      0.9954      5.8027     0.0160
X*Z           0      0.0000      0.0000         .          .
Z*Y           1      1.3863      0.8062      2.9566     0.0855
X*Y           1      2.3979      0.7687      9.7306     0.0018
```

10.8 GENMOD versus CATMOD

I've used PROC GENMOD exclusively in this chapter, but you can also estimate loglinear models with PROC CATMOD. I prefer GENMOD for three reasons:

- PROC GENMOD uses a dummy variable parameterization for CLASS variables while PROC CATMOD uses "effect coding." As I explained in Section 5.8, I find PROC CATMOD's parameterization difficult to interpret.
- PROC GENMOD can fit a wider range of loglinear models than PROC CATMOD. Most importantly, PROC CATMOD does not allow the device of treating a variable as both quantitative and qualitative in the same model.
- PROC GENMOD can correct for overdispersion when appropriate.
- PROC GENMOD can optionally produce likelihood-ratio hypothesis tests. PROC CATMOD only produces Wald tests.

There are two other noteworthy differences:

- PROC CATMOD can operate on individual-level data by constructing the minimal contingency table required for each model it estimates. PROC GENMOD requires the contingency table as input, although this is easily produced with PROC FREQ by using the OUT= option in the TABLES statement.
- PROC CATMOD assumes that any zeros it encounters in the contingency table are structural zeros and, therefore, deletes them before fitting the model. If you want to treat them as random zeros, you must replace the zeros with a very small number (see the *SAS/STAT User's Guide* for details).

Appendix

The ROBUST Macro

The ROBUST macro computes robust estimates of standard errors and Wald chi-squares for the coefficients from PROC LOGISTIC or PROC PHREG when the data is clustered. One common application is to longitudinal data with each individual treated as a cluster. It is adapted from a SAS/IML program written by Terry Therneau of the Mayo Clinic. SAS/IML is required.

For PROC LOGISTIC, you must specify the OUTEST=*name1* and COVOUT options in the PROC statement. You must also use the OUTPUT statement with the OUT=*name2* and DFBETAS=*namelist* options. *namelist* should have one name for each term in the model, including the intercept. There must also be a variable in the data set that contains a unique value (either character or numeric) for each cluster. The macro is invoked after running the LOGISTIC procedure.

For PROC PHREG, you must specify OUTEST=*name1* in the PROC statement. (COVOUT is unnecessary). You must also use the OUTPUT statement with the OUT=*name2* and DFBETA=*namelist* options. *namelist* should have one name for each variable in the model. There must also be a variable in the data set that contains a unique value (either character or numeric) for each cluster. This variable must be added to the OUTPUT data set by using the ID statement. The macro is invoked after running the PHREG procedure.

BE CAREFUL! In the OUTPUT statement, the option is DFBETAS in PROC LOGISTIC but DFBETA in PROC PHREG. (The former produces standardized dfbetas, the latter does not). Also PHREG does NOT have an intercept, so the list of variables in DFBETA=*namelist* should not have a name corresponding to the intercept.

The parameters are:

OUTEST=   Name of the data set used in the OUTEST= option

OUT=   Name of the data set used in the OUT= option

ID=   Name of the variable that contains a unique value for each cluster

DF =   List of names used in the DFBETAS or the DFBETA option

Examples

```
PROC LOGISTIC OUTEST=a covout;
  MODEL y=x z w;
  OUTPUT out=b dfbetas=dint dx dz dw;
RUN;
%ROBUST(outest=a, out=b, id=subjid, df=dint dx dz dw)

PROC PHREG OUTEST=a;
  MODEL y*d(0)=x z w;
  ID subjid;
  OUTPUT out=b dfbeta=dx dz dw;
RUN;
%ROBUST(outest=a, out=b, id=subjid, df=dx dz dw)
```

Program

```
%macro robust(outest=a, out=_last_, id=id, df=);
proc sort data=&out;
  by &id;
run;

proc means data=&out noprint;
  by &id;
  var &df;
  output out=_out1_(keep=&df) sum=&df;
run;
```

```
data _out1_;
set;
array d (*) &df;
if d(1)=. then delete;
run;

data _reduce_;
  set &outest;
  array abc(*) _character_;
  length name $8;
  call vname(abc(1),name);
  if name ne '_LINK_' and _type_ eq 'COV' then delete;
  drop  _lnlike_;
run;

proc iml;
  use _reduce_ where (_type_='COV');
  read all into cov;
  use _reduce_ where (_type_='PARMS');
  read all into b[colname=vname];
  if ncol(cov)=0 then se=1;
  else se=sqrt(diag(cov));
  use _out1_;
  read all into x;
  x=x*se;
  v=x`*x;
  se=sqrt(vecdiag(v));
  wald=(b`/se)##2;
  p=1-probchi(wald,1);
  chi=wald||p;
  c={"Chi Square" "p-value"};
  reset noname fuzz=.000001;
  print, "Robust Variance Matrix",,
      v[colname=vname rowname=vname];
  print, "Standard Errors",, se[rowname=vname];
  print, "Wald Statistics",, chi[rowname=vname colname=c];
quit;
run;


%mend robust;
```

The PENALTY Data Set: Outcomes for Murder Defendants

The PENALTY data set contains information about the outcomes of penalty trials for 147 defendants convicted of first-degree murder in New Jersey. This data is used extensively in Chapters 2 and 3. The variables are:

DEATH	1=death sentence; 0=life sentence
BLACKD	1=defendant was black; 0=otherwise
WHITVIC	1=victim was white; 0=otherwise
SERIOUS	Measure of the seriousness of the crime as evaluated by a panel of judges; based on rankings of cases, values range from 1 to 15
CULP	Measure of the "culpability" of the defendant, based on predicted values from a logistic regression of DEATH on many other variables; values range from 1 to 5
SERIOUS2	Alternative measure of seriousness based on judges' *ratings* of cases rather than rankings; values range from 1 to 5

The WALLET Data Set: Altruistic Behavior by College Students

The WALLET data set reports survey results from 195 undergraduates at the University of Pennsylvania. This data set is used as an example in Chapters 5 and 6. Variables are:

WALLET	Response to question, "If you found a wallet on the street, would you 1=keep the wallet and the money 2=keep the money and return the wallet, or 3=return both the wallet and the money?"
MALE	1=male; 0=female
BUSINESS	1=enrolled in business school; 0=otherwise
PUNISH	Variable describing whether student was physically punished by parents at various ages: 1=punished in elementary school but not middle or high school 2=punished in elementary and middle school but not high school 3=punished at all three levels
EXPLAIN	Response to question "When you were punished, did your parents generally explain why what you did was wrong?" 1=almost always; 0 = sometimes or never

The TRAVEL Data Set: Transportation Choices to Australian Cities

The TRAVEL data set has information on choices of travel mode between Australian cities for 210 people (Hensher and Bradley 1993). For each person, there was a separate record for each of the four possible choices (air, train, bus, or car), resulting in a total of 840 observations. The variables are:

ID	Unique identifier for each person
MODE	1=air, 2=train, 3=bus, 4=car
CHOICE	1=chose that mode; 0=didn't choose that mode
TTME	Terminal waiting time
COST	Total cost for all stages
TIME	Total time in vehicle for all stages
HINC	Household income in thousands of dollars
PSIZE	Size of traveling party

The JUDGERNK Data Set: Rankings of Seriousness of Murder Cases

The JUDGERNK data set contains information on rankings of the seriousness of 147 murder cases by 50 judges. Each judge ranked 14 or 15 cases by seriousness. The data set contains 736 observations, each corresponding to one ranking by one judge. The variables are:

JUDGID	ID number of the judge
RANK	Ranking given to the case. 1=most serious; 14 or 15=least serious.
BLACKD	1=defendant was black; 0=otherwise
WHITVIC	1=victim was white; 0=otherwise
DEATH	1=defendant received the death penalty; 0=otherwise
CULP	Measure of the "culpability" of the defendant, based on the predicted values from a logistic regression of DEATH on many other variables; values range from 1 to 5
CASE	ID number of the murder case

The PTSD Data Set: Psychological Distress among Fire Victims

The PTSD data set comes from a sample of 316 survivors of residential fires who were interviewed at 3 months, 6 months, and 12 months after the fire (Keane et al. 1996). There are 948 records in the file, one for each person at each point in time. The variables are:

SUBJID	Unique numeric identifier for each *person*
PTSD	1=person had symptoms of post-traumatic stress disorder at the interview; 0=otherwise
CONTROL	Scale of perceived control over several areas of life
PROBLEMS	Total number of problems reported in several areas of life
SEVENT	Number of stressful events since the last interview
COHES	Scale of family cohesion, measured only at first interview with values replicated for later time points
TIME	Values of 1, 2 or 3, corresponding to the three interviews

The POSTDOC Data Set: Postdoctoral Training among Biochemists

The sample consisted of 557 male biochemists who got their doctorates from 106 American universities in the late 1950s and early 1960s (McGinnis, Allison and Long 1982). The variables are:

PDOC	1=received postdoctoral training; 0=otherwise
AGE	Age in years at completion of the Ph.D.
MAR	1=married; 0=otherwise
DOC	Measure of the prestige of the doctoral institution in bioscience fields
UND	Measure of selectivity of the person's undergraduate institution
AG	1=degree is from an agricultural department; 0=otherwise
ARTS	Number of articles published while a graduate student
CITS	Number of citations to published articles
DOCID	ID number of the doctoral institution

The CASECONT Data Set: Women in Homeless Shelters

The CASECONT data set comes from a sample of 1582 women who stayed in family shelters in New York City for at least one 7-day period ending during 1992 (Metraux and Culhane 1997). This sample was constructed from a larger sample by taking 791 women who had a baby during their stay and matching them (by DAYS) to 791 women who did not have a baby. The variables are:

PUBHOUSE	1=woman exited to public housing; 0=otherwise
STAYBABY	1=woman gave birth during shelter stay; 0=otherwise
BLACK	1=black race, 0=nonblack
KIDS	Number of children in the household
DOUBLEUP	1=living with another family prior to shelter stay; 0=otherwise
AGE	Age of woman at beginning of shelter stay
DAYS	Number of days in shelter stay

The PROGNOSI Data Set: Physicians' Utterances about Prognosis

The PROGNOSI data set contains information about patient visits to 125 physicians (Christakis and Levinson 1998). The variables are:

LENGTHPX	Number of utterances about prognosis
PTAGE	Patient's age
PTSEX	Patient's sex (1=male; 0=female)
EZCOMPT	Doctor's rating of how easy it was to communicate with the patient; values range from 1 to 5
MDLIKEPT	Doctor's rating of how much he or she liked the patient; values range from 1 to 5
SURGEON	1=doctor was a surgeon; 0=otherwise
CLAIMS	Number of malpractice claims filed against the doctor
MINUTES	Length of the visit in minutes

References

Agresti, A. (1990), *Categorical Data Analysis*. New York: John Wiley & Sons.

Agresti, A. (1996), *An Introduction to Categorical Data Analysis*. New York: John Wiley & Sons.

Allison, P. D. (1987), "Introducing a Disturbance into Logit and Probit Regression Models," *Sociological Methods and Research*, 15, 355-374.

Allison, P. D. (1995), *Survival Analysis Using the SAS System: A Practical Guide*. Cary, NC: SAS Institute Inc.

Allison, P. D. (1999), "Comparing Logit and Probit Coefficients Across Groups." Forthcoming in *Sociological Methods and Research*.

Allison, P. D. and Christakis, N. A. (1994), "Logit Models for Sets of Ranked Items," in *Sociological Methodology 1994*, ed. P. V. Marsden, Oxford: Basil Blackwell, 199-228.

Begg, C. B. and Gray, R. (1984), "Calculation of Polychotomous Logistic Regression Parameters Using Individualized Regressions," *Biometrika*, 71, 11-18.

Breslow, N. and Day, N. E. (1980), *Statistical Methods in Cancer Research. Vol. 1: The Analysis of Case-Control Studies*. Lyon: IARC.

Bryk, A. S. and Raudenbusch, S. W. (1992), *Hierarchical Linear Models: Applications and Data Analysis*. Newbury Park, CA: Sage.

Chamberlain, G. (1980), "Analysis of Covariance with Qualitative Data," *Review of Economic Statistics*, 48, 225-238.

Christakis, N. A. and Levinson, W. (1998), "Casual Optimism: Prognostication in Routine Medical and Surgical Encounters," unpublished manuscript.

Collett, D. (1991), *Modelling Binary Data*, London: Chapman & Hall.

Cox, D. R. (1972), "Regression Models and Life Tables" (with discussion), *Journal of the Royal Statistical Society, Series B*, 34, 187-220.

Cox, D. R. and Snell, E. J. (1989), *Analysis of Binary Data*, Second Edition. London: Chapman & Hall.

Davis, C. E.; Hyde, J. E.; Bangdiwala, S. I.; and Nelson, J. J. (1986), "An Example of Dependencies Among Variables in a Conditional Logistic Regression," in *Modern Statistical Methods in Chronic Disease Epidemiology*, eds. S. H. Moolgavkar and Ross L. Prentice, New York: John Wiley & Sons.

Diggle, P. J.; Liang, K. Y.; and Zeger, S. L. (1994), *The Analysis of Longitudinal Data*, New York: Oxford University Press.

Everitt, B. S. (1992), *The Analysis of Contingency Tables*. Second Edition. London: Chapman & Hall.

Fienberg, S.E. (1980), *The Analysis of Cross-Classified Categorical Data*. Second Edition. Cambridge, MA: The MIT Press.

Fox, John (1991), *Regression Diagnostics*. Newbury Park, CA: Sage Publications.

Gail, M.H.; Wieand, S.; and Piantadosi, S. (1984), "Biased Estimates of Treatment Effect in Randomized Experiments with Nonlinear Regression and Omitted Covariates," *Biometrika*, 71, 431-444.

Glass, D. V., ed. (1954), *Social Mobility in Britain*. Glencoe, IL: Free Press.

Goodman, L. A. (1970), "Some Multiplicative Models for the Analysis of Cross Classified Data," *Proceedings of the Sixth Berkeley Symposium on Mathematical Statistics and Probability*, 649-696.

Greene, W. H. (1992), *LIMDEP User's Manual and Reference Guide, Version 6.0*. Bellport, NY: Econometric Software, Inc.

Hauck, W. W., and Donner, A. (1977), "Wald's Test as Applied to Hypotheses in Logit Analysis," *Journal of the American Statistical Association*, 72, 851-853.

Heckman, J. J. (1978), "Dummy Endogenous Variables in a Simultaneous Equation System," *Econometrica*, 46, 931-960.

Heckman, J. J. (1979), "Sample Selection Bias as a Specification Error," *Econometrica*, 47, 153-161.

Hensher, D. A. and Bradley, M. (1993), "Using Stated Response Data to Enrich Revealed Preference Discrete Choice Models," *Marketing Letters*, 4, 139-152.

Hilbe, J.(1994), "Log Negative Binomial Regression Using the GENMOD Procedure SAS/STAT Software," Proceedings of SUGI 19. Cary, NC: SAS Institute Inc.

Horney, J., Osgood, D. W., and Marshall, I. H. (1995), "Criminal Careers in the Short-Term: Intra-Individual Variability in Crime and Its Relation to Local Life Circumstances," *American Sociological Review*, 60, 655-673.

Hosmer, D. W. and Lemeshow, S. (1989), *Applied Logistic Regression*. New York: John Wiley & Sons.

Hout, Michael (1983), *Mobility Tables*. Beverly Hills: Sage Publications.

Jennings, D. E. (1986), "Judging Inference Adequacy in Logistic Regression," *Journal of the American Statistical Association*, 81, 471-476.

Kalbfleisch, J. D. and Sprott, D. A. (1970), "Applications of Likelihood Methods to Models Involving Large Numbers of Parameters" (with discussion), *Journal of the Royal Statistical Society, Series B*, 32, 175-208.

Keane, A.; Jepson, C.; Pickett, M.; Robinson, L; and McCorkle, R. (1996), "Demographic Characteristics, Fire Experiences and Distress of Residential Fire Survivors," *Issues in Mental Health Nursing*, 17, 487-501.

Kim, J. and Feree, G. D. (1981), "Standardization in Causal Analysis," *Sociological Methods and Research*," 10, 187-210.

Levinson, W.; Roter, D. L.; Mullooly, J. P.; Dull, V. T.; and Frankel, R. M. (1997), "Physician-Patient Communication," *Journal of the American Medical Association*, 277, 553-559.

Long, J. S. (1997), *Regression Models for Categorical and Limited Dependent Variables*. Thousand Oaks, CA: Sage Publications.

Maddala, G. S. (1983), *Limited Dependent and Qualitative Variables in Econometrics*. Cambridge, UK: Cambridge University Press.

McCullagh, P. (1980), "Regression Models for Ordinal Data" (with discussion), *Journal of the Royal Statistical Society, Series B*, 42, 109-142.

McCullagh, P. and Nelder, J. A. (1989), *Generalized Linear Models*. Second Edition. London: Chapman and Hall.

McCulloch, C. E. (1997), "Maximum Likelihood Algorithms for Generalized Linear Mixed Models," *Journal of the American Statistical Association*, 92, 162-170.

McFadden, D. (1973), "Conditional Logit Analysis of Qualitative Choice Behavior," in *Frontiers in Econometrics*, ed. by P. Zarembka. New York: Academic Press, 105-142.

McGinnis, R.; Allison, P. D.; and Long, J. S. (1982), "Postdoctoral Training in Bioscience: Allocation and Outcomes," *Social Forces*, 60, 701-722.

Metraux, S. and Culhane, D. P. (1997), "Family Dynamics and Recurring Homelessness Among Women in NYC Homeless Shelters," paper presented at Annual Meeting of the Eastern Sociological Society.

Morgan, S. P. and Teachman, J. D. (1988), "Logistic Regression: Description, Examples and Comparisons," *Journal of Marriage and the Family*, 50, 929-936.

Muthén, B. (1984), "A General Structural Equation Model with Dichotomous, Ordered, Categorical, and Continuous Latent Variable Indicators," *Psychometrika*, 49, 115-132.

Nagelkerke, N. J. D. (1991), "A Note on a General Definition of the Coefficient of Determination," *Biometrika*, 78, 691-692.

Neuhaus, J. M. and Kalbfleisch, J. D. (1998), "Between- and Within-Cluster Covariate Effects in the Analysis of Clustered Data," *Biometrics*, 54, 638-645.

Prentice, R. and Pyke, R. (1979), "Logistic Disease Incidence Models and Case-Control Studies," *Biometrika*, 66, 403-412.

Punj, G. N. and Staelin, R. (1978), "The Choice Process for Graduate Business Schools," *Journal of Marketing Research*, 15, 588-598.

Rodriguez, G. and Goldman, N. (1995), "An Assessment of Estimation Procedures for Multilevel Models with Binary Responses," *Journal of the Royal Statistical Society, Series A*, 158, 73-89.

Rosenbaum, P. R. and Rubin, D. B. (1983), "The Central Role of the Propensity Score in Observational Studies for Causal Effects," *Biometrika*, 70, 41-55.

SAS Institute Inc. (1995), *Logistic Regression Examples Using the SAS System*. Cary, NC: SAS Institute Inc.

SAS Institute Inc. (1996), *SAS/STAT Sofware: Changes and Ehancements Through Release 6.12*. Cary, NC: SAS Institute Inc.

SAS Institute Inc. (1989), *SAS/STAT User's Guide, Version 6, Fourth Edition*, Volumes 1 and 2. Cary, NC: SAS Institute Inc.

Seeman, M. (1977), "Some Real and Imaginary Consequences of Social Mobility: A French-American Comparison," *American Journal of Sociology*, 82, 757-782.

Sewell, W. H. and Shah, V. P. (1968), "Parents' Education and Children's Educational Aspirations and Achievements," *American Sociological Review*, 33, 191-209.

Sloane, D. and Morgan, S. P. (1996), "An Introduction to Categorical Data Analysis," *Annual Review of Sociology*, 22, 351-375.

Smith, H. L. (1997), "Matching With Multiple Controls to Estimate Treatment Differences in Observational Studies," in *Sociological Methdology 1997*, ed. A. E. Raftery. Oxford: Basil Blackwell, 325-353.

Stokes, M. E.; Davis, C. S.; and Koch, G. (1995), *Categorical Data Analysis Using the SAS System*. Cary, NC: SAS Institute Inc.

White, H. A. (1980), "A Heteroskedasticity-Consistent Covariance Matrix Estimator and a Direct Test for Heteroskedasticity," *Econometrica*, 48, 817-838.

Index

Call your local SAS® office to order these other books and tapes available through the Books by Users℠ program:

An Array of Challenges — Test Your SAS® Skills
by **Robert Virgile**.......................................Order No. A55625

Applied Multivariate Statistics with SAS® Software, Second Edition
by **Ravindra Khattree**
and **Dayanand N. Naik**..............................Order No. A56903

Applied Statistics and the SAS® Programming Language, Fourth Edition
by **Ronald P. Cody**
and **Jeffrey K. Smith**................................Order No. A55984

Beyond the Obvious with SAS® Screen Control Language
by **Don Stanley** ....Order No. A55073

Carpenter's Complete Guide to the SAS® Macro Language
by **Art Carpenter** ....Order No. A56100

The Cartoon Guide to Statistics
by **Larry Gonick**
and **Woollcott Smith**................................Order No. A55153

Categorical Data Analysis Using the SAS® System
by **Maura E. Stokes, Charles S. Davis,**
and **Gary G. Koch** ....Order No. A55320

Common Statistical Methods for Clinical Research with SAS® Examples
by **Glenn A. Walker**..................................Order No. A55991

Concepts and Case Studies in Data Management
by **William S. Calvert**
and **J. Meimei Ma**.....................................Order No. A55220

Efficiency: Improving the Performance of Your SAS® Applications
by **Robert Virgile**......................................Order No. A55960

Essential Client/Server Survival Guide, Second Edition
by **Robert Orfali, Dan Harkey,**
and **Jeri Edwards**.....................................Order No. A56285

Extending SAS® Survival Analysis Techniques for Medical Research
by **Alan Cantor**..Order No. A55504

A Handbook of Statistical Analyses Using SAS®
by **B.S. Everitt**
and **G. Der** ....Order No. A56378

The How-To Book for SAS/GRAPH® Software
by **Thomas Miron** ....Order No. A55203

In the Know ... SAS® Tips and Techniques From Around the Globe
by **Phil Mason** ....Order No. A55513

Integrating Results through Meta-Analytic Review Using SAS® Software
by **Morgan C. Wang** and
Brad J. Bushman ....Order No. A55810

Learning SAS® in the Computer Lab
by **Rebecca J. Elliott** ....Order No. A55273

The Little SAS® Book: A Primer
by **Lora D. Delwiche** and
Susan J. Slaughter ....Order No. A55200

The Little SAS® Book: A Primer, Second Edition
by **Lora D. Delwiche** and
Susan J. Slaughter ....Order No. A56649
(updated to include Version 7 features)

Logistic Regression Using the SAS System: Theory and Application
by **Paul D. Allison** ....Order No. A55770

Mastering the SAS® System, Second Edition
by **Jay A. Jaffe** ....Order No. A55123

Multiple Comparisons and Multiple Tests Using the SAS® System
by **Peter H. Westfall, Randall D. Tobias,**
Dror Rom, Russell D. Wolfinger,
and **Yosef Hochberg** ....Order No. A56648

The Next Step: Integrating the Software Life Cycle with SAS® Programming
by **Paul Gill** ....Order No. A55697

Painless Windows 3.1: A Beginner's Handbook for SAS® Users
by **Jodie Gilmore** ....Order No. A55505

Painless Windows: A Handbook for SAS® Users
by **Jodie Gilmore** ....Order No. A55769
(for Windows NT and Windows 95)

Painless Windows: A Handbook for SAS® Users, Second Edition
by **Jodie Gilmore** ....Order No. A56647
(updated to include Version 7 features)

PROC TABULATE by Example
by **Lauren E. Haworth** ....Order No. A56514

Professional SAS® Programmers Pocket Reference, Second Edition
by **Rick Aster** ....Order No. A56646

Professional SAS® Programming Secrets, Second Edition
by **Rick Aster**
and **Rhena Seidman** ....Order No. A56279

Professional SAS® User Interfaces
by **Rick Aster** ....Order No. A56197

Audio Tapes

JMP® Books

*Welcome * Bienvenue *Willkommen *Yohkoso * Bienvenido*

SAS® Publications Is Easy to Reach

Visit our SAS Publications Web page located at www.sas.com/pubs

You will find product and service details, including

- **sample chapters**
- **tables of contents**
- **author biographies**
- **book reviews**

Learn about

- **regional user groups conferences**
- **trade show sites and dates**
- **authoring opportunities**
- **custom textbooks**

Order books with ease at our secured Web page!

Explore all the services that Publications has to offer!

Your Listserv Subscription Brings the News to You Automatically

Do you want to be among the first to learn about the latest books and services available from SAS Publications? Subscribe to our listserv **newdocnews-l** and automatically receive the following once each month: a description of the new titles, the applicable environments or operating systems, and the applicable SAS release(s). To subscribe:

1. Send an e-mail message to **listserv@vm.sas.com**

2. Leave the "Subject" line blank

3. Use the following text for your message:

      subscribe newdocnews-l *your-first-name your-last-name*

    For example: subscribe newdocnews-l John Doe

    Please note: newdocnews-l ◄——— that's the letter "l" not the number "1".

For customers outside the U.S., contact your local SAS office for listserv information.

Create Customized Textbooks Quickly, Easily, and Affordably

SelecText® offers instructors at U.S. colleges and universities a way to create custom textbooks for courses that teach students how to use SAS software.

For more information, see our Web page at **www.sas.com/selectext**, or contact our SelecText coordinators by sending e-mail to **selectext@sas.com**.

You're Invited to Publish with SAS Institute's User Publishing Program

If you enjoy writing about SAS software and how to use it, the User Publishing Program at SAS Institute Inc. offers a variety of publishing options. We are actively recruiting authors to publish books, articles, and sample code. Do you find the idea of writing a book or an article by yourself a little intimidating? Consider writing with a co-author. Keep in mind that you will receive complete editorial and publishing support, access to our users, technical advice and assistance, and competitive royalties. Please contact us for an author packet. E-mail us at **sasbbu@sas.com** or call 919-677-8000, then press 1-6479. See the SAS Publications Web page at **www.sas.com/pubs** for complete information.

Read All about It in *Authorline*®!

Our User Publishing newsletter, *Authorline*, features author interviews, conference news, and informational updates and highlights from our User Publishing Program. Published quarterly, *Authorline* is available free of charge. To subscribe, send e-mail to **sasbbu@sas.com** or call 919-677-8000, then press 1-6479.

See *Observations*®, Our Online Technical Journal

Feature articles from *Observations*®: *The Technical Journal for SAS*® *Software Users* are now available online at **www.sas.com/obs**. Take a look at what your fellow SAS software users and SAS Institute experts have to tell you. You may decide that you, too, have information to share. If you are interested in writing for *Observations*, send e-mail to **sasbbu@sas.com** or call 919-677-8000, then press 1-6479.

Book Discount Offered at SAS Public Training Courses!

When you attend one of our SAS Public Training Courses at any of our regional Training Centers in the U.S., you will receive a 15% discount on any book orders placed during the course. Each course has a list of recommended books to choose from, and the books are displayed for you to see. Take advantage of this offer at the next course you attend!

SAS Institute Inc.
SAS Campus Drive
Cary, NC 27513-2414
Fax 919-677-4444

E-mail: sasbook@sas.com
Web page: www.sas.com/pubs
To order books, call Fulfillment Services at 800-727-3228*
For other SAS Institute business, call 919-677-8000*

* Note: Customers outside the U.S. should contact their local SAS office.